Sojourner Truth

Matthew Henson

Frederick Douglass

Phillis Wheatly

Roland Hayes

Paul Laurence Dunbar

Dr. Carter G. Woodson

ABC BOYS

Archie Moore

Thurgood Marshall

Frank L. Peterson

Clifton R. Wharton, Jr.

Whitney M. Young

Asa Philip Randolph

J. L. Moran

Paul R. Williams

Free at Last

Free at Last

E. E. Cleveland
D.D., L.L.D.

Published jointly by
REVIEW AND HERALD PUBLISHING ASSOCIATION
Washington, DC 20039-0555
Hagerstown, MD 21740

PACIFIC PRESS PUBLISHING ASSOCIATION
Boise, ID 83707
Oshawa, Ontario, Canada
Montemorelos, N.L., Mexico

E. Earl Cleveland, minister, evangelist, author of several books, and kindly counselor of those in need of spiritual help.

PRINTED IN U.S.A.

CONTENTS

Part III—PROPHECY

Part IV—THE OBEDIENCE OF FAITH

Inside the Cover

MARIAN ANDERSON, contralto concert singer of the Metropolitan Opera

MARY McLEOD BETHUNE, founder and president emeritus of Bethune-Cookman College

RALPH BUNCHE, undersecretary of the United Nations Organization

GEORGE WASHINGTON CARVER, scientist noted for research on the uses of peanuts

FREDERICK DOUGLASS, orator, abolitionist, and second minister to Haiti

PAUL LAURENCE DUNBAR, lyric poet, first to express the esthetic feelings of Negroes

ROLAND HAYES, concert tenor, widely acclaimed in Europe and America

MATTHEW HENSON, first man to reach the North Pole in the Peary expedition

MAHALIA JACKSON, well-known singer of gospel songs

Dr. CHARLES S. JOHNSON, president of Fisk University

Lt. Col. LEONARD JOHNSON, commander of a medical group in the Strategic Air Command

Dr. MORDECAI W. JOHNSON, president of Howard University

THURGOOD MARSHALL, Justice of the Supreme Court

ARCHIE MOORE, boxing champion, founder of the ABC Boys Club

J. L. MORAN, educator, president of Oakwood College

ROBERT R. MOTON, president of Tuskegee Institute

JESSE OWENS, holder of more world track records than any other American

FRANK L. PETERSON, denominational leader in Washington, D.C.

ASA PHILIP RANDOLPH, leader of march on Washington that encouraged President Roosevelt to launch the Fair Employment Practices Act

JACKIE ROBINSON, first black baseball player in the major leagues

SOJOURNER TRUTH, emancipated slave, preacher, and abolitionist

BOOKER T. WASHINGTON, founder of Tuskegee Institute

CLIFTON R. WHARTON, Jr., president of Michigan State University

PHILLIS WHEATLEY, slave poet, later emancipated, widely acclaimed in Europe

WALTER A. WHITE, executive secretary of the NAACP for 24 years, consultant at the United Nations

ROY WILKINS, executive secretary of the NAACP after Walter White

PAUL R. WILLIAMS, architect, and government adviser on housing

Dr. CARTER G. WOODSON, eminent scholar, superintendent of schools in Manhattan

WHITNEY M. YOUNG, executive director of the National Urban League

"Ye Shall Know the Truth,
and the Truth
Shall Make You Free"

John 8:32

PART I

A Saviour

"Free at Last"

THE HISTORY of the black man in America is inseparably intertwined with the Bible. During the dark night of the black man's servitude the preacher was the only public speaker allowed on the plantation, and the Scriptures were the only approved reading. Listening to the stories of the Hebrew slavery and the Exodus, the black man discerned a similarity of experience and made the message of the Bible the cradle of his hope. The church became the temple of hope, and the Negro spiritual reflected the ebb and flow of his dreams. Ranging from the abject pathos of "Nobody Knows but Jesus" to the triumphant notes of "Free at Last," the black man's music mirrors his history and his hopes. This book is dedicated to his hopes.

Reading the New Testament, the black man identified with Jesus. The act of Simon bearing the cross and relieving the suffering of our Lord, brings warmth and pride to our hearts. The

12

black man identifies with Christ in His crucifixion. He sings, "The world treat You mean, Lord; treat me mean too. But that's how things are down here." Then he captures the glorious hope of the resurrection with the words, "Were you there when He rose up from the grave? Oh, sometimes it causes me to tremble." He senses that if Christ rose from the dead his own future is sure.

And so through the long weary years he waited for his Moses. God did not disappoint him. Israel reached her Promised Land. The black man's Moses took many forms and colors. Ministers of the gospel, editors, politicians, and orators mounted the fiercest attack in history on human bondage, even when it was suicide to criticize this traffic in black gold. But courageous, determined men persisted. The underground railroad played its part. A praying people were getting their answer. The black man worked and waited on the Lord. It took only one plague to release him from the Egypt of Southern servitude—the Civil War. In that bloody struggle the black man was a participant. In the latter stages of the war the black soldier was a meaningful factor in the Northern victory. From Kansas came the first regiment of black troops to fight for their own freedom.

With the achievement of freedom there must be spiritual revival, mental and cultural development. We must worship and think as free men. To attain political freedom and remain a slave to immorality, intemperance, and self-indulgence is supreme folly. "Righteousness exalteth a nation: but sin is a reproach to any people." Sin like an albatross hangs about the neck of the human family, dragging down our hopes and dreams.

Israel reached her Promised Land. Will we reach ours? Recently a modern dreamer said, "Tonight I am not afraid. I have seen the promised land. You will cross over, but I may not be

13

able to go over with you." The next night his voice was stilled by
an assassin's bullet. The dreamer died; his dream must not. Fear
must not be allowed to mute the witness of Christ. The gospel of
Christ that fired our hopes through the long night of slavery
must guide us through the treacherous waters of the future. We
will reach the promised land if we go with God. If on the other
hand we succumb to the evils of our Canaanite environment and
like Israel forget the God who brought us thus far, then in us will
be fulfilled the dictum of the philosopher, "Whom the gods destroy, they first make mad." May we ever pray in the words of a
well-known anthem I have paraphrased:

> God of our weary years,
> God of our silent tears,
> Thou who hast brought us thus far on our way,
> Help us by Thy might to follow Thee to the light.
> Keep us forever in right paths, we pray,
> Lest our feet stray from the places, our God, where we met Thee;
> Lest our heart, drunk with the wine of the world, forget Thee.
> Shadowed beneath Thine hand,
> May we forever stand—true to
> Our God, true to our fellow man.
>
> Rugged the road we've trod
> Bitter the chastening rod
> Felt in the day when hope unborn had died,
> Yet with a steady heat
> Have not our weary feet
> Come to the place for which our fathers sighed.
> We have come over the way
> That with tears has been watered;
> We have come, treading our path
> Through the blood of the slaughtered;
> Out of the gloomy past
> 'Til now we stand at last near the
> White gleam where our bright star is cast.

He's got you and me, brother, in His hands;
He's got the whole world in His hands.

"He's Got the Whole World"

"IF I WERE HUNGRY, I would not tell thee: for the world is mine, and the fulness thereof" (Psalm 50:12).

Man—where did he come from, and where is he headed? And why is he here? Much of the delinquency, juvenile and adult, that plagues our planet stems from the fact that, for many, these questions remain unanswered. The Bible provides the only satisfactory answer to the problem of human origin and destiny. Moreover, it alone illumines the darkness that enshrouds the chaos of our troubled times.

Just how essential is this knowledge of the past? During the dark days of slavery an African stood proudly erect while others bent over their tasks. He was lashed repeatedly, but refused to bend. Though cursed and threatened, he refused to yield. When asked why, he answered, "I am the son of a chief." The knowledge of his background gave him a sense of identity and security. This

15

had a definite bearing on his behavior. Sociologists tell us that much of the root cause of social misbehavior is traceable to broken homes and lack of pride in one's origin. "The soil of human origin is discernible in her sons."

It is comforting to know that "the Lord God formed man of the dust of the ground, and breathed into his nostrils the breath of life; and man became a living soul" (Genesis 2:7). "So God created man in his own image, in the image of God created he him; male and female created he them" (chapter 1:27). "For thus saith the Lord that created the heavens; God himself that formed the earth and made it; he hath established it, he created it not in vain, he formed it to be inhabited: I am the Lord; and there is none else" (Isaiah 45:18).

Man can claim no greater dignity. He came from the hands of the Creator Himself. Man came not up from the slime pits as suggested by evolutionists, but from the life-giving hands of a loving God. Original man was never a one-celled amoeba nor the multi-staged mammal types created by anthropologists. He was created one day a whole man—complete, mature. "And God saw every thing that he had made, and, behold, it was very good. And the evening and the morning were the sixth day" (Genesis 1:31). The day spoken of here was not a long, mystical, geological age. It was a regular twenty-four-hour day. Whenever the Bible uses the word "day" with a numeral in front of it—such as first, second, third—it refers to a twenty-four-hour period. A casual glance at your concordance will confirm this. Furthermore, vegetation was created on the third day. If the nights were hundreds of years long, the vegetation would have died in the darkness. It takes sunlight to grow vegetation. Man, woman, and the beasts of the forest were created on the same day. That man is a product

2

The Christ of the centuries, and our Saviour today, invites people of all races and creeds to find true freedom in Him.

of divine intelligence is logical and reasonable. To try to account for man or this planet by natural law, while denying the existence of the One who made these laws, is self-contradictory. "For by him were all things created, that are in heaven, and that are in earth, visible and invisible, whether they be thrones, or dominions, or principalities, or powers: all things were created by him, and for him" (Colossians 1:16).

It is significant that the *image* of God is in man. Man was created Godlike. That he has lost much of his Godlikeness because of sin is the subject of another chapter. However, a knowledge of our exalted origin should lead us to seek anew that golden cord of character that links us with our Maker. The clay must reflect the character of the potter, as the moon glistens by the light of the sun.

During the dark days of slavery in America, use was made of the Biblical story of the curse on Ham to justify the enslavement of black men, and because of this Negroes were to be "hewers of wood, and drawers of water" forever, and "servants" unto their brethren (see Genesis 9:25). This story does *not* teach that the black race is cursed or condemned to an inferior place in world history. In fact, Ham was not cursed, but Canaan, one of Ham's sons. Furthermore, the curse was upon Canaan alone and not upon his sons. The first great cities were built by the Canaanites, and their subjugation by the Hebrew people was delayed for centuries. Nor is there any evidence that the Canaanites ever inhabited Africa. The sons of Cush did migrate to Africa and Western Arabia; in fact, the word *Cush* means "black" or "Ethiopian." But Canaan was the one cursed by his grandfather, not Ham or Cush. The Bible does *not* teach that Ham became black because he was cursed. No one knows the color of Ham's father, Noah.

We do know that "the whole earth was of one language, and of one speech" when men began to build the first skyscraper. You see, men were still flood shocked. It had rained forty days and nights until the waters had covered the earth. At the command of God, Noah had prepared an ark, and in this giant ship all his family was saved. When the floodwaters receded God promised that He would never again destroy the earth by water. The sons of Noah did not believe God, and set about to build "a city and a tower, whose top may reach unto heaven" (chapter 11:4).

"And the Lord came down to see the city and the tower, which the children of men builded" (verse 5). Any deed committed in unbelief is rebellion against God and requires His attention.

"And the Lord said, Behold, the *people is one,* and they have all one language" (verse 6). What a declaration! God Himself proclaims repeatedly the *oneness* of the human family. Of the whole human family, Malachi could proclaim, "Have we not all one father? hath not one God created us? why do we deal treacherously every man against his brother, by profaning the covenant of our fathers?" (Malachi 2:10).

Many centuries later Peter could add: "And hath made of one blood all nations of men for to dwell on all the face of the earth, and hath determined the times before appointed, and the bounds of their habitation" (Acts 17:26). The Bible teaches that all human kind is related and that all men—black, white, red, and yellow—are blood brothers. We are all descendants of Adam through Noah. What happened at Babel?

"Go to, let us go down, and there confound their language, that they may not understand one another's speech. So the Lord scattered them abroad from thence upon the face of all the earth: and they left off to build the city" (Genesis 11:7, 8). There is no evidence that the Lord did anything physiological to the people. He changed their languages, and those who could understand one another congregated together. Today there are well over 3,000 languages and dialects. Thus people were "scattered . . . abroad from thence upon the face of all the earth." And though in their individual geographical locations, personality, physical, and cultural differences developed, the basic kinship of each race to the others is, and will forever remain, a fact.

At different times in human history men have arisen proclaiming the inherent superiority of one race over another. Of such, Adolph Hitler was the most prominent in our century, but his myth was punctured by cannon fire and collapsed in a sea of blood. The record of history is open for all to see. Every continent has had its day, and all have experienced the deep sleep of primitive heathenism. The long-buried history of black African civilizations is now becoming common knowledge—the emergence of new nations on the continent guiding their own destinies—but the key to this change is the subject of another chapter. Perhaps Psalm 75:6, 7 is enlightening on this point: "For promotion cometh neither from the east, nor from the west, nor from the south. But God is the judge. He putteth down one, and setteth up another." Yes, "He's got the whole world in His hands."

Christianity is not the white man's religion. It had its beginning in Asia, not Europe. Christ was a Semite, not a European. But He demonstrated while on earth that He genuinely loved all men. Moreover, He taught that all men should love one another. The church of the living God is a house of prayer for all people. The gospel of the Lord Jesus proposes to reconcile man to God and to his fellow man. In it alone is the hope of the race—the whole human race.

In our world and in our land a dangerous polarization of human attitudes is developing, one that bodes ill for our hope for survival. The apostles of hate and violence of all races are having a field day, exploiting the ills that afflict our society. Hear these words while there is yet time! We can have change without violence, revival without hate, and reform without bloodshed. But it will be only if oppressor and oppressed will "hear the word of the Lord"! If not, this world will indeed become a vast valley filled with dry bones.

But man has a higher destiny than this. He is the crowning act of God's creation. Because of man more than anything else "the morning stars sang together, and all the sons of God shouted for joy." God will never let the world perish under the lethal fallout of the mushroom cloud. God Himself will purify the earth of sin and sinners in His own way. Believing, repentant, contrite men will be saved. For them, paradise will be restored. Then it will be understood that at no time in human history did God leave man or this planet unattended; in fact, "He's got the whole world in His hands."

"Trouble Won't Last"

ONCE ON EARTH there was plenty for everyone, but since the fall of man there has never been a time when all men ever had plenty. It did not take long to develop a dual society of the rich and the poor. Eventually there developed a middle class who were neither rich nor poor, but were well provided for. They later became what was called the backbone of society. In the field of economics it became evident that the larger the middle class, the healthier the state of society. But the population explosion has blighted man's hope of ultimate prosperity for all. Babies are simply being born too fast for the available material goods to keep pace with the expanding population. It is therefore evident that the poor will be with us always.

The Christian religion neither caters to the rich nor despises the poor. Jesus, while standing in the Temple one day, watched the pompous rich men giving of their wealth but made no comment until a woman, obviously poverty stricken, slipped in and quietly put in her mite. Calling attention to this, Jesus declared that she had put in more than the others, for she gave all she had. She was a sacrificial giver.

The words of the spiritual, "O, my Lord, what shall I do?" mirror the frustration of poverty, for many of the poor are trapped in a cycle of misery from which there seems to be no escape. The well-fed can easily pass judgment on the poor, but few really know much about benumbing poverty. In every society some are ground under by the system, and years of living at subsistence level breeds a new mode of thought, behavior, and conversation.

A recent President of the United States, in an effort to do something about the problem, launched what was called the war on poverty. Few can deny that many have been benefited, but in spite of this program and many others, poverty still seems to spread. It is clear that if indeed we are at war with poverty, we have not yet won a battle. In our times the bitterness of the alienated is expressing itself, in some instances, in violence. The cry of the poor, "What shall I do?" must have an answer soon if man is to survive on this planet.

Jesus Christ came to the earth as a very poor man, thus showing His esteem for the poor. He was not accorded the dignity of being born in a hospital or even at a hotel but among the calves in the stall. As a grown man He was heard to remark, "Birds of the air have nests; but the Son of man hath not where to lay his head" (Matthew 8:20). He was seen more often among the poor and common men than with the rich. Not that Christ did not love all men, but He had a special pitying tenderness toward the disadvantaged, and went out of His way while on earth

23

to reassure them. Christ knew the cycle of poverty was surrounded by a fence of steel and few born within this circle ever get out of it. Much of His energy was spent in uplifting the poor, and much of His teaching was designed to bring them inspiration, light, and hope.

It is ironic that in our age so little has been done for the poor by the possessors of great wealth. Nor may the middle-class man shake his finger in disdain, for he too has largely ignored the cry of poverty. But recently up from the ghettolike streets of some of the great cities himself, he has chosen to forget his less fortunate brother. Much of the sound and the fury that have echoed destructively across the face of the earth are the voice of rejection, and the cry of despair by the poor retreating to the security of anonymity. It is easy to get lost among one's fellows.

Too long have the poor been fed empty political promises. They have been treated to solutions that don't solve and cures that don't heal, and in agony their voice is heard crying out, "What shall we do?" To which the rich would answer, "Pull yourself up by your bootstraps"—and this to a man who has neither boots nor straps! "Why won't these people work?" is a question often heard concerning the poor. All such know little of the frustration of knocking on doors that never open and answering ads only to be told when confronting the advertiser that the position is "filled."

Many of the hopeless did not get that way overnight, but under the persistent pounding of rejection something inside just died and the flickering flame of faith faded out. How do you bring hope to the hopeless, inspiration to the hard of heart? There is but one solution. Christ must be brought to the attention of the

At times the problems of life seem more than anyone should be called upon to bear. Fortunately, troubles do not last forever.

poor, and they must come to look upon Christ as a "friend that sticketh closer than a brother." The church must minister to the needs of the poor as Christ did while He was on earth. Christians must reject the scornful attitude of the world toward the have nots. Men who represent Christ must understand that being poor is hard enough and that the insults daily heaped upon the poor often become unbearable. As a result, the poor often react with blind violence.

But Christ has spoken to the poor: "Come unto me, all ye that labour and are heavy laden, and I will give you rest" (Matthew 11:28). He wants to identify Himself with the man who is down and out. The wealthy and the affluent already know that God loves them. It is that rejected man whose clothes are disheveled, whose stomach is empty, and whose brain is untrained who is the test of the genuineness of our experience with Christ. The good Samaritan understood this, and unlike the Levites and priests who went by on the other side, he came near the man, bound up his wounds, and took him to a hotel and secured a room and paid for it. He showed kindness to the needy when it was needed most.

This is a hard world in which we live. We have stretched ribbons of concrete and steel through the cities providing rapid transit past the tenement shacks and the blight of the inner city. Affluent society finds such sights painful to the eye and wounding to the pride, so it seeks to speed by them, avoiding the painful day-to-day confrontation with them. Like the proverbial ostrich, society would bury its head in the sand and comfortably delude self until the reaction of the poor, like seismic shock waves, makes the whole structure of society tremble. Then there is a response, but this is not the answer.

The dreamer said it before he died, and Jesus had said it nineteen hundred years before that. Somehow the strong must act for the relief of the weak, and the weak must somehow find a better voice than violence to air their just claims on society. While it is true that some of the poor are not doing as much as they could to better themselves, it is equally true that with greater opportunity most of the poor would better their lot. Long ago Solomon said, "He that hath pity upon the poor lendeth unto the Lord" (Proverbs 19:17). And Jesus said, "For whosoever shall give you a cup of water to drink in my name, because ye belong to Christ, verily I say unto you, he shall not lose his reward" (Mark 9:41).

It is ironic that men spend millions probing outer space and building huge monuments to the pride of man, while the destitute camp at our doorsteps. The world has not traveled far from Jesus' parable of the rich man and Lazarus. To be sure, thousands of people have used their wealth unstintingly to relieve the destitute, but there are still covetous souls who eat in peace while the groans of the starving sound in ears that are deaf to the cries of their fellow men.

This chapter is an appeal to reason. Let not the fact that poverty will always be with us discourage us from ministering to the needs of the poor. As one philosopher put it: "Some men, staring at the jungle, become discouraged instead of taking their ax and felling one tree at a time." It is indeed possible to behold the jungle of human misery, and despair of doing anything because no one can do everything. But the true man of faith, like Jesus, goes to work by healing one at a time. It is remarkable how much misery can thus be relieved in the course of a lifetime. Of this we may be sure: There will be no genuine

27

happiness for any of us while we ignore the misery of some of us. We have literally come to the place in this nation—and in the world—where we must share what we have or lose it. Our survival, as a nation and as a world, hangs on our answer to this question: Are we Christian enough to share what we have with others?

They laid my pretty little Jesus
Down in the straw, . . .
And that's what make the glory manger.

"The Glory Manger"

ONE HAS QUOTED—very often and very thoughtlessly, I am inclined to believe—Richard Watson Gilder's poem:

> If Jesus Christ is a man—
> And only a man,—I say
> That of all mankind I cleave to him,
> And to him will I cleave alway.
>
> If Jesus Christ is a God—
> And the only God,—I swear
> I will follow him through heaven and hell,
> The earth, the sea, the air!

The Bible fact is that Christ was not either/or, but *both* God and man. He was unique in all of human history. He was divinity clothed with humanity. "And the Word was made flesh, and dwelt among us, (and we beheld his glory, the glory as of the only begotten of the Father,) full of grace and truth"

(John 1:14). By the incarnation Christ was indeed born of a woman, and thus could claim an earthly mother. Long before this grand event, however, He was the Word of God. He was divine, the second person of the Godhead. "For unto us a child is born, unto us a son is given: and the government shall be upon his shoulder: and his name shall be called Wonderful, Counsellor, The mighty God, The everlasting Father, The Prince of Peace" (Isaiah 9:6). "Behold, a virgin shall be with child, and shall bring forth a son, and they shall call his name Emmanuel, which being interpreted is, God with us" (Matthew 1:23). And so, with Gilder, let us prepare to cleave to Him alway, and to "follow him through heaven and hell, The earth, the sea, the air," for He is the God-Man.

Of Himself, Jesus said to the woman of Samaria: "If thou knewest the gift of God, and who it is that saith to thee, Give me to drink; thou wouldest have asked of him, and he would have given thee living water" (John 4:10). That phrase, "living water," is strangely reminiscent of John 3:16, which says, "For God so loved the world, that he gave his only begotten Son, that whosoever believeth in him should not perish, but have everlasting life."

Again Jesus said: "I came forth from the Father, and am come into the world: again, I leave the world, and go to the Father" (chapter 16:28). So, as we approach the "glory manger," we do so with a feeling of awe, for there is something supernatural here. God has come to tabernacle with man in the person of Jesus Christ. Bow down ye heavens and be astonished, O earth! Heaven's choicest Lily was planted in the soil of human flesh. The Pearl of Great Price was encased in the bosom of humanity. The Bread of Life made Himself available for human consumption. Shiloh was now here, and unto Him would the gathering of the people be. On this evening of our Saviour's birth the morning stars would again sing together, and all the sons of God shout for joy, for salvation is created. A great and effectual door is now open to all men everywhere.

"And the Spirit and the bride say, Come. And let him that heareth say, Come. And let him that is athirst come. And whosoever will, let him take the water of life freely" (Revelation 22:17).

"For ye know the grace of our Lord Jesus Christ, that, though he was rich, yet for your sakes he became poor, that ye through his poverty might be rich" (2 Corinthians 8:9).

Dr. C. C. Grubb was talking to a theatrical manager on board a ship going to Australia. The manager confessed that he was an agnostic, but he said, "I have been struck by some of your remarks, and I thought I would like to have a talk with you."

At the end of the talk he said, "Well, Mr. Grubb, I see one thing."

Mr. Grubb asked, "What do you see?"

He answered, "Well, I see that if Christ is anything, He must be everything."

But why was so fearful a price to be paid for man's redemption? Why must the Son of God Himself come down and pay with His life for man's sin? The apostle John suggests a partial answer in John 1:1-3: "In the beginning was the Word, and the Word was with God, and the Word was God. The same was in the beginning with God. All things were made by him; and without him was not any thing made that was made."

No less than the Creator would have to be the Redeemer, if

...r shows the infant Jesus to an adoring
...p of today's children. "May I hold
...?" asks the girl with hands outstretched.

man was to be saved. The sin of man was against the government of God, and if he was not to pay with his own life for his sins, then his Creator must assume responsibility for them and die as a substitute for sinful man. The love of Christ for man was such that He consented to take man's place, to die man's death that man might live. Also, skeptical man needed an example in human flesh that beings can live a life of obedience. This, Christ provided, from the cradle to the grave.

The devil has always argued that God's requirements are too high for man and that even divine grace is not sufficient to enable man to measure up to the standards of Jehovah. Christ spent thirty-three years on this earth in human form, giving the lie to this allegation. He not only proved that the life of obedience can be lived out in human flesh, but demonstrated just how this may be done. He began by reassuring us that our evil desires within can be subdued, and that external environmental pressures can be resisted. "For what the law could not do, in that it was weak through the flesh, God sending his own Son in the likeness of sinful flesh, and for sin, condemned sin in the flesh: that the righteousness of the law might be fulfilled in us, who walk not after the flesh, but after the Spirit" (Romans 8:3, 4).

Here is a plain promise that Christ will come into our hearts and take up His abode there, enforcing the claims of the law within the human heart so fully and completely that the righteousness of the law is fulfilled in us. Those who live at home with us will be aware of these changes. Those who work with us on the job will not understand us, and those who live in the neighborhood will see the change. It is real. "We have heard a joyful sound, Jesus saves." So Christ says to the sinner, "I can do in your flesh what I did in My own." He "is able to keep you from falling, and to present you faultless before the presence of his glory with exceeding joy" (Jude 24).

Christ then is our example. We are to follow in His steps. When we accept Him as our personal Saviour, obedience becomes the natural expression of a converted heart. We obey God because we love Him. "If ye love me, keep my commandments" (John 14:15).

The human family needed a Saviour who was akin to both God and man. The Mediator must understand thoroughly both the mind of God and the mind of man in order to bring them together. The reconciling of the world to God was no easy matter. Only divinity and humanity could accomplish this, and that is why Christ was the unique Being in all the universe qualified to undertake the task in man's behalf. As man, He was "in all points tempted like as we are, yet without sin," and yet as God He could raise the dead. Also, He can represent fallen human beings before an all-righteous, all-wise heavenly Father.

Christ became man to demonstrate at the lowest level that the government of God is just and that no more is required of man than he can give, with God's help. It is clear also that if Christ could live a pure life as a human being, on the very lowest level of existence, then there was no excuse for angel apostasy. Furthermore, the devil stands unmasked for what he was and is—a seducer, a deceiver, and a rebel.

Up to the cross the devil failed to induce Christ to sin. Christ died in triumph, and of that experience it is written: "And having spoiled principalities and powers, he made a shew of them openly, triumphing over them in it" (Colossians 2:15).

At the cross the devil missed his final opportunity to induce the Son of God to sin, and thus render hopeless the sacrifice being made for man's redemption. At the cross the devil was working against man, trying to destroy man's Saviour; but Christ triumphed even there. He did not sin, nor was a word of complaint found on His lips. This spoiled principalities and powers; this made a show of them openly. Thus Christ once again triumphed over Satan and in so doing made for man a way of escape, "that whosoever believeth in him should not perish, but have everlasting life."

Were you there when they crucified my Lord?
Oh! sometimes it causes me to tremble, tremble,
tremble,
Were you there when they crucified my Lord?

"Were You There?"

A DISSIPATED military officer, having become hopelessly involved in debt, sat down in desperation and wrote out a list of his indebtedness. Summing up the whole, he wrote in despair at the bottom: "Who can pay such a debt as this?" That night the emperor passed through the barracks in disguise. Seeing the paper beside the sleeping man, he read it and wrote at the end of the question the one word: Nicholas.

In the morning the officer wondered who had done it, but all doubts vanished when at ten o'clock the emperor sent the cash necessary for the heavy payment. Great was his joy at this unmerited favor. I need not add that this soldier, from that day forward, would willingly have laid down his life for the emperor.

Sin is a debt too enormous for any human being to pay, and "all have sinned" (Romans 3:23). In abject despair some have said, Who can pay this debt? to which I answer, Jesus.

"FREE AT LAST"

> Jesus paid it all,
> All to Him I owe;
> Sin had left a crimson stain:
> He washed it white as snow.

The Roman cross, a symbol of human shame, became a door of hope for millions, their only way of escape. The Roman cross was comparable to our electric chair. All who went there were supposed to be disgraced forever; but Jesus Christ, by hanging on a cross, is exalted forever. It is what put Him there that makes the difference. "For God so loved the world, that he gave his only begotten Son, that whosoever believeth in him should not perish, but have everlasting life" (John 3:16).

Old Testament prophets looked forward with mingled feelings to Calvary, that grand but awful event. The prophet Isaiah wrote, "Surely he hath borne our griefs, and carried our sorrows: yet we did esteem him stricken, smitten of God, and afflicted. But he was wounded for our transgressions, he was bruised for our iniquities: the chastisement of our peace was upon him; and with his stripes we are healed. All we like sheep have gone astray; we have turned every one to his own way; and the Lord hath laid on him the iniquity of us all" (Isaiah 53:4-6).

The prophet Daniel wrote: "And after threescore and two weeks shall Messiah be cut off, but not for himself" (Daniel 9:26). And in the fullness of time Old Testament prophecy became New Testament reality. Christ died for our sins. "Jesus, when he had cried again with a loud voice, yielded up the ghost" (Matthew 27:50). "For when we were yet without strength, in due time Christ died for the ungodly. . . . But God commendeth his love toward us, in that, while we were yet sinners, Christ died for us" (Romans 5:6-8). "Ye know the grace of our Lord Jesus

38

Christ, that, though he was rich, yet for your sakes he became poor, that ye through his poverty might be rich" (2 Corinthians 8:9).

> The sun grew dark with mystery;
> The morn was cold and chill
> As the shadow of a cross arose
> Upon a lonely hill.

And on that cross Christ died for our sins. He who knew no sin accepted, in His own person, the guilt and condemnation for the sins of the whole world. So heavy was this burden that it almost destroyed Him before He reached the cross, for in the Garden of Gethsemane, weighed down by the burden of the world's collective guilt, He cried out, "Father, if thou be willing, remove this cup from me." But, strengthened by the angel for the task that lay ahead, he added in submission, "nevertheless not my will, but thine, be done" (Luke 22:42).

Then began the longest journey any man has ever taken on this earth. He made His way over the torturous trail of human hate, submitted Himself to every indignity of man, suffered the dehumanizing agony of scourging, had His sensitive mind seared with the venom of false accusation. He who was God heard Himself called a devil.

Christ, the Friend of sinners, heard Himself described as an enemy of Caesar. I often wonder which was more painful for Him—living with us, or dying for us. Whatever the answer, Christ died for our sins, affording us infinite spiritual benefits we could not secure by any other means. "Who hath delivered us from the power of darkness, and hath translated us into the kingdom of his dear Son: in whom we have redemption through his blood, even the forgiveness of sins" (Colossians 1:13, 14).

39

It is because Christ died on the cross that I may find pardon, peace, and power at the throne of God. That death makes possible the reconciliation of man with God. "And you, that were sometime alienated and enemies in your mind by wicked works, yet now hath he reconciled" (verse 21).

Christ's death on the cross makes it unnecessary for any man to die in hell-fire. "The Lord is not slack concerning his promise, as some men count slackness; but is longsuffering to us-ward, not willing that any should perish, but that all should come to repentance" and "have everlasting life" (2 Peter 3:9; John 3:16). It is an encouraging fact that those who accept Christ as their Saviour, those who accept His sacrifice as an adequate atonement for their sins, those who accept His precious blood as their merit before God, those who accept the gift of Christ's life as their own payment of ransom, do not have to worry about the second death —the death in hell-fire. They will not perish; Christ has died for them.

The death of Christ at Calvary was a demonstration of His love. He knew the day would come when life would become too heavy a burden for all of His children, and they would need the encouragement of His companionship and love. So He gave Himself at Calvary as a constant and eternal reminder of His love. "God so loved the world, that he gave his only begotten Son," and "commendeth his love toward us, in that, while we were yet sinners, Christ died for us" (John 3:16; Romans 5:8).

Albert Buckner Coe tells the following incident: "When the body of Abraham Lincoln lay in state in Cleveland, Ohio, during the course of the sad funeral journey back to Illinois, an elderly black woman stood in line, holding a little child in her arms. After gazing a long time into the face of the emancipator of her

40

people, the woman whispered to her child, 'Take a long, long look, honey. That man died for you.' "

One of the most touching scenes in all of history is recorded in the third chapter of Genesis. After Adam and Eve sinned against God they ran and hid themselves. But the Bible says that "they heard the voice of the Lord God walking in the garden in the cool of the day. . . . And the Lord God called unto Adam, and said unto him, Where art thou?" (Genesis 3:8, 9).

What a picture! The Creator in search of His errant creatures. We might think that Adam would have sought God, in view of the fact that he had insulted God. But, no, the insulted seeks out the insulter. Erring man ran from God, but the love of God would not let him go. In the cool of the evening the voice of God is heard calling, "Adam, . . . Where art thou?" What further proof of love is needed? When man sinned, God came searching for him, and for thirty-three years Christ lived on this earth for him. On Calvary Christ died for him. No matter how dark the days may get, there is no excuse for doubting the deep, interested love of the Creator for all His creatures.

A little boy was the sole support of his invalid mother. He made a meager living by selling papers. Knowing that her birthday was near, he saved his money religiously and by her birthday he had thirty-five cents. With it, he ran to the florist for some flowers. He studied the floral arrangements, picked out the most expensive one in the house, and handed the florist thirty-five cents. In shocked disbelief the florist stared at the money and then at the little boy. He said, "Who are you buying these for, son?"

"I'm buying them for my mother," answered the boy. "This is her birthday. Is that enough money?" asked the little fellow.

Turning his back and wiping a tear from his eye the florist answered, "Yes, son, this is more than enough. You take these flowers to your mother."

Out of the store dashed the little boy, barely pausing to look to the right or the left. Suddenly there was a screeching of brakes, the smell of rubber, and the sickening crunch of metal hitting flesh. A torn little boy lay dying in his own blood, clutching the remnants of his floral wreath. Mike, the police officer, bent down over the dying form and said, "Is there anything I can do for you, son?"

"Yes," gasped the little boy. "Take these flowers to mamma. This is her birthday, and I don't want her to think that nobody thought of her. Give them to her and tell her that I love her." With that he died.

Hanging on the cross and soaked with His own blood, Christ bore the floral wreath of God's love for man. Even now He extends it to you and to me. However dark your path may be He wants you to know that He loves you, and He doesn't want you ever to forget that somebody is thinking of you.

Christ died at Calvary to expose Satan for what he really is. There's a poem that says,

> There are two guides for trav'lers, only two guides:
> One's the good Shepherd, e'en thro' the death tides;
> The other,—the serpent, beguiling with sin,
> Whose beauty external hides poison within,
> Hides poison within, death poison within.

Few men who follow the devil realize they are on the trail of the pied piper of hell, and that the glitter that gilds his rosy portrayals is fool's gold and tinseled silver. At Calvary Christ conquered, in that He forced Lucifer to lay bare the venom of his innermost nature for all the world to see. The universe witnessed the fury of men inspired by devils, and heard their bloodthirsty cry, "Let him be crucified. . . . His blood be on us and on our children." See the cruelty of the nails that pierce His hands and feet and the spear that rips open His side, the crown of thorns mercilessly pressed upon that innocent brow. Who can witness this scene and not love Jesus and better understand the nature of sin and Satan?

Yes, at Calvary the devil exposed himself for what he really was. He could not restrain his hellish enthusiasm in tormenting the Son of God. If Satan would treat the Son of God like that, what would he do to us?

So to the foot of the cross we go, for our ears and hearts have heard the invitation:

> Come, ye disconsolate, where'er ye languish;
> Come to the mercy seat, fervently kneel;
> Here bring your wounded hearts, here tell your anguish;
> Earth hath no sorrow that heaven cannot heal.

Christ died on the cross to vindicate His law. He knew the day would come when men would practice what is known as the new morality. Under this theory all external forms of discipline are to be cast aside and a man is to decide for himself what is right and what is wrong. This foolish proposition would make the human brain the court of final appeal, and man the source of ultimate authority. What more would a man need to declare himself God, if the new morality be true? Jesus died on the cross to say to the world that His law is forever binding, that God has jurisdiction over the earth, and that for his best good in this life and his entrance into the life to come man must submit himself to the mandates of Jehovah.

There is Someone who tells us what to do and that Someone is God. He has earned that right, both by Creation and redemption. He made us, and He paid with His life to buy us back from the enemy of our souls. The death of Christ on the cross was submission to the claims of the law of God. Man had violated the law of God and was thus a sinner. By taking man's place before the bar of justice and paying the penalty for breaking the law, Christ insured its perpetuity and made it clear to the human family that His commandments would be forever binding. He can point to the shedding of His own blood as evidence that the law is still in force, for it was the broken law that claimed the life of its transgressor. "Believe on the Lord Jesus Christ, and thou shalt be saved, and thy house" (Acts 16:31).

He arose, He arose, He arose from the dead,
And the Lord shall bear my spirit home.

"He Arose From the Dead"

THE TOMB of Joseph of Arimathea is now empty! "In the end of the sabbath, as it began to dawn toward the first day of the week, came Mary Magdalene and the other Mary to see the sepulchre" (Matthew 28:1).

In the steel-gray chill of dawn these believing women sought their Lord. A heavenly messenger met them with surprising news: "Fear not ye: for I know that ye seek Jesus, which was crucified. He is not here: for he is risen, as he said. Come, see the place where the Lord lay" (verses 5, 6).

After the resurrection Christ was careful to establish the fact of His living presence. "And that he was buried, and that he rose again the third day according to the scriptures: and that he was seen of Cephas, then of the twelve: after that, he was seen of above five hundred brethren at once. . . . After that, he was seen of James; then of all the apostles" (1 Corinthians 15:4-7).

C. C. Lorimer has thus described the resurrection: "Lo! from the distant south with gleeful and giddy wing, the birds return, the fragile flowers, with radiant hues and aromatic breath, revive with winter's cold embrace; and from fragrant climes the gentle winds come back, laden with odors sweet and quickening warmth; and thus may Jesus thrust aside the gateway of the stone before His clammy prison, and reappear to His rejoicing saints, bearing to them from the realms of the invisible, sweet messages of immortal blessedness. And thus He conquered; for as the Paschal sun arose from the chills and fogs of the somber night, filling the earth with lustrous beauty, so, on that morning, Jesus ascended from the realms of death, and dispersed the awful gloom that enshrouded the moral world."

And so Christ ascended on high, leading captivity captive, to begin a work for us that none but He could do. "For Christ is not entered into the holy places made with hands, which are the figures of the true; but into heaven itself, now to appear in the presence of God for us" (Hebrews 9:24).

Men and women throughout all human history have pondered the question of accountability. The majority of us believe that there is a God. Some men worship idols; others worship the true and living God. If there is indeed a God in this world—and the Bible clearly teaches that there is—then the question of accountability is a very real one. If a child has a parent, then that child is accountable to the parent for his behavior until he reaches the age of accountability. Likewise it is true that the great God of the universe, who is indeed the Father of us all, certainly has as one of His prerogatives the moral right to require of human beings an accounting of their stewardship. By that we mean, What are you doing with your life? What are you doing with your

47

The stone was rolled away, and Jesus arose from the grave, giving assurance that He can and will raise us from the dead also.

time? What about that brain of yours? How do you use it? And what about the talents God gave you? These are the great questions involved in the subject of the judgment.

In Acts 1:11 we encounter the ascension of Jesus Christ. He was born, as you know, of a virgin, walked the earth for approximately thirty-three years. He was crucified for our sins at Calvary, but rose again three days later, on the first day of the week. Where did He go? "Ye men of Galilee, why stand ye gazing up into heaven? this same Jesus, which is taken up from you into heaven, shall so come in like manner as ye have seen him go into heaven" (Acts 1:11). There is no question as to where Christ went or where He is. The Bible clearly teaches that He went to heaven. Hebrews 1:3 tells us that He is sitting at "the right hand of the Majesty" in the heavens. "The Lord is in his holy temple, the Lord's throne is in heaven" (Psalm 11:4).

Hebrews 8:1, 2 makes it clear that Christ entered the tabernacle in the heavens, the great temple in the sky, there to perform a work for human beings they cannot perform for themselves.

Revelation 15:5 makes it very clear that there is a temple in the sky—a great sanctuary in heaven. "And after that I looked, and, behold, the temple of the tabernacle of the testimony in heaven was opened." Verse 6 says: "And the seven angels came out of the temple, having the seven plagues, clothed in pure and white linen, and having their breasts girded with golden girdles." This text emphasizes that there *is* a temple in the sky, a tabernacle in heaven to which our Lord ascended on that great day, there to make intercession for us.

It will pay us, as we contemplate this great temple in the sky, to go back and examine God's temple on earth—a great sanctuary built as a type of the one that is in heaven. We read about it in Hebrews 9:1-3: "Then verily the first covenant had also ordinances of divine service, and a worldly sanctuary. For there was a tabernacle made; the first, wherein was the candlestick, and the table, and the shewbread; which is called the sanctuary. And after the second veil, the tabernacle which is called the Holiest of all."

Paul goes on to explain the significance of this earthly sanctuary. He makes clear in Hebrews 8:5 that it was patterned after the one in heaven. It was a figure of the one in heaven (Hebrews 9:9, 23). The earthly was patterned after things in the heavens, not an exact replica of it. A view of the earthly gives us a faint idea of what the heavenly tabernacle is like, but cannot equal it in glory. Nothing on earth can reveal the full splendor of heavenly things. When Christ left this earth He entered the temple in heaven, there to embark upon a most important phase of the work of salvation.

Hebrews 9:24 tells us that Jesus went into the heavenly temple: "For Christ is not entered into the holy places made with hands, which are the figures of the true; but into heaven itself, now to appear in the presence of God for us." What He is doing there is clear—He is appearing in the presence of God for us. His ministry there includes a work of judgment: "I beheld till the thrones were cast down, and the Ancient of days did sit, whose garment was white as snow, and the hair of his head like the pure wool: his throne was like the fiery flame, and his wheels as burning fire. A fiery stream issued and came forth from before him: thousand thousands ministered unto him, and ten thousand times ten thousand stood before him: the judgment was set, and the books were opened" (Daniel 7:9, 10). We have here a picture of Christ

4

entering the great temple in the sky to begin a work of intercession and judgment for the saints. This is the great work in which Christ even now ministers on behalf of His people.

1 John 2:1 states the nature of Christ's work in heaven: "My little children, these things write I unto you, that ye sin not. And if any man sin, we have an advocate with the Father, Jesus Christ the righteous." The initial phase of Christ's ministry in heaven was one of intercession, mediation, and substitution. But this eventually led to another aspect of His ministry—the work of judgment, of examining lives and records, of determining each person's eternal destiny. In Revelation 22:12 Christ says, "Behold, I come quickly; and my reward is with me, to give every man according as his work shall be." Even now He is determining what our reward will be. He does this on the basis of the merit He offers us under the divine provision of justification, and on the basis of the way we live. He takes into consideration every man's opportunity to know truth, and his faithfulness in responding to his opportunity. This is the broad spectrum of the judgment now going on in heaven for the sins of men and for the sake of the saints.

But Christ is doing even more than that: "Nevertheless I tell you the truth; It is expedient for you that I go away: for if I go not away, the Comforter will not come unto you; but if I depart, I will send him unto you" (John 16:7). Not only does Christ judge, not only does He intercede, not only does He substitute, not only does He mediate, He sent us the Holy Ghost. The second chapter of Acts relates how He fulfilled this promise, for on the day of Pentecost when the disciples were all together in one place and were of one accord, the Holy Ghost descended upon them and began His work for them.

50

So today, my friends, we have not been left comfortless. We have not been left to find our own way through the maze of this earthly existence, through this vale of wrath and tears. It is true that in every life the cup of sorrow runs over. Death, disease, sickness, and a million other ills plague the human family. How comforting to know that the third person of the Godhead is with us right here on earth, twenty-four hours a day. He takes our needs and petitions and presents them to our Master in heaven, and He in turn, as our advocate, mediator, and intercessor, presents them before the judgment throne. Thus God is reconciling the world unto Himself.

But God is doing something else very important for us, to which we now turn our attention. In John 14:1-3 He said, "Let not your heart be troubled: ye believe in God, believe also in me. In my Father's house are many mansions: if it were not so, I would have told you. I go to prepare a place for you. And if I go and prepare a place for you, I will come again, and receive you unto myself; that where I am, there ye may be also." That little phrase, "I go to prepare a place for you," is interesting because it relates definitely to the work of Christ as our intercessor (Hebrews 7:24), substitute (Romans 5:10), mediator (Hebrews 7:24), and judge (Daniel 7:9, 10). This sweeping divine operation is summarized in that phrase of Christ's "I go to prepare a place for you." It takes all of this for Him to establish our right to heaven.

A few years ago in this great nation people of darker skins were barred from some public accommodations such as eating places and hotels; but there came a change. Dr. Martin Luther King and his young followers began to enter these places and demonstrate against this evil. Then what happened? The law was changed, and today a man can make use of most of the public accommodations across the nation without regard to his color. Dr. King and those with him opened a way for black men to follow, establishing the equal rights of all men to enjoy all public accommodations. In a similar sense when Christ says, "I go to prepare a place for you," He establishes man's right to go to heaven.

When man sinned he was dispossessed and had no rightful home of his own. But Christ said not to let this trouble us: "I go to prepare a place for you. And if I go to prepare a place for you, I will come again, and receive you unto myself."

So today, even as we worship, Christ is interceding, substituting, offering His body and His perfect life as an atonement for our sins; He is mediating, reconciling God and man; He is judging on our behalf—in order to prepare a place for us and to establish our right to enter in through the gates into the city of our God.

It was important to us that Christ rose from the dead. We can better understand the statement of the apostle Paul in Romans 4:25 that He "was delivered for our offences and was raised again for our justification." What Christ is doing now in the heavenly tabernacle makes possible our justification. He is ministering as our high priest in the sanctuary, that He may declare us just on the merits of His shed blood. Had Christ not risen from the dead, all that He did before that event would have been meaningless. But His bursting of the tomb says to every Christian, You serve a living Saviour. The resurrection of our Lord ensures our own exodus from the grave. One day the dead in Christ shall rise first. In 1 Corinthians 15:17-20 the apostle Paul, however, bases the resurrection of the righteous dead on the resurrection of Christ: "And if Christ be not raised, your faith is vain; ye are yet in your sins. Then they also which are fallen asleep in Christ are perished. . . . But now is Christ risen from the dead, and become the first fruits of them that slept."

So, in a very real sense, the future of humanity trembled in the balance in the steel-gray haze of the Easter sunrise, as the earth awaited the resurrection of our Lord. Then came the sound of an angel as of a trumpet's blast, summoning the Creator from His earthly prison. As He came forth from the tomb He had the keys of death, hell, and the grave in His hands, having demonstrated before men and angels the truth of His declaration, "I am the resurrection, and the life."

I looked over Jordan, and what did I see? . . .
A band of angels coming after me. . . .
Swing low sweet chariot.

"Swing Low Sweet Chariot"

WILL JESUS CHRIST come back to earth? What will His coming be like? Can we have some idea of when His coming is near? Fortunately, the Bible answers all of these questions. According to 1 Thessalonians 4:16-18, "The Lord himself shall descend from heaven with a shout, with the voice of the archangel, and with the trump of God: and the dead in Christ shall rise first: then we which are alive and remain shall be caught up together with them in the clouds, to meet the Lord in the air: and so shall we ever be with the Lord. Wherefore comfort one another with these words."

The same Jesus who was born as a Babe in a manger because there was no room in the inn for Him; who walked the earth for thirty-three years, giving sight to the blind, speech to the dumb, and causing the lame to walk; the same Jesus who was crucified at Calvary for our sins; and who "was wounded

55

"The Lord himself shall descend from heaven with a shout, . . . with the trump of God: and the dead in Christ shall rise first."

for our transgressions" and was "bruised for our iniquities" (Isaiah 53:5); who was buried in the tomb and arose from the dead—this same Jesus has promised to come again. This is the significance of the expression "the Lord himself." There can be no case of mistaken identity here. The Christ who was crucified is alive today and has not forgotten His faithful children here on earth. He will return!

The apostle John wrote: "Behold, he cometh with clouds; and every eye shall see him, and they also which pierced him: and all kindreds of the earth shall wail because of him" (Revelation 1:7).

Nothing is more clearly taught in the Scriptures than that Jesus Christ will come again to the earth: "Our God shall come, and shall not keep silence: a fire shall devour before him, and it shall be very tempestuous round about him" (Psalm 50:3).

People often ask about the manner of Christ's coming. Some think He will come secretly and steal His people away, and that the wicked will know that Christ has come only after the righteous have been translated in a secret rapture. According to this theory a man driving a bus will suddenly disappear along with the righteous passengers, leaving the bus stalled on the street corner. Is this true? What does the Bible say?

"And then shall appear the sign of the Son of man in heaven: and then shall all the tribes of the earth mourn, and they shall see the Son of man coming in the clouds of heaven with power and great glory" (Matthew 24:30).

This is no secret rapture. This is not Christ stealing into the earth to take away the saints. This is a literal, visible, public event. The Bible says that every eye will see Him. The Scriptures say all the kindreds of the earth will mourn or wail because of Him. The Scriptures say that the sign of the Son of man will appear in the heavens. Jesus Himself said, "For as the lightning cometh out of the east, and shineth even unto the west; so shall also the coming of the Son of man be" (verse 27). A bolt of lightning cannot very well be hid from public view.

I think I know where the secret rapture theory got its origin. The Bible says that the day of the Lord will come as a thief in the night. We read that in 2 Peter 3:10. But it goes on to speak of the very visible shaking of the earth and the momentous events that will accompany the coming of Christ. Thieves sneak in quietly under cover of darkness and do their work, but robbers come at midday and publicly hold up a bank, take all the money, and walk out in full view of the citizenry. The word "thief" in 2 Peter 3:10 does not indicate that the coming of Christ will be a silent event, but that He will come unexpectedly, just as the thief does. Few will be looking for Him. It is in this sense that Christ will come as a thief.

Isaiah foretold a terrible shaking of the earth at Christ's coming, and he describes how men will react to it: "And they shall go into the holes of the rocks, and into the caves of the earth, for fear of the Lord, and for the glory of his majesty, when he ariseth to shake terribly the earth. In that day a man shall cast his idols of silver, and his idols of gold, which they made each one for himself to worship, to the moles and to the bats; to go into the clefts of the rocks, and into the tops of the ragged rocks, for fear of the Lord, and for the glory of his majesty, when he ariseth to shake terribly the earth" (Isaiah 2:19-21).

A little boy in a classroom was asked by his teacher, "Suppose you knew that the king of England was going to visit this classroom. What would you do?"

57

The little boy replied, "I'd get ready."

"Well," asked the teacher, "suppose you knew the king of England was coming and he told you exactly what time he was coming. What would you do?"

Said the little boy, "I'd get ready."

"Suppose you were told that the king was coming but you did not know exactly when he was coming. What would you do?"

"Well," said the little boy, "I'd get ready and stay ready."

In view of the earth-shaking events that will accompany the coming of our Lord, it behooves us all not only to get ready but to be in a constant state of readiness, for we know not the day nor the hour of His coming. The Bible does, however, clearly indicate that we may know when that event is near. We can know with certainty that the coming of the Lord is near, even though we cannot tell the year, the month, the day, or the hour.

In Matthew 24 and Luke 21 Christ gives us certain signs of the nearness of His second coming: "For nation shall rise against nation, and kingdom against kingdom: and there shall be famines, and pestilences, and earthquakes, in divers places" (Matthew 24:7). We need not pause long to analyze this text. It reads like the headlines of a modern-day newspaper. Someone will say that there have always been wars, famines, pestilences, and earthquakes. But never in the history of the world have wars been so violent, so continuous, and so devastating in their effects. There has always been hunger, but never before in the history of the world has the human family been threatened with a population explosion like that of our day and with the food shortage it portends. We have clearly come to the aggravated state of affairs Christ here foretells, and these signs indicate that the coming of our Lord Jesus Christ is at hand. Soon "he shall send his angels with a great sound of a trumpet" (verse 31).

We stand at the threshold of tremendous events, and we should pause at this point to examine the significance of the coming of Christ to the individual Christian and sinner: "Beloved, now are we the sons of God, and it doth not yet appear what we shall be: but we know that, when he shall appear, we shall be like him; for we shall see him as he is" (1 John 3:2). "When he shall appear, we shall be like him"—our bodies will be transformed to be like His own glorious body (Philippians 3:21). At the coming of the Lord, men all over the earth who suffer from disease and from the limitations of these sin-cursed human bodies will at last be delivered.

Our text also says that we shall see Him as He is. This side of the cross we have never had the privilege of seeing our Lord and Master. In that day we shall see Him face to face. In the language of the hymn writer:

> Face to face shall I behold Him,
> Far beyond the starry sky;
> Face to face in all His glory,
> I shall see Him by and by!

But the coming of the Lord will bring another advantage to the human family. It will mean the end of man's bungling administration of the affairs of this earth. For six thousand years men have tried to run this world without God, and in the process they have solved none of earth's major problems. To this very day we stand within the shadow of the war to end wars, and the extinction of the human family seems but a matter of time. The coming of the Lord will bring this process of self-destruction to a halt. God made this earth, and He will one day put an end to man's bungling reign of sin.

The coming of Christ will also mean adventures in space for all of us, for we "shall be caught up together with them in the clouds, to meet the Lord in the air: and so shall we ever be with the Lord" (1 Thessalonians 4:17).

This whole world is doomed to destruction, but the Christian will be taken out of it to a city that has foundations, whose builder and maker is God. The coming of Christ will mean reunion with loved ones. We have been separated from those we love by death. But at the coming of the Lord there will be a resurrection of the dead, and we who have been separated will be reunited and swept past the sun, moon, and stars to be forever with the Lord. Should we not then heed the injunction of Hosea 10:12: "Sow to yourselves in righteousness, reap in mercy; break up your fallow ground: for it is time to seek the Lord, till he come and rain righteousness upon you"?

"Seek ye the Lord while he may be found, call ye upon him while he is near: let the wicked forsake his way, and the unrighteous man his thoughts" (Isaiah 55:6, 7).

The coming of the Lord is near. It is even at the door.

> Lift up the trumpet, and loud let it ring:
> Jesus is coming again!
> Cheer up, ye pilgrims, be joyful and sing;
> Jesus is coming again!

All the signs that indicate His coming are fast being fulfilled. May we see in them a warning to prepare to meet our God!

During the Civil War, the forces of General Johnston were in retreat. Conditions were favorable for a Northern victory, so General Sheridan took a trip to Washington. While he was there the fortunes of the North sank to a new low, for a Southern counterattack split the Northern armies. News of this reached Washington, and Sheridan hastened south as rapidly as possible. As he rode along he came upon his bedraggled troops, and inquired what was going on. They told him that the Southern army had carried the field, and that his own army was in retreat. "But," they added hopefully, "everything will be all right when you get there."

As we look about us today, it would seem as though the enemy of the Lord has carried the field of battle. The wickedness of man is great in the earth. It appears that the flood tide of evil will completely bury the good, but we have faith that everything will be all right when Christ gets here.

General MacArthur was spirited away from the Philippine Islands in a submarine, but he vowed he would return. Long weary months of preparation passed before he could fulfill his promise. During that time the Philippine Islands echoed and reechoed with the sound of horrible atrocities, and it seemed that all hope was lost. During my visit to the Philippine Islands many of the inhabitants told me the one thing that kept them going was the hope that General MacArthur would keep his promise. He did return, and the Philippine Islands were liberated from the hands of the enemy.

The Bible says that Christ will return, that He will put His enemies under His feet, and that He will take those who have believed in Him and followed Him and loved Him, out of this world to a better place where there are better things. The dismal circumstances surrounding us must not dim our faith in His coming. Amid the encircling gloom our faith may shine even brighter, for Jesus said: "When these things begin to come to pass, then look up, and lift up your heads; for your redemption draweth nigh. . . . Behold the fig tree, and all the trees; when they now shoot forth, ye see and know of your own selves that summer is now nigh at hand. So likewise ye, when ye see these things come to pass, know ye that the kingdom of God is nigh at hand" (Luke 21:28-31).

Elijah stood talking to his friend Elisha. Both knew that soon Elijah was to be taken out of the earth without seeing death. They were rapt in earnest conversation when suddenly out of the sky came the flaming brilliance of a fiery chariot. It swung low and then swerved heavenward, bearing its precious earthly cargo with it. This scene will be repeated when the heavens are parted as a scroll and angels of God sweep low to gather the righteous and transport them to the paradise of God.

Ride on, King, ride on, King Jesus,
Ride on, conquering King,
I want to go to heaven in the morning.

"Ride On, King Jesus"

CHRIST, THOUGH ABSENT in the flesh, is still King of the earth. He has lost neither interest in nor control of human affairs. Man's attempt to assume control of his own destiny has succeeded only in making him a slave of sin and human tyranny. Six thousand years of history have glorified the warrior, the dictator, and the power-hungry emperor. Though often forgotten, the God of heaven still functions effectively on this planet. "The most High ruleth in the kingdom of men" (Daniel 4:17).

Sometimes it does seem that affairs get out of hand. When a war breaks out and carnage begins, we all wonder why God doesn't stop it. It apparently never occurs to us that God didn't start it. Out text says that the Most High ruleth in the kingdom and sets over it the basest of men. Why would God do that? Why would He allow the basest of men to take over the kingdom from time to time?

First of all, let us note that the Bible does not say that every man who becomes head of a nation is a base man. What it does say is that sooner or later God allows the basest of men to come to power. Why? The answer is simple.

Back when God created the earth, He ordained man to control himself. It was not His purpose that man should control other men. According to Genesis 1:28, God gave man his dominion—"over the fish of the sea, and over the fowl of the air, and over every living thing that moveth upon the earth." Notice that God gave man dominion over everything that moves on the earth except his fellow men. He created man in His own image, and only God can control a being in His own image. This explains why six thousand years of human authority have been a failure, and why sooner or later man rebels against his fellow man. This rule simply doesn't work. You see, God originally planned to rule man Himself. And today, only as God controls him is man able to live peacefully and in harmony with his fellow man. This is why, from time to time, wars break out. Men who are not under the control of God presume to assert their will over their fellow men. There is war on earth for the same reason there was war in heaven—the will of a created being struggling against the will of God. There can be no peace between men until the Prince of Peace rules in their hearts.

So, the Most High rules in the affairs of men and permits the basest of men to come to power from time to time in order to remind man of the days in the time of the Garden of Eden when God Himself ruled man. When God ruled man there was no war, no famine, no earthquake, no pestilence, no fighting, no divorce. None of the negative things that have come to pass since man took over his own affairs were in existence when man

5

Heaven opens and King Jesus rides forth in power and glory on a white horse, conquering and to conquer (Rev. 19:11-14).

submitted himself to God's rule. Now God allows the basest of men to come to power that we may realize how wonderful it will be when the kingdoms of this world become the kingdom of our Lord and of His Christ. Then the re-creation of the world will take place and man will be resettled in the paradise he once lost through sin.

But my message for you includes more than this. It says that the world is *not* out of control, even though things appear that way. It says that there is a divine hand on the wheel and that God will permit men and devils to go only so far and then He will bring them in check.

Three levels of authority concern man. First of all, let us talk about angelic authority. Yes, there are angels in this world—good angels and bad angels. The evil angels are trying to assert their authority over the human heart and there are men being controlled by devils, by evil spirits, right here on this earth.

Authority is the central question of Christianity. Who is going to control your life? Who is going to be your Lord? Who is going to be your master? Will it be a fallen angel? There are some men who have submitted their lives to fallen angels.

There is also what we call human authority, of which there are two kinds. First are those persons who are governed by current consensus. What society thinks of this or that is their basis for determining right and wrong. If society accepts it, it's right; if society condemns it, it's wrong. But that approach to the problem is totally out of harmony with the Scriptures. Right and wrong were determined before man was created. The Bible contains the only measuring stick by which we may determine what is right and wrong. It does not depend on what you or I think, or what our friends think, or even on a universal consensus. Right and wrong are determined by what God says. We will come to the question of divine authority in a moment.

I have pointed out that some people's lives are being ruled by other people through custom and tradition. The next type of human authority, I think, is that of our own minds and wills. Some people don't acknowledge God. They interpose their own thinking, their own wills between themselves and God. They want to have their own way. Their attitude is like that of a child who doesn't want to submit to the authority of a parent. Every time the parent tells him to do something, the child rebels. He has the will of a mule; he won't submit, he won't accept discipline, he won't come into line.

This is usurped authority. It is treasonable for a man to assert his will over the will of God. It is treasonable for a man to allow society to come between him and God or to allow evil angels to dictate his actions. The only legitimate authority on this earth is divine authority. Divine authority is legitimate because God created man, and then redeemed man—bought him back after he sinned. So divine authority is based on two foundations.

When you buy an automobile the factory sends a little book along that tells you how to treat the car. In a sense that is authority, and it is authentic authority, because the people who made that car know more about it than the man who buys it. They have every right to tell the buyer how to treat his car to receive the most service from it. Indeed, if those who made the car did not give this service, the buyer might be able to sue the manufacturer when something went wrong, on the assumption that the manufacturer should have explained how the car works and what has to be done to service it and keep it in good working order.

Now, divine authority is based on the fact that God created man and everything in the earth, indeed, in the universe. That's why He has a right to tell men what to do, to issue orders and expect man to obey. We read in Isaiah 45:12: "I have made the earth, and created man upon it: I, even my hands, have stretched out the heavens, and all their host have I commanded," and in chapter 46:9: "Remember the former things of old: for I am God, and there is none else; I am God, and there is none like me." You see, God bases His authority on the fact that He made everything, and the Maker alone knows what is best.

The apostle Paul asks if a created being has the right to argue with its creator. Should the potter be instructed by the pot? he asks.

The only authentic authority in the world is divine, for divine authority created and then redeemed man. "What? know ye not that your body is the temple of the Holy Ghost which is in you, which ye have of God, and ye are not your own? For ye are bought with a price: therefore glorify God in your body, and in your spirit, which are God's" (1 Corinthians 6:19, 20).

So we face the fact of divine authority—of God's right to define right and wrong, to command. No man can command without authority. Look at the army. The only people giving orders there are men in authority. The corporal, the sergeant, the major, the general, the colonel—all can give orders because they are in authority. So also the great God has the right to authorize, to command, to save, to condemn, to reward, to punish.

Some people wail when they get what they deserve. They don't like the principle in Galatians 6:7 that says, "Be not deceived; God is not mocked: for whatsoever a man soweth, that shall he also reap." They can't live with that. They question the right of God to bring back upon man's head the results of his deeds and his decisions. I never question it, because the great God is the Creator. He created man, and made the laws by which man is to live. Because God loves man He will never require anything impossible of man, and He will never direct man in a way that is not for his best good.

There often comes a conflict between divine authority and human authority. In Daniel 3 Shadrach, Meshach, and Abednego stood before King Nebuchadnezzar, who commanded that when the music went forth every subject of the kingdom should bow down to a golden image he had erected on the Plain of Dura. This order contravened the commandment of God that says, "Thou shalt not make unto thee any graven image, or any likeness of any thing that is in heaven above, or that is in the earth beneath, or that is in the water under the earth: thou shalt not bow down thyself to them, nor serve them: for I the Lord thy God am a jealous God, visiting the iniquity of the fathers upon the children unto the third and fourth generation of them that hate me; and shewing mercy unto thousands of them that love me, and keep my commandments" (Exodus 20:4-6).

The God of heaven has forbidden the worship of idols, the bowing down before images and statues, but that was precisely what the king commanded Shadrach, Meshach, and Abednego to do. They chose to obey God rather than man, and because of this they were cast into a burning, fiery furnace. But miracle of miracles! When the king came out to look with satisfaction upon the work of the flames, he saw four men walking untouched and unhurt. "And the form of the fourth is like the Son of God," he said (Daniel 3:25). This is double reassurance that whether we suffer the depth of deprivation or soar to the highest height of human privilege, we may be assured of the Master's presence with us—in sickness and in health, in prosperity and adversity.

When the time comes for you to lay aside this old world as a garment outworn, outgrown,

> . . . go not, like the quarry-slave at night,
> Scourged to his dungeon, but, sustained and soothed
> By an unfaltering trust, approach thy grave,
> Like one who wraps the drapery of his couch
> About him, and lies down to pleasant dreams.
> —WILLIAM CULLEN BRYANT

Sweet little Jesus Boy, they made You
be born in a manger;
Sweet little Glory Child, didn't know
who You were.

"Didn't Know Who
You Were"

FOR CENTURIES prophets looked forward to the coming of the Messiah, the Deliverer of God's people. Isaiah wrote: "For unto us a child is born, unto us a son is given: and the government shall be upon his shoulder: and his name shall be called Wonderful, Counsellor, The mighty God, The everlasting Father, The Prince of Peace" (Isaiah 9:6).

God was to take on the nature of a man and live among men, facing the problems that men face. Never again could Heaven be accused of not understanding men. In Christ, God would effect a reconciliation between man and God. In Christ, God would become a part of the human family by blood, a fact He would never change throughout a million eternities. So, "when the fulness of the time was come, God sent forth his Son, . . . to redeem them that were under the law, that we might receive the adoption of sons" (Galatians 4:4, 5).

71

Christ not only came, but it was announced in advance why He was coming. Man had violated the law of God, and it was this law that condemned him to death. Christ came to take man's place, to redeem man from the consequences of the law, to restore him to the position of an adopted son of God by grace through the Lord Jesus Christ. So it happened in far-off Judea some nineteen hundred years ago that shepherds were tending their flocks by night when the stillness was broken by the sweet strains of the angelic choir, singing, "Glory to God in the highest, and on earth peace, good will toward men" (Luke 2:14). The shepherds were told, "For unto you is born this day in the city of David a Saviour, which is Christ the Lord" (verse 11). They were directed to the manger in Bethlehem.

Christ was born in a stable, born as the poorest of the poor. During His ministry there is no evidence that He had a large wardrobe. Said He of Himself: "The foxes have holes, and the birds of the air have nests; but the Son of man hath not where to lay his head" (Matthew 8:20). So the most poverty stricken can look to Him and find an understanding heart and a sympathetic ear.

Furthermore, Christ was a citizen of Nazareth. To some this would mean that He grew up on the wrong side of the tracks. Nazareth had such a reputation that someone asked, "Can there any good thing come out of Nazareth?" (John 1:46). Yes, the Saviour grew up in Nazareth so that men and women, wherever they are, might know that in Christ they can find one who understands. Further, they may know that a man is valued not on where he is from but on what he is and where he is headed. Furthermore, Christ was rejected. "He came unto his own, and his own received him not" (verse 11).

72

Yes, Christ knew what it was to be an outsider. Segregation and discrimination were His daily fare. His many-sided teachings concerning man's relationship with his fellow man were designed to rid society of these ills, but He experienced them Himself, so that any man on earth, so treated, may know that in Christ he will find a sympathetic heart, an understanding mind, a listening ear.

There is no evidence that Christ ever attended school while on earth. Upon one occasion, some listening to Him were heard to exclaim in surprise at His wisdom, knowing that He had not attended the schools of the scribes and Pharisees. But in Him was all wisdom, for He was God as well as man. Yet in Christ, even the uneducated can find sympathy and understanding. He was courteous and gracious and cultured above all men, toward all with whom He came in contact. This was the manner of the King that He was, and is, though in His divine nature He had sat on the throne of the universe and received the obeisance of angels. All of this the men of His day little understood. The language of the spiritual is true—"didn't know who You were."

Society of His day ignored Him, and men of power avoided all contact with Him except that which they considered necessary. I read of none of the great banking interests of His day seeking His advice in fiscal matters, and Caesar seemed to be unaware of His existence. But He was here, and the world did not know then what it knows now, namely, that what He did for man would be told and retold years after the most haughty dictator was forgotten.

Of His birth the angel explained to Mary, "The Holy Ghost shall come upon thee, and the power of the Highest shall overshadow thee: therefore also that holy thing which shall be born of thee shall be called the Son of God" (Luke 1:35). Before He came to this earth in the form of a baby, Jesus Christ was God: "In the beginning was the Word, and the Word was with God, and the Word was God" (John 1:1). "And the Word was made flesh, and dwelt among us, (and we beheld his glory, the glory as of the only begotten of the Father,) full of grace and truth" (verse 14).

It is therefore clear that to share the experiences of the human family Christ had to take on human nature, and divine wisdom achieved this at the Incarnation. Christ as God in the womb of Mary partook of human nature and became the God-man, spirit and flesh. Man needed a savior who understood through experience both God and man. Jesus Christ was as truly God as if He were not man and yet as truly man as if He were not God. Christ tailored Himself to the needs of humanity, and stands today as our representative. At the same time He is what He has always been—"The mighty God, The everlasting Father, The Prince of Peace" (Isaiah 9:6).

It was Christ who created this world. He was before the world was: "O Father, glorify thou me with thine own self with the glory which I had with thee before the world was" (John 17:5), Jesus prayed.

Of Him John spoke, "This was he of whom I spake, He that cometh after me is preferred before me: for he was before me" (chapter 1:15). John was older than was Jesus, but he recognized in Jesus the Son of God and knew that Christ had existed long before he did. But in the same chapter of John, the third verse, we read, "All things were made by him; and without him was not any thing made that was made."

"For by him were all things created, that are in heaven, and that are in earth, visible and invisible, whether they be thrones, or dominions, or principalities, or powers: all things were created by him, and for him" (Colossians 1:16).

Considering the way that men treated Christ while He was here, we can but conclude that "they didn't know who You were."

Not only is Christ the Creator of this world, He is its Redeemer also. "Giving thanks unto the Father, which hath made us meet to be partakers of the inheritance of the saints in light: who hath delivered us from the power of darkness, and hath translated us into the kingdom of his dear Son: in whom we have redemption through his blood, even the forgiveness of sins" (Colossians 1:12-14).

By sinning against God, man separated himself forever from divine favor unless some means was devised for his ultimate restoration. Man needed a redeemer, a substitute, a friend who would take his place before the judgment bar of God and bear the guilt and penalty for transgression. Jesus did this willingly out of a heart of love.

"But God commendeth his love toward us, in that, while we were yet sinners, Christ died for us. Much more then, being now justified by his blood, we shall be saved from wrath through him. For if, when we were enemies, we were reconciled to God by the death of his Son, much more, being reconciled, we shall be saved by his life" (Romans 5:8-10).

The story is told of a little boy who was sailing his small boat on the city lake when a wind suddenly caught it and bore it away downstream. The little boy was heartbroken as he made his way home, for he didn't think he would ever see his little boat again. One day while walking downtown, he looked into a store window and there was his little sailboat, waiting for someone to buy it. He rushed in and claimed it. "Mister, please give me my boat."

The man said, "Son, you'll have to pay five dollars for this boat or somebody else will. You have no proof that this is your boat."

The little boy said, "Will you hold it for me for a week?"

The proprietor said, "I'll do that," and he took the boat out of the window.

The little boy got himself a job, worked hard, and earned the five dollars. With great joy he went down on Friday, bought his boat, and as he walked down the street, clutching it to his bosom, he said, "Little boat, you're mine twice now. You are mine because I made you. Then I lost you, but now you are mine again because I bought you back."

It was Christ who made us, and after we were lost He bought us back. We are His twice now. Let us live for Him.

My God is real, real in my soul,
My God is real for He has washed and made
  me whole;
His love for me is like pure gold,
My God is real for I can feel
Him in my soul.

"God Is Real"

A FEW MONTHS AGO a magazine cover with black background and red letters trumpeted the question, "Is God Dead?" Thousands of believing Christians shout their answer, "No!" Plant and animal kingdoms answer, "No!" Millions of planets, galaxies, and solar systems say, "No!" The mighty ocean hurls its waves against the shore with a resounding "No!" The song of the mockingbird, the scream of the leopard, and the roar of the lion add their volume to the chorus, "No!" God is real, not imaginary; alive, not dead!

The atheist says there is no God. The infidel is against God. The agnostic says that he doesn't know whether there is a God out there after all. Some theologians say God used to be alive but that He is dead now. Others say that He is on sabbatical leave or that He's lost His power and authority over the world or that He is so busy that He doesn't have time for us down here.

The Word of God teaches something different, however. If you should wish to learn about electricity, you would read a book on electricity by a well-known authority. If you wanted to learn about cooking, you would read a book on cooking by an authority on cooking. If you want to know about God, you read the only authoritative Book in the world about God—and that's the Bible. What does the Bible say about God?

"The fool hath said in his heart, there is no God" (Psalm 14:1). I'm not going to comment on that verse, because I don't want to be insulting. The only point I want to make is that there is a God somewhere, and the man who denies it is labeled with a very uncomplimentary term. Think about that for a moment. This world on which we live is probably only one of millions of planets spinning through space. Who figured out the order and the harmony in this universe—the fact that planet does not collide with planet, the fact that our world orbits the sun and turns on its own axis? Who designed the order on this planet itself— the design of the flower, the blade of grass, the multi-systemed human being who walks the earth, every system working in perfect balance with every other system? It took a brain to figure all this out.

The Bible says that God did it, and that makes sense to me. "And hath made of one blood all nations of men for to dwell on all the face of the earth, and hath determined the times before appointed, and the bounds of their habitation; that they should seek the Lord, if haply they might feel after him, and find him, though he be not far from every one of us: for in him we live, and move, and have our being; as certain also of your own poets have said, For we are also his offspring" (Acts 17:26-28).

So man is the offspring of God, and God is the great power that holds the universe together. He is the Conceiver of the universe. No wonder He says, "Thou shalt have no other gods before me" (Exodus 20:3). We reject Pantheism, idolatry, and the worship of substitute gods.

The first thing we should know about God is that He is personal. He is not just an influence. He is a being. "And they saw the God of Israel: and there was under his feet as it were a paved work of a sapphire stone, and as it were the body of heaven in his clearness" (chapter 24:10). You see, the great God we serve has a body. He is a person. In Daniel 7:9 we read about His hair being like pure wool. Isaiah 6:1 speaks of God sitting upon a throne, and Revelation 1:12-18 describes Him as a personal being.

John 5:26 makes it clear that in Christ is original life, unborrowed, underived. "As the Father hath life in himself; so hath he given to the Son to have life in himself." 1 Timothy 6:16 tells us that only God has immortality. He alone is not subject to death.

Now the big question: Is this God we serve one person or three persons? As Christians we serve one God in three persons. But to establish this we must first discover whether or not God the Father and God the Son are one and the same. "I can of mine own self do nothing," Jesus said. "As I hear, I judge: and my judgment is just; because I seek not mine own will, but the will of the Father which hath sent me" (John 5:30). It is obvious from this that God the Father and God the Son are separate and distinct personalities. Both are God; both share the title God, but they are certainly separate and distinct.

What about John 8:42? "Jesus said unto them, If God were your Father, ye would love me: for I proceeded forth and came from God; neither came I of myself, but he sent me." Isn't it perfectly clear that one could not have sent the other were they not separate and distinct persons? Add to this John 16:28: "I came forth from the Father, and am come into the world: again, I leave the world, and go to the Father." One person cannot leave himself and then go back to himself. Obviously two distinct persons are involved. The person He came from and returned to had to be another person. Jesus called this person the Father.

There is additional evidence in John 16:16: "A little while, and ye shall not see me: and again, a little while, and ye shall see me, because I go to the Father." I think these texts sufficiently prove that the Father and the Son are separate and distinct personalities, both sharing the title God.

What about the Son and the Holy Spirit? Are they wrapped up in one body or are they separate and distinct? One text will make this clear: "Nevertheless I tell you the truth; It is expedient for you that I go away: for if I go not away, the Comforter will not come unto you; but if I depart, I will send him unto you" (verse 7).

Obviously the Holy Spirit and the Son are separate and distinct persons or Christ could never have said, "If I go not away, the Comforter will not come," nor could He have said, "If I depart, I will send him." A person does not send himself, nor can a person be coming and going at the same time. So, obviously, the Son and the Holy Spirit are separate and distinct.

It remains for us to determine whether the Father and the Holy Spirit are separate persons. Jesus told His disciples, "When the Comforter is come, whom I will send unto you from the Father, even the Spirit of truth, which proceedeth from the Father, he shall testify of me" (chapter 15:26).

It appears that the Holy Spirit and God the Father are

separate and distinct persons, for the Bible says that the Spirit of God proceeds from the Father and testifies of Him. Furthermore Christ said, "I will send unto you from the Father." It is clear then that the Father, the Son, and the Holy Spirit are separate and distinct persons.

The question of the Godhead may now be answered with great conviction and assurance of truth. We serve one God in three Persons—Father, Son, and Holy Spirit. These three are one, but they are not one in body. They are one in essence, they are one in purpose, they are one in power. When you deal with one, it is as though you are dealing with the other. They are equally divine, equally powerful, equally wise. Just as Genesis 2:24 speaks of two people becoming one in marriage, so may we understand that the Father, Son, and the Holy Spirit—in a very different sense and on a higher plane—are one though three. They are one in purpose, in essence, and in power. A husband and wife, though they are separate and distinct beings, must be one in purpose, or their marriage will not last.

The name of God is variously mentioned in the Bible. We read of Him as the "Lord," the "Holy Ghost," the great "I AM." Isaiah 9:6 says, "For unto us a child is born, unto us a son is given: and the government shall be upon his shoulder: and his name shall be called Wonderful, Counsellor, The mighty God, The everlasting Father, The Prince of Peace." He is the Lily of the valley, the Bright and Morning Star. He is called Shiloh, and the patriarch Jacob said, "The sceptre shall not depart from Judah, nor a lawgiver from between his feet, until Shiloh come; and unto him shall the gathering of the people be" (Genesis 49:10).

The names for God in the Bible are legion. The important

thing to remember is that the Godhead is one in purpose, one in the purpose of creating man and one in the purpose of redeeming man.

Let's talk about Creation. "In the beginning God created the heaven and the earth. And the earth was without form, and void; and darkness was upon the face of the deep. And the Spirit of God moved upon the face of the waters. And God said, Let there be light: and there was light" (chapter 1:1-3). In John 1:1-3 the Bible makes it clear that Christ was present at Creation too: "In the beginning was the Word, and the Word was with God, and the Word was God. The same was in the beginning with God. All things were made by him; and without him was not any thing made that was made." So the Father, the Son, and the Holy Spirit were one in the creation of man.

What about salvation? "For God so loved the world, that he gave his only begotten Son, that whosoever believeth in him should not perish, but have everlasting life" (John 3:16). Yes, God the Father loves us too. He loves us so much that He gave His Son. But what about the Son? "He was wounded for our transgressions, he was bruised for our iniquities: the chastisement of our peace was upon him; and with his stripes we are healed" (Isaiah 53:5). The Son gave Himself. But what about the Holy Spirit? "It is expedient for you that I go away: for if I go not away, the Comforter will not come unto you; but if I depart, I will send him unto you" (John 16:7). The Holy Spirit is the Comforter. He is the Great Enabler. He is the Strengthener. He is the one who accomplishes conversion in our hearts. It is He who gives us power to live the Christlike life.

So Father, Son, and Holy Spirit were united in Creation

and united in redemption. Let us therefore come boldly to the throne of grace, in order to find grace to help in time of need.

It is said that when Mrs. Einstein, wife of the great scientist, reached America after her flight from Germany, reporters clustered around her and one asked, "Do you know all about relativity?"

Replied Mrs. Einstein, "No, I know very little about it, but I know my husband."

It may well be that many of you who read this chapter know little about the Bible from its theological aspect, but if you know Christ pardons your sins, you have found that central point around which all else clusters. We serve a risen Saviour. Let us seek Him while He may be found.

I've just come from the fountain,
His name's so sweet.

"His Name's So Sweet"

IS THERE SOMETHING greater than the name of Jesus? Speaking of Him Paul wrote, "Who, being in the form of God, thought it not robbery to be equal with God: but made himself of no reputation, and took upon him the form of a servant, and was made in the likeness of men: and being found in fashion as a man, he humbled himself, and became obedient unto death, even the death of the cross. Wherefore God also hath highly exalted him, and given him a name which is above every name: that at the name of Jesus every knee should bow, of things in heaven, and things in earth, and things under the earth; and that every tongue should confess that Jesus Christ is Lord, to the glory of God the Father" (Philippians 2:6-11).

No, there is no name on earth above the name of Jesus. The many references to Christ, both in the Old and New Testaments, make a fascinating study. For instance, Genesis 3:15

"The Lord is my rock, and my fortress, . . .
my high tower, my refuge, my saviour."
Amidst troubles of life He will protect us.

calls Jesus the seed of the woman. Genesis 49:10 calls Him Shiloh. Exodus 3:14 calls Him the great "I AM." In Leviticus we read of the sacrifices of the lamb, and of the star of David. Deuteronomy 18:15 calls Him the "Prophet." Joshua 5:13-15 speaks of Him as the "captain of the host of the Lord." In Isaiah 9:6 He is called "Wonderful, Counsellor, The mighty God, The everlasting Father, The Prince of Peace." In second Samuel chapter seven He is called the "seed" of David. In Psalm 110 He is called a "priest for ever." In Isaiah 53 He is represented as the "righteous servant." In Jeremiah 23:6 He's called "The Lord our Righteousness." Ezekiel 21:27 calls Jesus the coming Prince. In Daniel 7:13 He is "The Son of man," and in Zechariah 6:12, "The Branch." In Malachi 3:1 He's called "the messenger of the covenant." We could go on and on.

Every name is significant in that it explains some aspect of Christ's character, life, and work. Christ was not on earth for the first time when He was born in the manger. He had been here long before. As a matter of fact, before the world was Christ was. In John 17:5 Jesus prayed, while here on earth, "O Father, glorify thou me with thine own self with the glory which I had with thee before the world was." Many people don't understand this. They feel that Christ, when born as a baby, was making His first visit to this world. This is not so. John 1:1-3 makes it clear that Christ created heaven and earth. Again and again He appeared to the Old Testament prophets and patriarchs. He was with the children of Israel when they made their famous exodus out of Egypt. When He was born as a babe in Bethlehem's manger He came as man's Redeemer. He was preparing Himself to be the Lamb sacrificed without spot. He spent thirty-three years of selfless living among men.

Those thirty-three years said to man, "I am your Saviour; I am your Redeemer, and as I have lived this life in My flesh, I can live it in yours."

Christ was also the deliverer of Israel, as we have said, for they "did all drink the same spiritual drink: for they drank of that spiritual Rock that followed them: and that Rock was Christ" (1 Corinthians 10:4). Christ was the great Lawgiver of Exodus 20:1, 2: "And God spake all these words, saying . . ." Jesus' names and titles in the New Testament—the Word, Christ, Emmanuel, the root and offspring of David—all refer to Him of whom it was said in Old Testament times that He was the seed of the woman, Shiloh, the Prince of Peace, the great I AM. Jehovah of the Old Testament is Jesus of the New Testament, and Christ in all the Bible is a revelation of God.

The words of Acts 4:12 are certainly true today: "Neither is there salvation in any other: for there is none other name under heaven given among men, whereby we must be saved." Therefore, we should not take that name in vain, according to Exodus 20:7. According to Acts 16:16, 18, demons fear that name, and John 14:13 says that we ought to pray in the name of Jesus. Acts 2:38 says that we ought to be baptized in His name. O what exalted excellence resides in that great name: "Thou shalt call his name Jesus: for he shall save his people from their sins. . . . And they shall call his name Emmanuel, which being interpreted is, God with us" (Matthew 1:21-23).

I ask again, is there something greater than the name of Jesus? Listen to Psalm 138:2: "I will worship toward thy holy temple, and praise thy name for thy lovingkindness and for thy truth: for thou hast magnified thy word above all thy name." Yes, God has set His word above His name.

But what does this mean? If you go down to the bank to borrow some money, they ask you to fill out an application form and sign your name, but you can't get that money on your name. What the bank clerk will do is to tell you to come back in a couple of days after he checks out your references, and he'll let you know if you can have the money. What is he really doing when he checks out your references? He is trying to find out if you are a man of your word. Indeed, he honors your word above your name. If you haven't been paying your bills, no matter what your name is, you're not going to get that money.

Jesus makes this point very clear in Luke 6:46, where He says, "Why call ye me, Lord, Lord, and do not the things which I say?" There isn't any magic in the name. Indeed, there isn't any help in the name for a man who will not obey God's word. He has magnified His word above His name. We take the name of the Lord in vain when we accept the name Christian but do not live like a Christian ought to live. "Thou shalt not take the name of the Lord thy God in vain; for the Lord will not hold him guiltless that taketh his name in vain" (Exodus 20:7). We are supposed to match our profession with our deeds. Why call on His name and neglect His word?

A young man left home and went to work. He went to work on the same job his father had taken over years before. The foreman came to him and said, "Is your name Thompson?"

"Yes."

"Well, you've got a lot to live up to here, for your father was with the company for forty years, and we never had a better worker."

What that foreman really said was, "Be sure your deeds match your name, because that name stands for something."

When I was a young boy I said to my father, "There are some things I think I'd like to go out and do," but the things I mentioned were not in harmony with my father's principles. He looked at me and said, "Son, go ahead and do anything you want to do, but before you go, be sure and change your name." As I thought that over, and thought of the significance of the name, I decided that my behavior would have to conform, for I wouldn't sacrifice the family name for anything. I must match the name with appropriate deeds or forfeit the name.

So, I repeat again, there is no name in heaven or on earth greater than the name of Jesus. It is in His name that we pray, and it is because of that name that God answers our prayers. We pray, "Our Father which art in heaven, Hallowed be thy name" (Matthew 6:9). The name of Christ is a holy name and should therefore not be taken lightly upon the lips. There are men who curse and swear and blaspheme, and to give force to what they say they invoke that Name that should not be taken upon profane lips or used in common, ordinary speech. How we speak a name says something about the person bearing the name. We don't toss around lightly the names of people in high office for whom we have great respect. We speak those names with respect, even with awe. When in our hearts there is reverence and awe for the majesty of Christ, if there is love for Him, we will speak His name with great respect, with tenderness, and with awe. We demonstrate our respect and love for God when we obey Him, when we do what He says.

"If ye love me, keep my commandments" (John 14:15). "Ye are my friends, if ye do whatsoever I command you" (chapter 15:14).

I appeal to you, don't use the name of Christ as a smoke

screen to cover your sins. Don't use it as a badge of respectability. That holy name means nothing to a man who does so. The name of Christ moves Heaven only when it covers a Christ-actuated life. This, and this alone, makes the name of Christ meaningful.

What is your name? I don't mean the name you received from your father and mother. Do you bear the name of Christian? The name of Christ is the one door of hope and salvation for needy man. Have you walked through that open door? The name of Christ puts demons to flight, brings peace to the soul, and light to the heart.

PART II

Salvation

Good news, chariot's coming
And I don't want it to leave me behind.

"Good News"

THE HISTORICAL SKETCH of an
Ohio church records that in 1863 a Bible
with raised letters was presented to the blind organist, William L.
Campbell. In making the presentation, the pastor said, "May the
precious truths of the gospel of Christ be your comfort in life,
your support in death, and your portion in eternity."

The apostle Paul wrote, "For I am not ashamed of the gospel
of Christ: for it is the power of God unto salvation to every one
that believeth; to the Jew first, and also to the Greek" (Romans
1:16). What is this gospel? It is the good news that man need no
longer wander about in this world a lost person. It is the good
news that Christ has come into the world to save sinners and
that His grace is sufficient. The gospel tells about the birth of
Jesus. It talks about His life. It talks about His death. It speaks
of His resurrection and His ascension to heaven. It talks about
His priestly ministry, and it speaks of His second coming to the

earth. Finally it talks about the earth made new—Paradise restored and regained.

But the gospel does more than this. It not only recites the aforementioned facts, but relates these facts to human experience. It says that a man who believes the gospel will experience inner transformation and outward reformation. It says that the gospel of Christ is effectual in forgiving, pardoning, and cleansing sin, and that the man who accepts it begins to live a new life in this present world. We read this in Titus 2:11, 12: "For the grace of God that bringeth salvation hath appeared to all men, teaching us that, denying ungodliness and worldly lusts, we should live soberly, righteously, and godly, in this present world." You see, the gospel of the Lord Jesus Christ does not wait to begin its work until we've reached another world, but begins right here on earth. The gospel of the Lord Jesus does its full and effectual transforming, reforming work upon the sinful hearts of men. The Bible says that it is the power of God unto salvation.

The word "salvation" is interesting. It means, "a salvage operation." A few years ago I was in the Philippine Islands. Standing on the shores of Manila Harbor a friend recited the following events: He said that not long ago that harbor was blocked by sunken American ships that had been bombed by Japanese fliers during the war. For years the harbor was unusable because of these sunken ships. One day someone brought cranes to the harbor and raised those sunken, rusted, good-for-nothing ships. They were brought to the surface, and taken back to the foundry and melted down. They reappeared as automobiles, kitchen utensils, stoves, and refrigerators. Furthermore, the harbor was cleaned so that boats were now able to come in and use its facilities.

This is what God does for man. Lives like the sunken ships in Manila Harbor—rusted, lost, unusable—are transformed by the grace of God, and even their own neighbors do not recognize them anymore. Such is the power of the gospel in this present world.

Surely what I have just discussed is nothing to be ashamed of. Why, then, did the apostle Paul feel it was necessary to affirm that he was not ashamed of the gospel of Christ? The apostle had three reasons.

At the time Paul wrote this statement, Christianity was a new religion. The Roman Empire was the great dictatorship of Paul's day. Anybody who talked about another king more powerful than Caesar was bound to get into trouble with the state. He put himself on collision course with earthly governmental administration. That is exactly what Christianity did. It announced the coming of another king, a King from another world. It even said that that King would one day take over the entire earth. The Roman emperors regarded this as a threat to their security. This is understandable, considering their pagan background. So they resolved to blot out the fledgling church and put its King out of existence. That is why Herod issued an order shortly after the birth of Christ that all male babies two years old and under were to be put to death.

Didn't Pilate say that day in his judgment hall, "Behold your King"? What he really meant was, He may be your king but He is not mine. And what did the Jews reply? "We have no king but Caesar!" They understood that to acknowledge another king was treason against the Roman state. But the Christian understood that to acknowledge an earthly king above the King of kings was treason against God. That is why Paul said, "I am not ashamed."

Second, established religion was against Christianity. Judaism had become sterile because it accepted the law of God in principle but not in practice. It refused to acknowledge the divinity of Christ, and does so to this day. For that reason the apostle Paul, having been converted to Christianity, was under extreme pressure from his former colleagues. Indeed, when he went back to the synagogue and tried to convert them to his new faith, he was more than once stoned and left for dead. We can understand why he would declare expressly, "I am not ashamed," in the face of an intransigent, persecuting, dictatorial government and established religious persecution. We can understand his reasoning when he says that he is unashamedly proclaiming a new King, that he is proclaiming the sovereignty of God.

But there is a third reason that led him to say he was not ashamed. There were the social pressures that followed acceptance of a new faith. All of his old friends tried to reason with him. Doubtless they gave him a thousand reasons why he should not be a Christian. These pressures were real then, as they are real now. When a man bucks the flood tide of the world, begins to swim upstream, literally accepts Christ in a world that has rejected Him—from every human point of view he really could be ashamed. But when Christ comes into the heart, all fear and all reticence are wiped away and a new, courageous boldness born of faith and hope takes possession of the life. We become new creatures in Christ Jesus.

The text says all this is conditional—"it is the power of God unto salvation to every one that believeth." It is no simple thing to believe, but it is not complicated either. It is not simple because it offers so much for so little. It is very difficult for a

95

man to believe that he is going to get a bargain in a day like this when economic head-hunters abound on every hand. Whenever a salesman says something is a bargain, immediately our defenses go up, and we begin to look for the hidden gimmicks.

That is what makes the gospel so difficult to believe. It offers so much for so little. What it really says is that eternal life is mine for the asking and for the believing. It says Christ came all the way from heaven to bring eternal life to me, and that I can have it without money and without price. We're so used to either doing things to earn what we get, or paying money to get them, that it's hard to believe that something as great as being saved from sin is absolutely free. But that is what the gospel offers. You can't earn it and you can't buy it. You must accept it by faith or you won't get it. These are the simple terms of the gospel.

How can a man afford to believe it? How can a man afford to doubt it, with all of the evidence in? You must remember that nineteen hundred years ago Christ undergirded all His promises with the sacrifice of Himself. He shed His blood, and we say that a man has to be sincere if he is willing to die for what he stands for. Christ stands for salvation of every human being, and He puts His life on the line to prove it. Who can deny the sincerity of His offer? Who can deny the validity of His promises now that He has shed His blood? So it should be easy to believe. The problem is that some people don't read about His sacrifice. They don't even read about His humble beginnings, His sacrificial life, let alone the efficacy of His death. No wonder they cannot accept the shedding of His blood for the remission of their sins. They do not know Him personally as their Saviour.

96

We are not hopelessly lost. "Come unto me, all ye that labour and are heavy laden, and I will give you rest. Take my yoke upon you, and learn of me; for I am meek and lowly in heart: and ye shall find rest unto your souls" (Matthew 11:28, 29). "Ye shall be gathered one by one" (Isaiah 27:12). Procopius reported that in the Far North, where the light of day is not visible for months each year, the inhabitants climb the mountains when it is time for the sun to appear, striving for the first glimpse of the rising sun. At its appearance they deck themselves in their best apparel, embrace one another with joy and cry, *Ecce sol,* "Behold the sun."

But what greater joy accompanies the dawning of the glorious light of the gospel upon the human soul. Does that not bring from our lips the cry, Behold the Son! The gospel brings genuine hope to the human heart. It tells man what God has done for him and what God can do to him and through him. This revelation makes man a new creature in Christ. It opens before his eyes fresh avenues of service. Instead of being ashamed of the gospel of Christ, we should spread it without reserve to the ends of the earth.

O, my good Lord, show me the way
To enter the chariot—travel along.

"Show Me the Way"

THESE ARE tension-filled days. The drive for equal rights and equal opportunities against the prohibitions of over three hundred and fifty years has at last reached a climax. The nation stands at that point in history when it will either climb upward to the excellence and the full realization of the American dream, or it will tumble amid the ruin and rubble of arson, looting, and riot. Which way will the nation go? The question of the black man is inseparably tied to the question of the destiny of America.

"In the year that king Uzziah died I saw also the Lord sitting upon a throne, high and lifted up, and his train filled the temple" (Isaiah 6:1). Uzziah was a righteous king. Israel had had so many evil kings that Uzziah was a welcome relief. The prophet Isaiah looked upon Uzziah as a personal friend, and this old prophet was especially pleased with the righteous character of the young king. When Uzziah died Isaiah lost a personal

99

To those who are confused on the highway of life, Christ is the "way, the truth, and the life." He will guide us to life eternal.

friend. There was great mourning in Israel, for this young king had worked his way into the hearts of the people. What he did was best for them, and they knew it. When he died it seemed as though the end of the world had come. But our text gives us an encouraging word: "In the year that king Uzziah died I saw also the Lord." In vision the prophet was lifted to the very throne of God.

In this day of trial and trouble and deep hurt for the Negro people and for the nation—a day when men remember with pain the assassination of a great man who did much to benefit this nation, Dr. Martin Luther King—in this day we need Isaiah's view of God. The end of the world is not yet, and we must go on living courageously, purposefully, and meaningfully, and we must go on building a nation, building a church, and living for God.

"I saw also the Lord sitting upon a throne, high and lifted up, and his train filled the temple." What a vision to have in a dark day like this! This speaks of a God who is an authority. It speaks of a God who is still in control, however chaotic things may look down here. It speaks of a God of order, a God of security, a God of power, a God of ability, a God we can trust. What a God to serve in a time like this! To be pitied above all men is a man who does not believe in such a God, in a personal God who can see, who can hear, who can understand; a God who can rescue, a God who can build, who can heal, and who can save. This is the Isaiah vision of God. This the black man needs now more than ever.

God sits on His throne at the very center of the universe. He is the great Father of the whole human family, for in the beginning God created the heavens and the earth. Genesis 2:7 says that the Lord God formed man of the dust of the ground and breathed into his nostrils the breath of life, and that man became a living soul. The human family can look back beyond Adam to God Himself as the Father of all mankind, for He is the great Creator.

God says, "I have made the earth, and created man upon it: I, even my hands, have stretched out the heavens, and all their host have I commanded" (Isaiah 45:12). "Thus saith the Lord that created the heavens; God himself that formed the earth and made it; he hath established it, he created it not in vain, he formed it to be inhabited: I am the Lord; and there is none else" (verse 18).

Verse 22 of that chapter says, "Look unto me, and be ye saved, all the ends of the earth: for I am God, and there is none else." The Isaiah vision of God speaks of a great Creator who in the beginning made all things and then created man for His own glory—"and there is none else." There is no other Creator, no other God and Saviour besides the God of heaven.

By contrast, there is abroad in our land, the theory of evolution, proposing that life just developed spontaneously, without any Creator. It takes a lot of faith to believe a theory like that. The Darwinian theory of evolution is widely accepted among intellectuals, but not by fundamentalists, for, basic to every man is the need for a father. For example: A man with a mental disorder goes to a psychiatrist, who for twenty-five to fifty dollars an hour asks him among other things questions about his childhood relationship to his father. These men who know the human mind have discovered that the desire for a father is basic in human nature. The Bible leads us to believe that God built this sense of need into man when He created the human race. This hungering and thirsting after the great universal Father is a part of our very being. It often goes unrecognized for what it is, and men sometimes wander into interesting bypaths in order to satisfy this craving. But the Bible tells us just what it is. It is a search for God, a desire to have a father and a desire to be like Him.

The Isaiah vision of God does this for the Negro. It identifies him with God. It says to him that he was created like every other man. It says to him that he is equal with all other men. It tells the Negro that he is one with his fellow citizens of the earth, whether they be white, red, or yellow. It says to the black man, "Lift up your head, for God is your Father." What should this do for the black man? It should elevate his thinking. It should refine his character. It should discipline his life. It should ennoble him. It should make of him a new creature. It should make of him more than a good citizen of this world, it should prepare him for citizenship in the world to come. This is the significance of the Isaiah vision of God—"I saw also the Lord sitting upon a throne, high and lifted up." Marian Anderson sings it this way: "He's got the whole world in His hands." Yes, it is comforting to know in an age when war ravages the earth, when famine and pestilence stalk the land, that there is a God whose heart of love follows even the sparrow in its zigzag wounded flight to the ground. And of how much more value we are than one of these, as Jesus said.

The Isaiah vision of God gives me a sense of security, and therefore emotional stability. What the black man and the white man both need more than anything else is this vision of God "sitting upon a throne, high and lifted up."

But there is a second vision of God that I would recommend,

and it is found in 1 Timothy 3:16: "Great is the mystery of godliness: God was manifest in the flesh." We need not only the Isaiah manifestation of God which speaks of a God who is exalted, a God who is King, a God who sits on a throne, a God who is surrounded by thousands and thousands of angels, but we also need the revelation of God as found in the writings of John: "The Word was made flesh, and dwelt among us" (John 1:14). Yes, God was manifest in the flesh.

A few years ago I stood in Trafalgar Square in London and saw the monument to Lord Nelson. At the top of it is a beautiful sculpture of Nelson, but one can't see it too well because it is so high. One wouldn't know who it is except the name is in block capital letters at the bottom of the giant column. When you read the inscription you know that this is a monument to the hero of Trafalgar and many another successful British naval engagement. Then, on the anniversary celebration for Lord Nelson, somebody got an idea. They made an exact replica of this great sculptured work away up there almost out of sight, and stood it on the ground next to the tall monument so that men could see and appreciate it. They could see what was at the top of the tall pillar by looking at the replica down on the level where they were. This is the meaning of "the Word was made flesh." Oh, yes, we need a God who sits upon a throne, high and lifted up, surrounded by the Shekinah glory that no man can approach unto. We need a Father like that. But we also need the Word made flesh. We need Jesus Christ—God in the flesh—who for thirty-three years walked the earth as a man, healed the sick, raised the dead, gave sight to the blind, unstopped deaf ears, and enabled the dumb to speak and the lame man to leap as an hart. In His path was the sweet aroma of a flower-filled, fruitful life, and we should follow in His steps.

There is a spiritual that says, "If we ever needed the Lord before, we sure do need Him now." We cannot afford the heady elixir of hot tempers and quick tongues. The days ahead are crucial for the black man, for the nation, and the world. Christ has the solution to every human problem, and by following Him we will find our way out of the night.

A poet has said:

> One ship drives east and another drives west
> With the selfsame winds that blow.
> 'Tis the set of the sails
> And not the gales
> Which tells us the way to go.
>
> Like the winds of the sea are the ways of fate,
> As we voyage along through life:
> 'Tis the set of a soul
> That decides its goal,
> And not the calm or the strife.

And so in the days ahead, though fraught with peril and problems that seem insoluble, we may negotiate these perilous rapids if we go with God.

Run, sinner, run—find
You a hiding place
In that morning—O my Lord—
In that morning when the Lord says, "Hurry."

"Run, Sinner, Run"

REALLY, our subject is a misnomer. It should be titled, "The Old Immorality." We've come to a time when some people want to throw off all moral restraints, and declare anything a man can get away with is all right. People who study the Bible know better. Romans 12:1 makes it clear that good religion applies not only to the spirit of a man; we are to present our bodies as living sacrifices, holy and acceptable unto God. This, Paul says, is a reasonable request. You see, body, mind, and spirit are really all one unit.

When God made man, He made him an integrated personality. Mind and spirit were perfectly balanced; furthermore, you cannot harm the body without affecting the mind and the spirit. Conversely, you cannot harm the mind without affecting the spirit and the body, nor can you neglect the spiritual nature of man and expect to prosper mentally and physically.

Let's concentrate on what we do with these bodies of ours.

We'll discover that our minds have a great influence on how we treat our bodies. In 1 Corinthians 6:19, 20 we're told that our bodies are the temples of the Holy Spirit, which is in us, and that if we defile the temple of God, He will have to destroy us. In Titus 2:11, 12, we read: "For the grace of God that bringeth salvation hath appeared to all men, teaching us that, denying ungodliness and worldly lusts, we should live soberly, righteously, and godly, in this present world." By "worldly lusts" the apostle refers to the lusts of the flesh, to immorality—which poses as the new morality, the privilege young people take of acting like married people while they are still single. This is the subject of our text: "Present your bodies a living sacrifice, . . . unto God."

Mass media has produced a threefold negative state of mind with reference to sex:

1. It is said that everybody is violating the commandment, "Thou shalt not commit adultery."

2. This, it is said further, should convince us that it is the thing to do.

3. It produces what we might call the bandwagon effect— "You will do it eventually, why not now?"

Number one: Everybody is *not* violating the seventh commandment.

Number two: It is *not* the thing to do.

Number three: It is *not* necessary for anybody ever to do it. But the movies, television, the newspapers, and certain magazines seemingly have conspired to glorify the violation of the seventh commandment of God's law. Indeed, we have come to a time in our practice of Freudian principles when we have thrown off all restraint, and deny that any externally originated law is binding on our internal purpose or thought, or on our external deeds. So today we are witnessing a generation on the loose, virgin clubs that are not virgin, things happening in drive-ins and other places that shame the sensibilities of the decent. The words of our text come back most appropriately, "Present your bodies a living sacrifice, . . . unto God."

In Proverbs 6:26-29 we discover just what effect the violation of the seventh commandment has on a person. "For by means of a whorish woman a man is brought to a piece of bread: and the adulteress will hunt for the precious life. Can a man take fire in his bosom, and his clothes not be burned? Can one go upon hot coals, and his feet not be burned? So he that goeth in to his neighbour's wife; whosoever toucheth her shall not be innocent."

Verse 32 reads, "But whoso committeth adultery with a woman lacketh understanding: he that doeth it destroyeth his own soul."

When we realize that we cannot violate the seventh commandment of God's law without paying a fearful price, it will give us pause for sober thought. I've listed a few things that happen to the man who tosses caution to the wind, who thinks he can do what he wants and get away with it.

1. There is a loss of innocence. The man who runs around in a promiscuous way not only loses innocence but he becomes brazen, hard, and careless toward other people.

2. There's also a loss of self-respect, and when a man loses respect for himself he loses respect for everybody else and is inclined to look upon everybody else as being like himself. Because he is going the way of all flesh, he naturally assumes that everybody else is as weak as he is.

3. There is a loss of spirituality. Man can't court the devil and worship God at the same time.

4. There's a loss of influence. Men who know him lose confidence in him.

5. The commission of adultery stimulates an insatiable appetite, one that cannot be satisfied. Men who live like this cannot love their own wives because they've been bitten by the bug of insatiability.

6. It has a negative effect on a later marriage. Young men who run around and develop habits such as this have a difficult time settling down once they get married.

But there are three risks a man runs in addition to these. First, there is the risk of venereal disease—syphilis and gonorrhea. Some people count on the wonder drugs to deliver them —penicillin and others—but the syphilitic strain is now defying penicillin, and there is a strain that penicillin cannot control. Don't fool yourself into thinking that the doctor can fix you up. Second, there is the danger of unwanted motherhood. Now I've heard about the pill, but the pill can't do what self-restraint and discipline should do for one, neither does it always preclude motherhood.

Third, there is the threat of violence. Violence seems to stalk the loose man, the danger of losing your life over a woman who will yield herself to you is certainly very real, and many men are pushing up daisies who should still be walking around —healthy, happy, and enjoying life.

But the central question is not what men are doing, but what the remedy is. James 4:7 clearly indicates that if we submit ourselves to God and resist the devil, he will flee from us. Now, this resistance takes the form of prayer. A man has to pray at the beginning of the day that God will keep him, keep his impulses, keep his thoughts under control, help him live a disciplined life. That word "resist" is an important word. It means to fight. The Word of God is like a vitamin to the body. A man who reads it gets strength from it, power to overcome evil. The song says, "Yield not to temptation, For yielding is sin, Each victory will help you, Some other to win." Win today's battle, and you are strengthened to win tomorrow's battle. "Fear thou not; for I am with thee: be not dismayed; for I am thy God: I will strengthen thee; yea, I will help thee; yea, I will uphold thee with the right hand of my righteousness" (Isaiah 41:10).

Yes, Christ is willing to come into our hearts and give us the power to say No when we feel like saying Yes to temptation. Christ, who mastered the tempest in a boat on the Sea of Galilee, can certainly master human nature within our hearts if we will let Him. So I appeal to you to believe that God will give you power over the impulses of the body, and enable you to present your body a living sacrifice acceptable to Him. We ought to respect our bodies too much to do some things with them and to them. We must respect our wives too much to disgrace them by living double lives, and youth must respect its own future too much to indulge prematurely in privileges that are sacred to the married state.

There is a disintegration of the personality that results from breaking the seventh commandment, a depraving of the thoughts, the purposes, and the will. May God give us the strength to turn to Him with all of our hearts and daily submit our lives to Him, that even in the areas of deep emotion and basic sexual desire we may know discipline and the strength that comes only with submission to Christ.

The nature of this problem must be thoroughly understood if it is to be met successfully. "For we wrestle not against flesh and blood, but against principalities, against powers, against the rulers of the darkness of this world, against spiritual wickedness in high places" (Ephesians 6:12).

Loose morality is more than the normal expression of fleshly desire. Demons loose in this world, bent on the ruin of the human family, fan the flames of desire until they become a raging inferno, if we do not resist. Resistance involves guarding the avenues to the mind. This is why passion-arousing movies and fiction should be rejected altogether. The pornographic literature flooding the newsstands of the nation is no accident. There is a deliberate campaign to promote an immoral and dissolute life. Everything that can be done is being done to glamorize the subnormal and to stigmatize the decent.

The wise will recognize this worldwide campaign for what it is—a money-making scheme, pure and simple, one that is heedless of the dire consequences to the morals of the human family. The excuse is made that the purveyors of filth are merely catering to the appetites of the masses. I would counter that they have in part created these appetites to which they minister, and thus the cause becomes a part of the effect and then parades as the remedy. The sad fact is that this condition is getting worse instead of better, as the prophet wrote, "Evil men and seducers shall wax worse and worse, deceiving, and being deceived" (2 Timothy 3:13), but, thank God, we are not helpless before surging, internal passions. We may exclaim in triumph with the apostle Paul, "And the Lord shall deliver me from every evil work, and will preserve me unto his heavenly kingdom: to whom be glory for ever and ever. Amen" (chapter 4:18).

Something within me that holdeth the rein;
Something within me that banishes pain;
Something within me I cannot explain;
All that I know, there is something within.

"Something Within Me"

"BUT YE SHALL receive power, after that the Holy Ghost is come upon you: and ye shall be witnesses unto me both in Jerusalem, and in all Judaea, and in Samaria, and unto the uttermost part of the earth" (Acts 1:8).

Many years have passed since the apostle lamented, "For the good that I would I do not: but the evil which I would not, that I do. . . . O wretched man that I am! who shall deliver me from the body of this death?" (Romans 7:19-24). In these verses he expresses mankind's supreme dilemma—how to do right, how to bridge the gap between profession and performance, how to make our deeds match our words.

The world has a right to expect the power of God in the church. The church has a right to expect it, and as individual members of the church we too have a right to expect it. Perhaps Jesus had this in mind when He said, "Let your light so shine before men, that they may see your good works, and glorify your Father, which is in heaven" (Matthew 5:16).

It is said that when Thomas Aquinas visited Rome and saw the magnificence of the papal palace, the pope remarked to him: "Well, Thomas, the church in our day cannot say, 'Silver and gold have I none.'"

"No," replied Thomas, "neither can she say, 'In the name of Jesus of Nazareth, rise up and walk.'"

There is an appalling lack of spiritual power evident among many of God's people today. This untapped source of divine power stands ready to assist in any emergency and to help perform every task. God has made no promise He cannot fulfill, but we must claim His grace, accept His promises, and act on His Word. Jesus compared the Holy Spirit to air; but we must breathe the air if it is to do us good. The Holy Spirit is compared to water, but a man must drink if he would quench his thirst. He is compared to fire, but a man must approach unto Him if his heart is to be warmed.

Why do we need divine power? First, to live the life that Christ has commanded. "I can do all things through Christ which strengtheneth me" (Philippians 4:13). "Now unto him that is able to keep you from falling, and to present you faultless before the presence of his glory with exceeding joy," wrote Jude (Jude 24).

Yes, man is powerless of himself to live the life that Christ has commanded, but with Christ all things are possible. Huge dynamos generate millions of watts of power, but one flick of a switch can cut off the power and plunge whole areas into darkness. Wind, water, and electrical energy have been harnessed to perform services for mankind on a global scale. Cut man off from these sources of power, and the whole fabric of civilization will collapse of its own weight. Spiritual power is even more vital to the child of God. Said the apostle, "For in him we live, and move, and have our being; as certain also of your own poets have said, For we are also his offspring" (Acts 17:28).

Second, we need power to serve others. All about us lies a world of human need. Again and again Jesus commissioned His disciples to help those who were helpless. The sick must be treated, the hungry fed, the naked clothed, the homeless housed. Thus those who have are obligated to assist the have-nots. When Jesus Christ was on earth He spent more time helping people than He did preaching to them. This is a practical lesson to His church on earth.

Sitting in the plush office of an economic adviser to an African government recently, I asked him what he thought a church might do to make itself meaningful to a newly developing nation. He said to me, "Your church will always be welcome in my country, for you build hospitals to treat our sick and schools to educate our young. I think every nation would welcome folk like you."

Yes, every Christian must serve as well as preach. Christ's example of the good Samaritan carries this message clearly. We are neighbors without regard to our national origin, and neither suspicion nor fear must hinder us from serving our needy fellow men. From Helsinki to Cape Town and from Bombay to Washington, there is a chain of human need. Into these endless fields of service, God has sent His servants. We must not fail Him.

Third, we need power to witness. "Go ye into all the world, and preach the gospel to every creature," said Jesus (Mark 16:15).

"Go ye therefore, and teach all nations, baptizing them in

8

the name of the Father, and of the Son, and of the Holy Ghost: teaching them to observe all things whatsoever I have commanded you: and, lo, I am with you alway, even unto the end of the world. Amen" (Matthew 28:19, 20).

A complete rehabilitation of the spirit and the mind as well as the body is needed, and only the gospel of the Lord Jesus Christ can completely undo the work that sin has done. So, by the mysterious art of preaching the message of salvation, men are brought into covenant contact with God. Their spirits are made whole. Their minds are made strong, and they are rendered capable of meeting the day-to-day problems of life. Faith, repentance, and conversion describe the mysterious transformations that take place in human lives. These words describe a God-captured heart; they speak of a man surrendering his stubborn will to Christ. Faith, repentance, and conversion state that a soul has been saved by grace through faith in the Lord Jesus Christ, and that the vast resources of heaven are now available to all who put their trust in Him. This power is available to all who will ask for it. "Ask, and it shall be given you; seek, and ye shall find; knock, and it shall be opened unto you" (chapter 7:7). Someone has said, "Little prayer, little power; much prayer, much power."

In his book, *How Jesus Won Men,* L. R. Scarborough says: "Jesus probably did as much praying while on earth as He did preaching or teaching or healing. His life of public ministry was a life of prayer. He not only prayed, He interceded. He was a great supplicator and intercessor. He was man's intercessor while on earth and our intercessor at the right hand of the throne of God. All of our petitions evidently pass to the Father in His name. He set us an example to pray while on earth. He prayed in public, He prayed in secret, He prayed in the mountain fastness

114

in the hours of darkness, He was a strenuous worker and a more strenuous intercessor by night. He was on earth probably God's top-most prayer. It would be profitable for all soul winners to study and re-study and seek to copy Christ's ministry of prayer."

It is clear, then, why Christ in His human nature exhibited such great power. He did not take advantage of His divine nature to resist the temptations of this life, or to render an effective public ministry. Christ overcame as we may overcome, through the power of prayer.

Dr. Scarborough also quotes Dr. H. C. Moore, who in a great baccalaureate address in 1917 classified the prayers of Christ on earth. Dr. Moore listed twenty-five different types of prayers that Christ prayed. If Christ in His human nature felt this deep need of dependence upon His Father, how much more should we!

I had just finished delivering a gospel message when a man staggered down the aisle toward the altar. He grabbed me by the arm, obviously under the influence of alcohol. He said, "Save me, save me. If you can't do something for me tonight, I'm lost. I'm lost."

We knelt in the sawdust there beside the platform, and there I committed this man to God in simple, childlike faith. It was not an emotional scene, but verily the Spirit of God came upon the man, and he was instantly healed of his desire for alcohol. He told me later that he had no home or job when he approached me that night, but today he is a well-respected family man with a good job, and a worshiper of the Lord Jesus Christ. Only the power of God can perform such miracles in human lives, and only the exercise of the high privilege of prayer can bring this type of power into the individual life.

A wealthy American spent years and a small fortune on what

was to be the largest plane that had ever flown. Top-secret procedures were established. No one except the builders was allowed to enter, and the builders were sworn to secrecy. As the day neared for the plane's completion and test flight, little leaks began to appear in the newspapers, and the general public was built up gradually to a state of excitement as the day approached. When all was in readiness the reporters and spectators assembled to watch the trial. There was a revving of engines and the thrilling noise of whirling propellers, as the giant lumbered down to the end of the runway for the take-off. The engines raced, the throttle was opened, and the giant lurched forward. Faster and faster it sped. Then suddenly the motors were cut and the plane slowed down. It was underpowered. It never left the ground.

How like this experimental airplane are many men and women who read these pages. Because of little prayer, they have little power. One of these days sons and daughters of God are going out of this world into the world to come, but the spiritually underpowered will never get off the ground.

Hold on, hold on;
Keep your hand on the plow,
Hold on.

"Hold On"

NEBUCHADNEZZAR, king of Babylon, built an image of gold on the Plain of Dura approximately ninety feet tall. At the dedication service he proclaimed, "Whoso falleth not down and worshippeth shall the same hour be cast into the midst of a burning fiery furnace" (Daniel 3:6). This command to worship the image of gold has an interesting background. In Daniel 2 Nebuchadnezzar had a dream of the statue of a man whose head was of gold, its breast and arms of silver, its belly and thighs of brass, its legs of iron, and its feet of iron mixed with clay.

Interpreting the vision, the prophet Daniel revealed to Nebuchadnezzar that the head of gold represented his kingdom, which, however, would pass away and be followed by a kingdom of silver, which history records was the kingdom of Medo-Persia. But that too would pass away and yield to the kingdom of Greece, and Greece in turn would yield to the iron mon-

117

archy of Rome, after which the nations of the world would be partly strong and partly weak. But Nebuchadnezzar rejected Daniel's interpretation that his own kingdom would pass away, and so—possibly as a reaction to this revelation—he built an image of gold from top to bottom, indicating his determination that *his* kingdom would last forever. He rejected the idea implicit in the metallic image of his dream, that Babylon would pass away. So he made an image entirely of gold, indicating his intention that Babylon should last forever.

When he called all his governors together to kneel before the statue, Nebuchadnezzar was asking them to share his dream of Babylon's lasting forever as a world empire. But the act of kneeling before the image was idolatrous, and in the distinguished audience gathered on the plain were Shadrach, Meshach, and Abednego, who were well aware of the issues involved. They knew Daniel's interpretation of the vision of Daniel 2, and that the head of gold meant that one day the kingdom of Babylon would fall. So for them, to kneel would be a denial of faith in a revelation from God. They were also familiar with the Ten Commandments, the second of which says, "Thou shalt not make unto thee any graven image, or any likeness of any thing that is in heaven above, or that is in the earth beneath, or that is in the water under the earth: thou shalt not bow down thyself to them, nor serve them" (Exodus 20:4, 5).

Their belief in God was so deep that they could not submit to the twin blasphemies demanded of them, even under the threat of death. So when the music sounded and the great host fell on their faces, Shadrach, Meshach, and Abednego stood like three giant oaks. They had made their decision. They would obey God rather than man even if it cost them their lives.

119

To the three Hebrew youth in Babylon, loyalty to the God of their fathers was more important than a heathen king's command.

This is the true spirit of Christianity, and those who have this spirit are truly Christians. It would have been an easy thing for Shadrach, Meshach, and Abednego to fall on their knees but refuse to worship. They would have escaped the fiery furnace, they would have enjoyed the favor of the king and the applause of their colleagues, for earthly advantage. They could have compromised their principles, but they would have lost their souls. No less is demanded of us today who profess the name of Christ. We must be willing to stand true to principle no matter what the risk or the cost.

For their act of civil disobedience, Shadrach, Meshach, and Abednego were haled before an angry King Nebuchadnezzar. His attitude is described as one of "rage and fury" (Daniel 3:13). "Is it true, O Shadrach, Meshach, and Abednego, do not ye serve my gods, nor worship the golden image which I have set up?" (verse 14).

In verse fifteen he offered to give them another chance and further challenged "that God that shall deliver you out of my hands." When will we followers of Christ awaken to the true nature of sin? While it may yield a temporary sensual pleasure, all sin is against God and an insult to His government. In these remarks King Nebuchadnezzar reveals the true nature of his command, and his arrogance in pitting himself against the God of heaven. But Shadrach, Meshach, and Abednego were no less adamant in their stand for right; "We are not careful to answer thee in this matter," they replied. "If it be so, our God whom we serve is able to deliver us from the burning fiery furnace, and he will deliver us out of thine hand, O king" (verses 16, 17).

Here the three heroes state their faith in God in no uncertain terms. They certify His ability to deliver them and imply that He loves them enough to be willing to do so. To us today comes the message, "Believe on the Lord Jesus Christ, and thou shalt be saved, and thy house" (Acts 16:31).

This means we must believe that Christ is able to save us, and that He loves us enough to be willing to save us. We must believe in His divinity, His love, and His power. All of this Shadrach, Meshach, and Abednego believed. But their faith had yet another dimension: "But if not, be it known unto thee, O king, that we will not serve thy gods, nor worship the golden image which thou hast set up" (Daniel 3:18).

It is this that separates true Christians from pretenders. What if God does not exercise His divine favor at a given moment? What if we have to wait for deliverance? What if the clouds hang low, the lightning flashes, and our whole sky of hope seems overcast, with not a break in the clouds? What will we do then? This is the test of the strength of our relationship with Christ.

"Then was Nebuchadnezzar full of fury, and the form of his visage was changed against Shadrach, Meshach, and Abednego: therefore he spake, and commanded that they should heat the furnace one seven times more than it was wont to be heated" (verse 19).

The three young men were thrown into the burning fiery furnace, to be consumed in a white-hot hell of searing flame. But in their soul was the message so accurately pictured in the Negro spiritual, "Hold on, hold on; Keep your hand on the plow, Hold on." They did hold on, and their faith saved them, for when the king in his lordly chariot rode out to the furnaces to witness the spectacle he cried out: "Did not we cast three men bound into the midst of the fire? . . . Lo, I see four men loose, walking in the midst of the fire, and they have no hurt; and the form of the fourth is like the Son of God" (verses 24, 25).

How right he was! Christ has never deserted His people. When we keep His commandments, He will keep us under the most hazardous circumstances. Even though death be our portion we will be able to say with David, "Yea, though I walk through the valley of the shadow of death, I will fear no evil: for thou art with me" (Psalm 23:4).

I watched my father die. He had given all his life to Christ in the service of the church, but now his summons had come. Just how would he die? I wanted to know. On the last day of his life he talked with us about our past lives, and we reviewed his own for him. Then he began to weaken. I saw a smile playing about his face as his older son folded his hands on his chest for the last time, and I read, " 'The Lord is my shepherd; I shall not want. He maketh me to lie down in green pastures: he leadeth me beside the still waters. He restoreth my soul: he leadeth me in the paths of righteousness for his name's sake. Yea, though I walk through the valley of the shadow of death, I will fear no evil: for thou art with me; thy rod and thy staff they comfort me. Thou preparest a table before me in the presence of mine enemies: thou anointest my head with oil; my cup runneth over. Surely goodness and mercy shall follow me all the days of my life: and I will dwell in the house of the Lord for ever' " (Psalm 23).

With the look of heavenly peace upon his brow he lapsed into unconsciousness from which he never returned. He realized in death the fulfillment of the Lord's promise, "Lo, I am with you alway, even unto the end of the world" (Matthew 28:20).

So, "It pays to serve Jesus, it pays ev'ry day, It pays every step of the way; Tho' the pathway to glory may sometimes be drear, You'll be happy each step of the way."

A group of scientists was in the mountains searching for a rare flower. As they looked down the side of one of the precipitous cliffs, there was their prize in a very dangerous spot, waiting to be plucked. The men looked at one another. Each of them was too heavy to be let down on the rope. Nearby there was a little boy playing. They called him and offered him money and said, "Son, if we tie this rope around you, we'll hold you. Can we let you down to pluck that flower for us?"

"Just a minute," said the little boy, and he raced into the distance and disappeared. Shortly he reappeared, holding a large man by the hand.

"All right, you can tie me up and let me down," he said.

"But who is this?" asked the scientist.

"That's my daddy, and I don't mind your letting me down on the rope as long as his hand holds it."

We may all be sure that in sickness and in health, in prosperity and adversity another hand holds us, and the power of God overshadows us. We must come to the place that we will do right for the sake of doing right and let Heaven take care of the consequences. This must be our profession of faith, our declaration of loyalty.

Follow, follow, rise up, shepherd, and follow.
Follow the star of Bethlehem,
Rise up, shepherd, and follow.

"Follow the Star"

"AND JESUS, walking by the sea of Galilee, saw two brethren, Simon called Peter, and Andrew his brother, casting a net into the sea: for they were fishers. And he saith unto them, Follow me, and I will make you fishers of men" (Matthew 4:18, 19).

These disciples, and all of the millions since then who have answered this call, became known as followers of Christ. In the intervening years, with the development of the Christian church, its adherents were sneeringly referred to as Christians first at Antioch, and this because those who truly follow Him so imitate Him as to remind their fellows of Christ Himself.

In this command to those who would become His disciples, Christ risked all. He had lived for over thirty years on this earth, and had set a habit pattern that gave Him confidence to issue such a bold invitation. Up until this point He had not sinned, and the record shows that from this point on also He

124

lived a sinless life. His life provides the only perfect pattern ever exhibited in human flesh by which we may mold our lives. Sinful man needs just such an example, for Satan argues that God cannot be obeyed. This is his contention, and with this lie he "deceiveth the whole world." But so widespread is the influence of this teaching that it took no less than the Son of God Himself in human flesh to provide a demonstration of man's ability to please God by faith in Christ. So the life of Christ has a message for us. It says that God can be obeyed in human flesh, and the Bible cites Christ as an example.

It is said that the wife of Dr. Judson, thinking to amuse him, read some newspaper notices in which he was compared to one or another of the apostles. He was exceedingly distressed and then he added, "Nor do I want to be like them. I do not want to be like Paul nor Apollos nor Cephas, nor any other man. I want to be like Christ. We have only one perfectly safe Exemplar; only one, who tempted like as we are in every point, is still without sin. I want to follow Him only, copy His teachings, drink in His Spirit, place my feet in His footprints, and measure their shortcomings by these and these only. Oh, to be more like Christ."

And significantly, this is exactly what the Scriptures teach. "Let this mind be in you, which was also in Christ Jesus" (Philippians 2:5).

My son and I often play table tennis together in the basement of our home. There have been times when I could have exerted pressure on him and defeated him, but so as not to discourage him, I would ease up and not play my best game. He would detect this immediately, and dispiritedly he would say, "Daddy, I don't want to play unless you do your best, for how can I improve if I play someone whose game is inferior to mine?" How right he was! His game could improve only in contest with someone of superior ability. Our example must excel us in all things, and this Christ does.

Man needs an example to encourage him in the face of his own recurrent delinquency. Again and again man tries and fails to live as perfectly as Christ did, and is likely to be discouraged in the effort. In spite of all the improvements we make, tendencies inherited and long cultivated often recur. This leads to self-depreciation and depression and ultimate discouragement. But to all such Christ is a door of hope, for in His flesh He did not avail Himself of His divinity to maintain His spirituality but overcame through dependence on the Father, as we must.

Christ spent long hours on His knees in prayer, and through this constant contact with the divine source of strength, He maintained His victorious stance from the cradle to the grave. This is meaningful because it shows us how to live victorious lives. Further, He offers the encouragement that is needed for erring man. His treatment of Zacchaeus, Judas, Peter, Mary Magdalene—all indicates that He sympathizes with us and is willing to help us.

"What do you do without a mother to tell all your troubles to?" asked a child who had a mother of one who had none.

"Mother told me what to do before she died," answered the little orphan. "I go to the Lord Jesus. He was mother's Friend, and He's mine."

"But," answered the other child, "Jesus is in the sky. He's away off and has a great many things to attend to in heaven. It is not likely that He can stop to listen to you."

"I do not know anything about that," answered the orphan. "All I know is that He says He will, and that's enough for me."

We are faced with the problem of environment. All about us we have examples of delinquency and outright transgression. If one should read the book of human nature he would cry out with the disciples, "Who then can be saved?" Apostasy in this world knows no profession, rank, or state of affluence. It ignores race, geographical locale, and wealth. Sin has infected the very nature of humanity, and the seeker after righteousness can get no encouragement from his environment. If he is to be helped, it must be from above.

As someone has said, "Except that which is above us comes into us, that which is within us and about us will destroy us." But Christ as our example helps us in two ways:

1. As a standard by which to measure our own need. "But we all, with open face beholding as in a glass the glory of the Lord, are changed into the same image from glory to glory even as by the Spirit of the Lord" (2 Cor. 3:18). It is a fact of human nature that whatever claims our most intense attention tends to mold our thinking and our behavior. Therefore, by beholding Christ we partake of His nature and become like Him. We behold Him by studying the Word of God. "Search the scriptures; for in them ye think ye have eternal life: and they are they which testify of me" (John 5:39). The Bible testifies of Christ. As we study the Scriptures, we come face to face with His righteous character. We begin to discern more clearly what He is like, and this in turn molds us.

2. We behold Him through prayer. As we address ourselves to Him day by day and hour by hour, He shares Himself with us. Christ also helps us as an Example, by coming into us and

enforcing the claims of His law with our consent. "For it is God which worketh in you both to will and to do of his good pleasure" (Philippians 2:13). So the example of Christ, far from being some detached, unattainable expression of the arbitrary will of God, is to the contrary an available experience to which all who believe in Him will attain. He does not demand blind obedience. The thousands of martyrs who paid with their lives for their faith in Christ knew what they were doing. Like Moses they chose to endure and suffer affliction with the people of God rather than to enjoy the pleasures of sin for a season. They coolly calculated the risks involved in choosing between the allurements of this world and the blessings of the hereafter. Christians are the most aware people on the face of the earth, for they not only become masters of their area of competence in this life; they become students of the greatest of all sciences —the science of salvation, which pertains to life here and hereafter.

Christianity, then, is an instrument of highest culture, for it creates in man an insatiable passion for knowledge and goodness. At the age of twelve Christ exhibited this quality in His conversation with the learned men of His day. They marveled at His wisdom in spite of the fact that He had not previously sat at their feet. They were unaware that they were in the presence of the one source of all wisdom, and that those who follow Him become recipients of the insights of heaven. A person thus endowed becomes a credit to humanity and to God.

In view of the spiritual and temporal benefits, is it not a mystery that more people do not follow the star of Bethlehem?

We shall overcome, we shall overcome,
We shall overcome some day.
Deep in my heart I do believe,
We shall overcome some day.

"We Shall Overcome"

"LIKEWISE RECKON ye also yourselves to be dead indeed unto sin, but alive unto God through Jesus Christ our Lord. Let not sin therefore reign in your mortal body, that ye should obey it in the lusts thereof" (Romans 6:11, 12).

We know what sin is. It is the transgression of God's law (1 John 3:4). It is rebellion against God (Genesis 39:9). It is loveless neglect of our fellow man (James 1:27). Sin as rebellion against God began in heaven in the heart of an angel. In Ezekiel 28 this angel is spoken of under the name "prince of Tyrus," but he is the same angel known as Lucifer, and later as the devil and Satan. We read, "Son of man, say unto the prince of Tyrus, Thus saith the Lord God; Because thine heart is lifted up, and thou hast said, I am a God, I sit in the seat of God, in the midst of the seas; yet thou art a man, and not God, though thou set thine heart as the heart of God" (verse 2).

"Thou wast perfect in thy ways from the day that thou wast created, till iniquity was found in thee" (verse 15).

God did not put iniquity into Lucifer, but created him perfect: "Thou sealest up the sum, full of wisdom, and perfect in beauty" (verse 12). God did not put sin into Lucifer; He found it there. Before Lucifer there was no sin. It began with him, and in the fires of hell it will end with him. God had to deal with the rebellion that began in heaven. "And there was war in heaven: Michael and his angels fought against the dragon; and the dragon fought and his angels, and prevailed not; neither was their place found any more in heaven. And the great dragon was cast out, that old serpent, called the Devil, and Satan, which deceiveth the whole world: he was cast out into the earth, and his angels were cast out with him" (Revelation 12: 7-9).

It was the devil's purpose to establish a beachhead on this planet from which he could fight his way back to the very throne of God. The devil by seducing our first parents, Adam and Eve, intended to turn this world into the seat of his rebel government, and ultimately to challenge the authority of God Himself at the very gates of glory. Viewed in this light, the temptation and fall of Adam and Eve assume even greater significance, for in seducing man the devil has merely used him as a pawn in his great struggle with God. This is the supreme deception. Our archenemy has convinced many that he, the devil, has man's interests at heart, that the laws of God are too strict and prohibitive, and that to rebel against them is a legitimate expression of man's desire for freedom.

So Satan entered the Garden where man held dominion under God. "And God blessed them, and God said unto them,

Be fruitful, and multiply, and replenish the earth, and subdue it: and have dominion over the fish of the sea, and over the fowl of the air, and over every living thing that moveth upon the earth" (Genesis 1:28).

The devil's scheme was simple—rob man of this dominion and then God would have to deal with him, Lucifer, as the god of this world, rather than with Adam. Genesis 3 reveals that to accomplish man's downfall, he attacked on a broad front.

"Yea, hath God said, Ye shall not eat of every tree of the garden? And the woman said unto the serpent, We may eat of the fruit of the trees of the garden: but of the fruit of the tree which is in the midst of the garden, God hath said, Ye shall not eat of it, neither shall ye touch it, lest ye die. And the serpent said unto the woman, Ye shall not surely die: for God doth know that in the day ye eat thereof, then your eyes shall be opened, and ye shall be as gods, knowing good and evil. And when the woman saw that the tree was good for food, and that it was pleasant to the eyes, and a tree to be desired to make

PAINTING BY VERNON NYE

© BY REVIEW AND HERALD

one wise, she took of the fruit thereof, and did eat, and gave also unto her husband with her; and he did eat" (Genesis 3: 1-6).

The devil first directed his attack at the mind, for the Bible says that the woman thought the tree was to "make one wise." He is still deluding men and women into thinking that they are somehow wiser and intellectually superior when they express their doubts about God and about the Bible and about the church and the Christian life. It has become fashionable to be skeptical. One of the chief premises of the new morality is that it would throw off all externally imposed laws and requirements, and make the human intellect the sole judge of what is right and wrong. This subtle lie began with the father of lies—the devil himself. The Creator and great God of all mankind is a God of justice, and there can be no justice without divine law. Sin is the transgression of divine law, and those who break that law are not very intellectual, they are not wise, they are not smart. Sin doesn't pay. It always collects.

The devil also attacked Eve's emotional nature. The Bible says that Eve saw "that it was pleasant to the eyes." Having become estranged from God intellectually, Eve became emotionally unbalanced, and what she had been able to pass by daily without being affected, suddenly became irresistible to her. The long fingers of temptation now gripped her soul. Such is the sure consequence of doubt. Only those who trust in God and who believe His Word are safe.

The devil attacked Eve's physical nature: "The woman saw that the tree was good for food." He appealed to her physical appetites. Today Satan has made more slaves by appealing to man's animal nature than in any other way. The Bible speaks again and again of the lust of the flesh and its destructive powers. "Now these things were our examples, to the intent we should not lust after evil things, as they also lusted. Neither be ye idolaters, as were some of them; as it is written, The people sat down to eat and drink, and rose up to play. Neither let us commit fornication, as some of them committed, and fell in one day three and twenty thousand" (1 Corinthians 10:6-8).

And so, over the thousands of years that have passed since the temptation and fall of man, the devil has not altered his strategy. Indeed, he has not needed to, for it is working too well. But thank God, no man needs to be victimized by sin. Sin can be dealt with successfully. It can be overcome. "Repent ye therefore, and be converted, that your sins may be blotted out, when the times of refreshing shall come from the presence of the Lord" (Acts 3:19).

"Wash you, make you clean; put away the evil of your doings from before mine eyes; cease to do evil; learn to do well; seek judgment, relieve the oppressed, judge the fatherless, plead for the widow. Come now, and let us reason together, saith the Lord: though your sins be as scarlet, they shall be as white as snow; though they be red like crimson, they shall be as wool. If ye be willing and obedient, ye shall eat the good of the land: but if ye refuse and rebel, ye shall be devoured with the sword: for the mouth of the Lord hath spoken it" (Isaiah 1:16-20).

Yes, it is within our power to choose to be free. Every man is born a slave to sin, but God has given us all the power of choice. We are free moral agents. We do not have to *remain* slaves of sin, and once we decide to be free, all of the powers of heaven are at our disposal to make freedom an accomplished fact. "Fear thou not; for I am with thee: be not dismayed; for

133

I am thy God: I will strengthen thee; yea, I will help thee; yea, I will uphold thee with the right hand of my righteousness" (chapter 41:10).

When Jesus Christ suffered, bled, and died at Calvary, He did it for all men's sins. He lifted the gates of heaven from their hinges, leaving forever an open door to the repentant sinner.

At Tunbridge, England, there is a monument erected to the memory of a group of gypsies. Gypsy Smith, a noted evangelist, tells us the meaning of that monument. Thirty gypsies, workers in the harvest fields, were driving rapidly and carelessly, singing and laughing, across a bridge when the wagon crashed into the railing, and wagon, horses, and gypsies were thrown into the river. One young gypsy seized a horse drifting downstream, and, mounting him, watched earnestly and anxiously for his mother. At length he saw her and laid hold upon her, but she struggled in such a way that he was not able to save her. When the gypsies were being buried in the churchyard, the boy who had tried in vain to save his mother knelt down in the trench containing the coffins and cried out, "Mother, Mother, I tried to save you. I did all that a man could do, but you would not let me."

Christ has done all that He can to save us, and He will save us if we will but let Him. Yes, we can overcome. We can overcome today.

Amazing grace! how sweet the sound
That saved a wretch like me!
I once was lost, but now am found;
Was blind, but now I see.

"Amazing Grace"

"THOUGH he were a Son, yet learned he obedience by the things which he suffered; and being made perfect, he became the author of eternal salvation unto all them that obey him" (Hebrews 5:8, 9).

This text refers to Jesus Christ. Any discussion of the subject of salvation, of being saved, of being redeemed by the precious blood of the Lamb, that does not center itself in Him is a fruitless discussion, for He is the Author of eternal salvation.

As we have said, the word *salvation* literally means "a salvage operation." It is that act whereby God takes nothing and makes something out of it. It is that act whereby God rescues a sinner from his sins and converts him into a child of the King. We have already mentioned the salvage of the many ships scuttled in Manila Harbor during World War II, and how the rusting metal was converted into useful things such as washing machines and stoves. This is exactly what happens when Christ saves a sinner. It is an act of creation. He takes a man who is dead in trespasses and sin—as the apostle Paul describes it— literally brings him back to life, and refits him, rejuvenates him, renews him, and then launches him anew upon the sea of life to be of service to his fellow men. This, in essence, is the definition of salvation.

Just how are men saved? The question before us is: What must I do to be saved? The answer is simple. We can do nothing to save ourselves. If the Bible teaches anything, it teaches this —the helplessness and hopelessness of man to save himself. "For I know that in me (that is, in my flesh,)," wrote Paul, "dwelleth no good thing" (Romans 7:18).

Human beings are like a drowning man going down for the third time. The best he can do is to throw up his hands and cry, "Help!" Unless someone dives in, makes his way to the stricken swimmer, and pulls him out, he is a lost man. This describes salvation better than anything I know.

We read in Acts that the jailer approached Paul and Silas on his knees, asking, "What must I do to be saved?" (Acts 16: 30). They answered, "Believe on the Lord Jesus Christ, and thou shalt be saved, and thy house" (verse 31).

There are two types of belief. Belief is either active or passive. Here is a man sitting in a house that is on fire. You go by and shout to him, "Mister, your house is on fire! Get out!" He says, "I believe you," but he doesn't move. This is what we call passive belief, and I don't need to tell you what would happen to the man who acted in such a way.

Let us suppose you go by his house and shout, "Mister, your house is on fire! Get out!" If he really believed you he would jump up and run out of the house as fast as possible.

This is active belief. Passive belief is mere intellectual assent. It says, "I know Jesus Christ died for my sins. So what?" Active belief embraces this cardinal doctrine of the Bible. Active belief embraces it as a personal experience. It accepts the death of Jesus Christ at Calvary in atonement for personal sin. I not only believe Him, but I believe *on* Him and *in* Him. He becomes a part of my life, for active belief claims Him by faith.

It is in this sense, then, that the apostles answered the jailer truthfully when they said, "Believe on the Lord Jesus Christ, and thou shalt be saved, and thy house."

Nineteen hundred years ago at a place called Calvary, Jesus Christ paid the supreme sacrifice for our sins. It is that act of unselfish sacrifice at Calvary that makes possible our salvation, and it is in the cross of Christ that we are to center our faith and our belief. We are to believe that because He died for us, we may be pardoned for our sins.

"Come now, and let us reason together, saith the Lord: though your sins be as scarlet, they shall be as white as snow; though they be red like crimson, they shall be as wool" (Isaiah 1:18). This literally happens to men and women who accept the sacrifice of Christ personally for their sins. We must believe that Christ died, not only to pardon, but also to cleanse. We must believe that Christ is able to break our sinful habit patterns and to take away those things that destroy the body and damn the soul. We must believe that there is power in the blood of the Lamb, wonder-working power, to pardon and cleanse. We must also believe that in the sacrifice of Christ for us peace is possible to all mankind. "Come unto me, all ye that labour and are heavy laden, and I will give you rest" (Matthew 11:28).

There are a lot of miserable people in this world today. Very few people are genuinely happy. They have what is called a guilt complex, based on their own unconfessed sins, which they have not laid on Jesus by faith. Christ says, "Bring your sins to me and though they be as scarlet, they shall be white as snow; though they be red like crimson, they shall be as wool." This is a reasonable proposition, for Christ gave His life for our lives and is therefore qualified to invite us to lay our sins on Him.

As to the ability of Christ to do this, let none be in doubt. Again and again we read in the Bible of sinners who came to Christ and received pardon, peace, and power to rise above their weaknesses. There was Mary Magdalene, the prostitute, who became a moral woman. There was Peter, the cursing, swearing fisherman, who became a calm, dignified, self-possessed Christian. There were James and John, the sons of thunder, who became so angry on one occasion that they asked the Lord to rain down fire upon the guilty inhabitants of a certain city. They later became docile, patient, quiet, tender, and loving sons of the Most High God.

Christianity works. Salvation is real. Redemption is possible. Conversion is a living experience. What must I do to be saved? Believe on the Lord Jesus Christ and you will be saved.

This question is asked again in Acts 2:38: "Then Peter said unto them, Repent, and be baptized every one of you in the name of Jesus Christ for the remission of sins, and ye shall receive the gift of the Holy Ghost." The men listening had asked, "Men and brethren, what shall we do?" This is virtually asking the same as "What shall I do to be saved?" But here we face a different answer. "Peter said unto them, Repent, and be baptized." Repentance is that act whereby man expresses to God, from his heart, a willingness to be changed, a willingness to surrender his sins, a willingness to allow God to do in his heart what needs to be done. Repentance is cooperation with God. It is relaxing our grip on our sins.

In South America an interesting method is used to catch monkeys. Men tie a container to the limb of a tree where there are monkeys, and put peanuts in the bottom of the container. The neck of the container is very narrow, while the bottom is very wide. The monkey goes to the container, forces his hand through the narrow neck into the wide bottom, spreads out his fingers, gets a handful of nuts, and, of course, can't pull his hand out again. Now if the monkey were smart, he would simply empty his hand of the nuts, make his hand as small as he did to put it in, pull it out and be safe, happy, and free. But the hunter knows that the monkey is a fool. He will not turn the peanuts loose. He will be there all night, trying to pull that handful of nuts through the narrow neck. The monkey will sacrifice his liberty for a handful of nuts.

Repentance is a willingness to relax one's hand or his grip on sin, as the monkeys would not do. This letting go is what is required of all who would be saved. Christ will not save a man with his sins. "Thou shalt call his name Jesus: for he shall save his people *from* their sins" (Matthew 1:21). Repentance, then, is a prime requisite for God to save a man.

Peter used another word in Acts 2:38—"baptized." After repentance, conversion comes automatically. As soon as we express our willingness to be changed, God steps in and changes us as of that very moment. We who were aliens from the commonwealth of Israel, without hope and without God in the

world, are made nigh by the blood of Christ. He accepts us as his sons, He adopts us into the royal family, He makes us children of the great King. All of this is based on our faith in Him and our repentance for sin.

In Matthew 19:16 we face the problem again. "Good Master, what good thing shall I do, that I may have eternal life?" asked a young man of Jesus. "If thou wilt enter into life," Jesus replied, "keep the commandments" (verse 17). Here Christ speaks of obedience.

Now let us summarize the steps man must take if God is to save him from sin:

1. Believe.

2. Repent. It is at that point that Christ converts the man, or saves him, before the man does a thing beyond simply believing. But in consequence of this salvation, he will obey. Obedience is the fruit of salvation, it is the natural outgrowth of the converted human heart, it is the fruit of the great change. An apple tree does not grow apples in order to become an apple tree. It grows apples because it is an apple tree. A man obeys God not in order to be saved; he obeys God because he has been saved. Said Jesus, "Ye shall know them by their fruits" (chap. 7:16). What we do is the outward evidence of what He has done within our hearts. The saved man obeys. Living faith works, for Titus 2:11 and 12 says, "For the grace of God that bringeth salvation hath appeared to all men, teaching us that, denying ungodliness and worldly lusts, we should live soberly, righteously, and godly, in this present world."

The grace of God within makes obedience the natural expression of divine love springing from within the man. "For it is God which worketh in you both to will and to do of his good

141

The rich young man turned away in sorrow. He wanted eternal life, but could not bring himself to give all and follow Christ.

pleasure" (Philippians 2:13). Thus the discipline of God is not regarded as oppression or suppression, but is exalted to the realm of privilege, so that the very appetites of man are brought into harmony with the will of God. Then we can say with Christ, "I delight to do thy will, O my God: yea, thy law is within my heart" (Psalm 40:8).

A friend of mine was imprisoned in the Philippines by the Japanese. He was completely cut off from all hope of rescue. The Allied armies were pressing rapidly north and south on the island, but the most optimistic prisoner expected to be shot before he could be rescued. One day, unexpectedly, the drone of airplane engines was heard overhead. The white star of the United States Army was plainly visible on the sides. Then the sky was darkened by hundreds of black dots as paratroopers leaped for the dense foliage beneath. The guards at the prison were taken completely by surprise, and in panic they scattered in all directions, leaving their prisoners, unharmed, to be liberated by United States Army paratroopers. They were saved, but not by any effort of their own. Help came at the proper time from above, and their safety was secured.

Nineteen hundred years ago help came to sinful man from above. Though lost and alienated from God, mankind is "made nigh" by the blood of Christ. Reconciliation is effected, security is assured.

Free grace and undying love,
Ring those golden bells.

"Free Grace"

THE QUESTION of salvation has been debated again and again throughout the ages, with men drawing one conclusion and then another as to how salvation comes to lost man. If the Bible is clear on anything—and it is—this question stands out abundantly clear, and the Bible's answers are full and complete. Let us examine the way men are saved, in hope that some reader will accept by faith the saving grace of the Lord Jesus Christ and find this blessed experience for himself.

In Ephesians 2, verse 8, we read: "For by grace are ye saved through faith; and that not of yourselves: it is the gift of God." Grace is the unmerited favor of God. It is an expression of the love of God for man, an unselfish love; a love that reaches out and embraces the ungrateful, the unholy, and the sinful and lost. But there are three perversions of this act of grace. We call them the three roads to hell:

1. Salvation by works. It is natural to the human heart to desire to do something to be saved. If salvation could be earned by good works, there would be a lot more people in the kingdom of God than will be there. But works alone cannot save man. In Psalm 51:5 we read, "Behold, I was shapen in iniquity; and in sin did my mother conceive me." It is clear, then, that salvation cannot come by inheritance, for in sin and iniquity is man conceived. It is further clearly indicated that man is not saved by what he does, for Galatians 5:4 says, "Christ is become of no effect unto you, whosoever of you are justified by the law; ye are fallen from grace." There are those who believe that by obeying the law of God they are justified and saved. Galatians 5:4 makes it clear that the most circumspect obedience to law is not sufficient of itself to save a man: "Christ is become of no effect unto you, whosoever of you are justified by the law; ye are fallen from grace."

This does not negate obedience to the law of God, neither does it condemn obedience. What it says is simply that obedience to law does not save a man, and that people who think it does, have fallen from grace. Now, is it possible to merit the grace of God by purchase? We find this in 1 Peter 1:18-20: "Forasmuch as ye know that ye were not redeemed with corruptible things, as silver and gold, from your vain conversation received by tradition from your fathers; but with the precious blood of Christ, as of a lamb without blemish and without spot: who verily was foreordained before the foundation of the world, but was manifest in these last times for you."

Yes, without blemish and without spot Christ offered Himself freely for our sins. So the grace of God cannot be purchased by corruptible things such as silver and gold.

In Zechariah 4:6 we are informed that the grace of God cannot be merited by the possession of earthly power. There is thus a total negation of human effort as a sufficient means of salvation. We are told that we cannot inherit salvation naturally from our parents, we cannot earn it by our obedience, we cannot purchase it with silver and gold, and we cannot receive it by the assumption of earthly power. So salvation by works alone is not a valid means of salvation.

2. Faith without works. In James 2:20 we are told that faith without works is dead. That's understandable. A man who says to his wife, "Darling, I love you," and doesn't prove it by getting a job and contributing to her support clearly indicates that his love is hypocritical. In 2 Timothy 3:5 we are warned against "a form of godliness" that denies the power of Christ. This describes the man who says, I believe in Christ, but does not demonstrate it by his daily life. This man has a mere form of godliness, but in him there is verily no exhibition of divine power. Such a man misrepresents Christ to sinners.

In Hebrews 6:4-6 it is clear that we not only misrepresent Christ, but ourselves as well: "For it is impossible for those who were once enlightened, and have tasted of the heavenly gift, and were made partakers of the Holy Ghost, and have tasted the good word of God, and the powers of the world to come, if they shall fall away, to renew them again unto repentance; seeing they crucify to themselves the Son of God afresh, and put him to an open shame." So we put God to an open shame when we profess with our lips the faith of our hearts, while doing the works of the devil in our daily lives. This is the second road to hell. But there is a third, and it is even more deceptive.

3. Faith and works. Some people believe they are saved by

10

faith in Christ and by doing what God says. This denies the fact that salvation is an act of God. We read in Romans 5:8: "But God commendeth his love toward us, in that, while we were yet sinners, Christ died for us." You see, man is totally helpless, in the face of his own sinfulness, to right his own wrongs. By faith and works this is impossible. This ignores the sinner's total unfitness. "For I know that in me (that is, in my flesh,) dwelleth no good thing," Paul wrote (chapter 7:18). This is our situation. We're like a lost man going down for the third time, and there isn't anything we can do but call for help. We're not saved by works. We're not saved by faith *and* works. We're not saved by faith without works. Then what is the one road to glory? How are men really saved? The answer is simple. We're saved by grace through faith in the Lord Jesus Christ, but that faith we exercise in the Lord Jesus Christ works. So we might say that *we are saved by grace through faith that works.*

James 2:18, 19 makes this clear: "Yea, a man may say, Thou hast faith, and I have works; shew me thy faith without thy works, and I will shew thee my faith by my works. Thou believest that there is one God; thou doest well: the devils also believe, and tremble." You see, faith works. Faith works in and through the heart and life of the individual. Works are a demonstration of faith. Obedience is a manifestation of grace. It is as natural as a man who, having eaten food and acquired energy, wakes up in the morning, and with that energy goes to work. He doesn't go to work in order to eat. He goes to work because he has eaten. He goes to work because of the energy that has come into his body from the food he ate. In short, food with its energy is the strength with which man is enabled to work. Even so, faith powers a man to keep God's commandments.

146

In Acts 10:35 we read that in every nation he who respects God and does right "is accepted with him." You see, man must fear (believe) in Christ, and if he does so genuinely, that fear and belief impels man to obey God and work righteousness. The Bible says that such is accepted with God; accepted on the basis of a man's faith and that alone. For by this a man is saved—through grace by faith. That faith is obedient, active, saving faith. That faith is resisting faith. It is working faith. So when you see a son of God, you see an active, obedient, compliant child of God. You see a man who is about his Father's business, not in order that he might become a son of God but because by grace through faith he already is. What he does simply tells the world what he is.

We must follow that road. The Shepherd of Israel has trod its narrow way before us. It is the way of service, service to God and fellow man. The prayer of our hearts should be:

> If they have sinned, yet lay Thy hand
> On me who at Thine altar stand;
> Ah Thou, who tendest this poor vine,
> Tread out the grapes; and all the wine
> Be theirs—and Thine!
> —RICHARD ROBERTS

"Petty men take the way of revolt; smash their way through and leave a trail of wreckage and fears behind them. Strong men show the quality of their strength by remembering those that are weak. The wise man hears the voice and follows the footsteps of our loving Lord who said, 'I am the way, the truth, and the life.'"

> Free grace and undying love,
> Ring those golden bells.

147

Thank you, Jesus;
Thank you, Lord;
For you brought me
From a mighty long way.

"Thank You, Jesus"

JESUS CHRIST is a friend of sinners, and that's good news. Whenever He approached a community, a quiver of excitement thrilled the needy as they realized that help was near at hand. Christ took the hardest cases. He sought out the most hopeless and ministered to their needs—the men possessed with demons who dwelt among the tombs, Mary the prostitute, the despised tax collectors, Zacchaeus and Matthew. It was said of Him, He eateth with sinners. Were Christ on earth today He would shock many of the middle-class concepts of today's church members. Many are too afraid of getting their clothing soiled or subjecting their olfactory senses to the stench of poverty to ever come to the areas of deepest need. This is where Christ would be found today—among people who need Him most.

Let us first consider Him in action with the woman of ill fame. It is early in the morning, according to John 8, and

148

He is sitting and teaching the people when the scribes and Pharisees appear, bringing with them a woman taken in adultery. It is significant that they knew where to go to find this woman. It has been suggested that perhaps they were among her old customers. In any event, they confronted the Master with a difficult question. They quoted the law with reference to one caught in the act of adultery and then asked the Master what His judgment would be. According to John 8:6-8, "Jesus stooped down, and with his finger wrote on the ground, as though he heard them not. So when they continued asking him, he lifted up himself, and said unto them, He that is without sin among you, let him first cast a stone at her. And again he stooped down, and wrote on the ground."

Apparently this was effective as far as her tormentors were concerned, for "they which heard it, being convicted by their own conscience, went out one by one, beginning at the eldest, even unto the last: and Jesus was left alone, and the woman standing in the midst. When Jesus had lifted up himself, and saw none but the woman, he said unto her, Woman, where are those thine accusers? hath no man condemned thee?" (verses 9, 10).

Notice that Jesus does not begin by condemning the woman for what she had done. She stood condemned already. What this woman needed was help, encouragement. Her own conscience was already condemning her. She didn't need harsh words from someone else to add to her misery. How much of our Christian ministry is a ministry of condemnation and hard words? The woman's answer to Him is significant.

"She said, No man, Lord" (verse 11). She did not say that God did not condemn her. In her own soul, standing in the

149

presence of the only begotten Son of God, her heart had felt the convicting power of His pure gaze, and her mind was open to His saving grace. But she did say, "No man, Lord."

The next words that fell from the lips of our Lord were as dew distilling on the tender green blades of young grass, "Neither do I condemn thee; go, and sin no more."

These are the words of a friend, and as you read this page, my brother, know that in those darkened corners of your own life that need light, those not-so-tidy portions of the heart that need rearrangement, that this same Friend of sinners stands ready to pardon, cleanse, and empower—in short, to make of you a new creature. And that's good news!

Let us watch Jesus in action with a thieving tax collector by the name of Zacchaeus. This little man heard that Christ was coming, so he ran and climbed into a sycamore tree to see Him, "for he was to pass that way" (Luke 19:4). "And when Jesus came to the place, he looked up, and saw him" (verse 5). This is typical of the Friend of sinners. He is responsive to the slightest movement toward Him. The most primitive inclination of the heart to reach out to Him finds its response in the great heart of God. Christ interpreted this act on the part of Zacchaeus in climbing the tree as reflecting a deep interest in Him. Christ did not ignore this man of a hated profession. He did not, as some might, look upon him with scorn, but respected him as a soul to be saved.

Jesus then "said unto him, Zacchaeus, make haste, and come down; for today I must abide at thy house" (verse 5).

What surer way to break a sinner's heart than to treat him with such deep interest and love! Zacchaeus became the envy of the neighborhood, for he who was despised and hated—and with some justification—was now the object of the Saviour's supreme regard. This would be a most unforgettable day for him. Christ was going to abide at his house! "And he made haste, and came down, and received him joyfully" (verse 6).

Certainly there were better homes in the area and more reputable hosts who would have been happy to have entertained our Lord. There were the righteous, the wealthy, the powerful, and the educated, and their feelings were injured that such respectable people had been bypassed. "And when they saw it, they all murmured, saying, That he was gone to be guest with a man that is a sinner" (verse 7).

If Christ had spent all His time among the respectable people, then the kingdom of God would have come to a quick and certain end, for "the common people heard him gladly." There seems to be a tendency on the part of the affluent to trust in their affluence, whether it be financial, social, or educational. Many of these people find it hard to follow the Man of Galilee. The reaction of Zacchaeus to the Master's thoughtful consideration brought repentance to his soul. "And Zacchaeus stood, and said unto the Lord; Behold, Lord, the half of my goods I give to the poor; and if I have taken any thing from any man by false accusation, I restore him fourfold" (verse 8).

Christ hadn't said a thing about stealing, though He knew that Zacchaeus was a thief. He treated the man with kindness and respect. This broke his heart and brought him to the feet of the Master in true repentance. "And Jesus said unto him, This day is salvation come to this house" (verse 9).

Jesus Christ is a friend of sinners, and that's good news.

The demoniacs presented a difficult problem. The two men involved were isolated from society. They were "possessed with devils, coming out of the tombs, exceeding fierce, so that no man might pass by that way" (Matthew 8:28). Christ knew that they were there, but He deliberately came that way, and immediately nature began to take its course. They rushed out, but the voices that cried to Him were the voices of demons: "What have we to do with thee, Jesus, thou Son of God? art thou come hither to torment us before the time?" (verse 29).

These men were so under the influence of Satan that he used their voices, and they were powerless to speak for themselves. This looks like an impossible case if ever there was one, but I have news for you. The impossible becomes possible under the touch of the Master's hand. There is something curiously reminiscent about these words of demons, "Art thou come hither to torment us before the time?" You see, they had met Christ before. He was their Creator. According to Revelation 12:7-9, He had cast them out of heaven. So when they met Him they knew that He would put them to flight.

In the presence of Jesus the demons' wail was an expression of fear. It is the question of a defeated person in the presence of his conqueror. When will we understand that Christ has already defeated the devil, and that if we will put our hand in His, He will accomplish for us what He has done already for Himself? "Submit yourselves therefore to God. Resist the devil, and he will flee from you" (James 4:7).

The song writer says, "Yield not to temptation, For yielding is sin, Each victory will help you some other to win; Fight manfully onward, Dark passions subdue, Look ever to Jesus, He'll carry you through. Ask the Saviour to help you, Comfort, strengthen, and keep you; He is willing to aid you, He will carry you through."

152

Christ didn't even bother to answer the demons that shouted from the lips of these two needy souls. "The devils besought him, saying, If thou cast us out, suffer us to go away into the herd of swine" (Matthew 8:31).

It was then that Christ spoke His first and only word to the demons that had enslaved two souls for whom He was about to die: "And he said unto them, Go" (verse 32). And they were expelled so violently that they caused the herd of swine to plunge down a steep place into the sea and perish in the waters. But Christ's mission had been accomplished. He had saved two souls.

What does this miracle say to us? Christ is a friend of sinners! He can be trusted with our lives. It is an open invitation to any man anywhere, living under any circumstance, however dismal, to look up and lift up his head, put his hand in the hand of God and commit his will to the will of God, and allow Christ to control his life.

> You've been my mother,
> You've been my father;
> You've been my sister, my brother too;
> Yes, You brought me from a mighty long way.

We are climbing Jacob's ladder, . . .
Every round goes higher, higher,
Soldiers of the cross.

"Jacob's Ladder"

"FOR BY GRACE are ye saved through faith; and that not of yourselves: it is the gift of God: not of works, lest any man should boast" (Ephesians 2:8, 9).

Essentially, the whole problem of sin may be summarized by the one word, *unbelief,* for the saved are the true believers. It is not easy to believe that we are saved from the power, presence, and guilt of sin by the sacrifice of another. It is deeply ingrained in human nature that we pay for every benefit. Historically man has been trained to merit his privileges. We are taught from childhood the doctrine of self-reliance. But in the truth of the gospel we are brought face to face with that which is humanly impossible. The great gulf between God and man can never be bridged by human merit. Sin has separated man from God, according to Isaiah 59:2. Therefore, without the divine approach man cannot even establish communication with

Daily prayer and Bible study enable us to make progress in Christian living and to prepare ourselves thoroughly for life eternal.

his Maker. We are reduced, therefore, to the one means of salvation open to man—that is, by grace through faith in the Lord Jesus Christ.

The word *grace* means "unmerited favor." A loving God must confer upon His children the privilege of sonship, and this He promises to all who put their faith in Him. But even this—man's faith—is a gift of God according to our text, but this gift God has generously shared with the human family.

In Romans 12:3 we read: "For I say, through the grace given unto me, to every man that is among you, not to think of himself more highly than he ought to think; but to think soberly, according as God hath dealt to every man the measure of faith."

Mysteriously ingrained in the heart of every new-born babe is the faintly flickering flame of faith. This focal point of past and future lies casually embedded in the nature of embryonic innocence. The development of faith and the placement of that faith will determine the destiny of each soul.

While it is true that a merciful Creator bountifully shares living faith with all His creatures, He leaves it to a man's choice as to where he will place his faith and whether or not he will develop it. Faith placed in Christ is never misplaced. It is when we trust ourselves and others with our salvation that we are doomed to disappointment.

"That at that time ye were without Christ, being aliens from the commonwealth of Israel, and strangers from the covenants of promise, having no hope, and without God in the world: but now in Christ Jesus ye who sometimes were far off are made nigh by the blood of Christ" (Ephesians 2:12, 13).

The human concept is, If I do I shall live. The gospel concept is, In Him I live, for Christ has done and is doing and will do in me and for me the will of God.

As we look about the religious world today, we see the sure results of two errors conceived and perpetuated over the centuries: 1. The error of the Hebrew nation, of strict obedience to the law while rejecting Christ. 2. The error that when a person accepts Christ he is no longer obligated to obey Christ. According to a third, and still more confusing, theory a man is saved by faith in Christ and obedience to His law. All three are erroneous concepts.

The Bible teaches that a man is saved by faith in Christ and that alone, and that his obedience is a consequence of that salvation.

"Thou shalt call his name Jesus: for he shall save his people from their sins" (Matthew 1:21).

Salvation by grace through faith in Christ involves justification and sanctification. "Therefore being justified by faith," wrote Paul, "we have peace with God through our Lord Jesus Christ: by whom also we have access by faith into this grace wherein we stand, and rejoice in hope of the glory of God" (Romans 5:1, 2).

It is an act of grace that changes man's standing before God. A man walks into the presence of God guilty, but if he puts his faith in Christ, he is immediately declared not guilty. Christ is able to do this because He became man's substitute in life and death. He became man's Sin Bearer. "He was wounded for our transgressions, he was bruised for our iniquities: the chastisement of our peace was upon him; and with his stripes we are healed" (Isaiah 53:5).

The moment we accept this priceless offer we are declared

just before God. We have made the transition from aliens to sons, from foreigners to citizens, from darkness to light, from sin to salvation. But the work of God in behalf of man at this point has only begun. What follows, we call sanctification.

Let us study that word. Sanctification is the process whereby God separates a man from his sins. Sanctification is the outgrowth of justification. There is no such thing as a justified, unsanctified man. A justified man must be separated from his sinful practices, and the process by which God accomplishes this is called *sanctification*.

"Wash you, make you clean; put away the evil of your doings from before mine eyes; cease to do evil; learn to do well; seek judgment, relieve the oppressed, judge the fatherless, plead for the widow. Come now, and let us reason together, saith the Lord: though your sins be as scarlet, they shall be as white as snow; though they be red like crimson, they shall be as wool" (Isaiah 1:16-18).

"What shall we say then? Shall we continue in sin, that grace may abound? God forbid. How shall we, that are dead to sin, live any longer therein?" (Romans 6:1, 2).

So there does occur in the life of a Christian a transformation, a change: "And be not conformed to this world: but be ye transformed by the renewing of your mind, that ye may prove what is that good, and acceptable, and perfect, will of God" (chapter 12:2).

Yes, sinful habits can and must be broken.

"Let not sin therefore reign in your mortal body, that ye should obey it in the lusts thereof. Neither yield ye your members as instruments of unrighteousness unto sin: but yield yourselves unto God, as those that are alive from the dead, and your members as instruments of righteousness unto God" (chapter 6:12, 13).

The degree of our yielding is determined by the state of our faith. A man's state of grace is dependent upon his state of faith. The more perfect our faith in Christ is, the more perfectly we will obey Him. That obedience, however, springs from within. God's requirements become privileges when they are lovingly and willingly obeyed, out of a converted heart. Sanctification, then, is the perfection of faith, and faith is perfected through testing day by day.

Yes, day by day through prayer and the study of the Word of God and the exercise of the will a man does battle with human nature and the temptations of the evil one. He is victorious if his faith is firm. We cannot win tomorrow's battle today. Each confrontation is individual, and we will be tested as long as we are in the flesh. But what if, during a given test, we fail? Are we then lost? Thank God, the answer is a resounding No! "If we confess our sins, he is faithful and just to forgive us our sins, and to cleanse us from all unrighteousness" (1 John 1:9).

"My little children, these things write I unto you, that ye sin not. And if any man sin, we have an advocate with the Father, Jesus Christ the righteous" (chapter 2:1).

This marvelous provision of forgiveness is not given to encourage us to continue to indulge our weaknesses, but rather as an encouraging instrument of deliverance. We must not ask forgiveness under the false assumption that the blood of Jesus Christ will cover the deliberately unrepentant sinner. What this text does say is that if I, at any given time, disappoint my Master and myself by transgressing His holy law, He stands ready to pick me up and launch me anew toward the kingdom of God in the ship of divine forgiveness.

No, we do not fall in and out of the heavenly family by individual acts of transgression. It is when our faith fails that we are lost. It is when we no longer believe that we are sons and daughters of God by His saving grace that we have closed the door of hope in our own faces. It is when we lose faith in His power, not only to forgive but to destroy sin in us and to enable us to live victorious lives, that we have joined that unfortunate group known as the legions of the damned. Only prayer and the study of the Word of God can feed our faith and keep it from failing under the pressures of environmental evil as well as internal inclination. Thus we "fight the good fight of faith." If we falter or fail, we pray for strength to believe and strive, and we rise to fight again. This is the history of the overcomer.

In the life of the apostle Peter we find much encouragement, for over a period of years he was transformed from a cursing, self-confident fisherman into a man so powerful that he could lead thousands to the foot of the cross, and at the same time so meek that at his crucifixion he would request to be crucified upside down because he felt unworthy to die as his Master had died. So—

> Have faith in God;
> In Him you stand perfected;
> Have faith in God;
> From sin thou art protected;
> Have faith, dear friend, in God.

And having put your foot on Jacob's ladder, continue your journey to the kingdom.

All night, all day,
The angels are watching over
me, my Lord.

"Angels Watching Over Me"

"WHEN I CONSIDER thy heavens, the work of thy fingers, the moon and the stars, which thou hast ordained; what is man, that thou art mindful of him? and the son of man, that thou visitest him? For thou hast made him a little lower than the angels, and hast crowned him with glory and honour" (Psalm 8:3-5).

Angels are created beings of a higher order than man. They are intelligent, powerful agents of the Lord, performing His purposes in heaven and earth. There are different orders of angels. There are the cherubim and the seraphim. Cherubim were placed to guard the way to the tree of life, to prevent men expelled from the Garden of Eden from eating of the tree (Genesis 3:24).

The seraphim had six wings. Isaiah heard them chanting, "Holy, holy, holy, is the Lord of hosts: the whole earth is full of his glory" (Isaiah 6:3). These heavenly beings are most

11

numerous, for when Peter sought to defend Jesus in the Garden of Gethsemane, he was sternly told to put up his sword. Jesus could pray the Father, and twelve legions of angels would come to His rescue.

Daniel 7:10 says: "A fiery stream issued and came forth from before him: thousand thousands ministered unto him, and ten thousand times ten thousand stood before him." There are so many angels in heaven that, after the expulsion of Lucifer and his cohorts, there were still enough to do the Master's biddings in heaven and in earth and throughout the universe. The devil is an angel himself, and was once in heaven. Of him the Bible says, "Thou art the anointed cherub that covereth; and I have set thee so: thou wast upon the holy mountain of God; thou hast walked up and down in the midst of the stones of fire. Thou wast perfect in thy ways from the day that thou wast created, till iniquity was found in thee" (Ezekiel 28:14, 15).

In Revelation 12:7-9 we read: "And there was war in heaven: Michael and his angels fought against the dragon; and the dragon fought and his angels, and prevailed not; neither was their place found any more in heaven. And the great dragon was cast out, that old serpent, called the Devil, and Satan, which deceiveth the whole world: he was cast out into the earth, and his angels were cast out with him."

The work of evil angels has been treated in another chapter. God's unfallen angels are active in the world today. We read in Hebrews 1:13, 14: "But to which of the angels said he at any time, Sit on my right hand, until I make thine enemies thy footstool? Are they not all ministering spirits, sent forth to minister for them who shall be heirs of salvation?"

These special messengers of the Lord are sent into the

earth as man's helpers in his struggle against evil. "The angel of the Lord encampeth round about them that fear him, and delivereth them" (Psalm 34:7). Not only are angels sent for our protection, they help us to understand the Word of God and the will of God. Daniel relates such an experience: "Yea, whiles I was speaking in prayer, even the man Gabriel, whom I had seen in the vision at the beginning, being caused to fly swiftly, touched me about the time of the evening oblation. And he informed me, and talked with me, and said, O Daniel, I am now come forth to give thee skill and understanding" (Daniel 9:21, 22).

Angels have been known to deliver God's people on the field of battle, and when the prophet Elijah was faint from a long day's journey, asleep under a juniper tree, the Bible says that an angel touched him and bade him arise and eat. "And he looked, and, behold, there was a cake baken on the coals, and a cruse of water at his head. And he did eat and drink, and laid him down again" (1 Kings 19:6).

This personal interest taken by spiritual beings in the welfare of humanity is but another revelation of the love of God for man. How comforting it is to know that even when asleep we are protected by guardian angels! Only when we enter the kingdom of God will we know the full extent of God's care for His people. The prophet Daniel gives a graphic description of what happened to him in the lions' den. He was flung there because of his faithfulness to God. These lions had not been fed for some time. The next morning Daniel was still alive, and when the king inquired as to his physical well-being, Daniel answered, "My God hath sent his angel, and hath shut the lions' mouths, that they have not hurt me: forasmuch as before him innocency was found in me; and also before thee, O king, have I done no hurt" (Daniel 6:22).

Whenever a minister stands up to proclaim the Word of God unseen angels stand by to assist him and to give effectiveness to his words. "And I saw another angel fly in the midst of heaven, having the everlasting gospel to preach unto them that dwell on the earth, and to every nation, and kindred, and tongue, and people" (Revelation 14:6). The angel doesn't do the actual preaching. Men do that. But angels are there to assist in the delivery of the message.

When God gets ready to destroy evil men, He will send angels upon that mission of destruction. "And I heard a great voice out of the temple saying to the seven angels, Go your ways, and pour out the vials of the wrath of God upon the earth" (chapter 16:1). And when Jesus comes back to this earth to receive His children, He will send the angels to gather them together and to escort them to meet Him in the clouds. "And he shall send his angels with a great sound of a trumpet, and they shall gather together his elect from the four winds, from one end of heaven to the other" (Matthew 24:31).

Angels had a part in the giving of the Scriptures: "The Revelation of Jesus Christ, which God gave unto him, to shew unto his servants things which must shortly come to pass; and he sent and signified it by his angel unto his servant John" (Revelation 1:1).

Angels have administered the justice of God: "And immediately the angel of the Lord smote him, because he gave not God the glory: and he was eaten of worms, and gave up the ghost" (Acts 12:23).

Angels are the protectors of our lives: "For he shall give his angels charge over thee, to keep thee in all thy ways. They shall bear thee up in their hands, lest thou dash thy foot against a stone" (Psalm 91:11, 12).

Angels are powerful beings. According to Matthew 28:2, 3: "There was a great earthquake: for the angel of the Lord descended from heaven, and came and rolled back the stone from the door, and sat upon it. His countenance was like lightning, and his raiment white as snow." So powerful was this mighty being that the earth shook at his presence.

Angels can fly with blinding speed. According to Daniel 9:21, 23, the angel Gabriel informed Daniel that he had been dispatched from heaven when Daniel began to pray, only a few minutes earlier.

Now the sun is 93 million miles away, and the casual reading of the prayer of Daniel takes just three minutes. Figuring only the distance from the earth to the sun, the angel Gabriel would have been traveling 31 million miles per minute. But he traveled farther than that, and so must have been traveling much faster. What blessed assurance this is to all who pray to God for help! Before we call He will answer, and while we are yet speaking God will hear.

An angel bore the announcement to Mary that she was the fortunate woman selected to be the mother of our Lord. Angels brought the announcement to the shepherds who watched their flocks by night, and angel voices were heard lifted in singing at the birth of the only begotten Son of God. You will never know until you get into the kingdom of God what dangers you have survived and what problems have been avoided, due to the intervention of holy angels. They have to obey God to remain in His good favor, just like human beings.

"The Lord hath prepared his throne in the heavens; and his kingdom ruleth over all. Bless the Lord, ye his angels, that excel in strength, that do his commandments, hearkening unto the voice of his word. Bless ye the Lord, all ye his hosts; ye ministers of his, that do his pleasure" (Psalm 103:19-21).

A few years ago I knelt in the Garden of Gethsemane, that sacred spot where our Lord spent His night of agony, the weight of the world's sins pressing upon Him, exercising such great pressure on His heart that great drops of sweat like blood oozed from His pores. The cup of human salvation trembled in the balance as the Saviour weakened physically under the load of the world's guilt. He prayed, "Father, if thou be willing, remove this cup from me," but instead, an angel was dispatched from heaven to strengthen Him and to encourage Him in this great mission of salvation. "Not my will, but thine, be done" (Luke 22:42), was the final decision.

An angel of the Lord appeared at the side of our Saviour at a very crucial time for Him and for us all, and strengthened Him to walk the torturous trail to Golgotha. The ministry of angels is another manifestation of God's love for us, and I take comfort in the words of the spiritual:

> All night, all day,
> The angels are watching over
> me, my Lord.

Don't worry about him, don't worry
about him;
God will work a wonder. Don't worry
about him.

"God Will Work a Wonder"

SOMEDAY SOON civilization as we now know it will come to an abrupt and catastrophic end. "The day of the Lord shall come as a thief in the night; in the which the heavens shall pass away with a great noise, and the elements shall melt with fervent heat, the earth also and the works that are therein shall be burned up" (2 Peter 3:10).

Joel's prediction of a great outpouring of God's Spirit in his day appropriately describes what God would do for us today: "It shall come to pass afterward, that I will pour out my spirit upon all flesh; and your sons and your daughters shall prophesy, your old men shall dream dreams, your young men shall see visions" (Joel 2:28).

The final work of the Holy Spirit in the lives of the saints will constitute the most glorious chapter in the history of the church. The program of God will end in a blaze of glory. God's side is going to win. The secret of that triumph is contained in

167

the words of the text: "I will pour out my spirit upon all flesh." The Holy Spirit of God, the third person of the Godhead, is in charge of the work of God in human hearts on the earth today. In the words of Hosea 6:3: "Then shall we know, if we follow on to know the Lord: his going forth is prepared as the morning; and he shall come unto us as the rain, as the latter and former rain unto the earth."

Here an agricultural figure of speech is used to describe the work of the Holy Spirit. Any good farmer knows that without the former rain the plant is likely to wither and die, and a tender blade of grass would barely clear the surface of the earth before it became discolored and faded away. So the early rain enables the newly planted seed to grow and flourish. Later comes what is called the latter rain, which ripens the grain and prepares it for harvest. This is what we face—the baptism of the Spirit compared to the latter rain to ripen the spiritual experiences of God's people all over the world, preparing them for the final conquest of the gospel and the coming of the Lord.

"Ask ye of the Lord rain in the time of the latter rain; so the Lord shall make bright clouds, and give them showers of rain, to every one grass in the field" (Zechariah 10:1). Men and women all over the world should be praying for the baptism of the Holy Spirit, but some are afraid of Him. They have seen some people supposedly under the influence of the Holy Spirit wallow on the ground, foaming at the mouth, their bodies contorted, their eyes wild and staring, making utterances that no one understands, and they say, "If this is what the Spirit of God does, I don't want Him in my life." This, dear reader, misrepresents God. The work of the Spirit of God is far deeper. John 16:13 says that it is the Spirit of God who guides man into a knowledge of truth. It is the Holy Spirit who converts us and who spreads the love of God abroad in our hearts. It is His love that softens and subdues and converts us. Far from making us shriek like madmen, the Holy Spirit cultures and refines us as we receive Him, and we become true representatives to our fellow men of what God is like.

But what about unknown tongues? There are those who contend that unless you can speak in a language nobody understands, you do not have the Holy Spirit. Nothing could be farther from the truth. According to Acts 1:8, people who witness to the love of Christ in a language that can be understood give clear evidence that they have been filled with the Spirit of God. "But ye shall receive power, after that the Holy Ghost is come upon you: and ye shall be witnesses unto me both in Jerusalem, and in all Judaea, and in Samaria, and unto the uttermost part of the earth."

But what of the unknown tongue of the Bible? Why was it given and what purpose did it serve? According to Acts 2, on the day of Pentecost when men from every nation gathered at Jerusalem, the disciples were filled with the Spirit and began to speak with other tongues as the Spirit gave them utterance. But what they were saying could be understood, according to verse 6: "Now when this was noised abroad, the multitude came together, and were confounded, because that every man heard them speak in his own language."

In 1 Corinthians 14 Paul exhorts Christians to speak with tongues that can be understood: "So likewise ye, except ye utter by the tongue words easy to be understood, how shall it be known what is spoken? for ye shall speak into the air" (verse 9). In verse 2 Paul makes it clear that no man will listen to one who speaks in an unknown tongue, therefore the speaker will be talking to God alone. Further, the apostle exhorted those who spoke in foreign languages to be sure that someone was present who could interpret what they were saying! "If any man speak in an unknown tongue, let it be by two, or at the most by three, and that by course; and let one interpret. But if there be no interpreter, let him keep silence in the church; and let him speak to himself, and to God" (verses 27, 28).

Several things are indicated here. A man who is under the control of the Spirit of God is not out of his senses. He has self-control, or he would not be able to obey the injunction of the prophet. He wouldn't know what he was doing, which is the case with many today who claim to be under the Spirit of God while speaking in unknown tongues. Further, the apostle states that not more than two or three should speak at any given service, and one at a time. The reason for this is that God is not the Author of confusion but of peace in all the churches of the saints (verse 33). "Even things without life giving sound, whether pipe or harp, except they give a distinction in the sounds, how shall it be known what is piped or harped?" (verse 7).

It is interesting to note that all the gifts of the Spirit were manifest while Christ was here, except the gift of tongues. This gift was withheld until the coming of the Holy Spirit at Pentecost, so believers and unbelievers would have a distinct sign that Christ had kept His promise and that the third person of the Godhead was now on earth. It is significant that this gift was first manifested when the Spirit of God entered the room where the 120 were gathered after Pentecost (Acts 2:1-4). Ignorant and unlearned men were suddenly possessed with the power to speak in languages other than their native tongue. Both those who spoke and those who listened had to give credit to God, for this was a Heaven-born miracle.

But what of today? Is everyone expected to manifest this gift if the Spirit of God is in him? The Bible gives an answer in 1 Corinthians 12: "For to one is given by the Spirit the word of wisdom; to another the word of knowledge by the same Spirit; to another faith by the same Spirit; to another the gifts of healing by the same Spirit; to another the working of miracles; to another prophecy; to another discerning of spirits; to another divers kinds of tongues; to another the interpretation of tongues: but all these worketh that one and the selfsame Spirit, dividing to every man severally as he will" (verses 8-11).

"And God hath set some in the church, first apostles, secondarily prophets, thirdly teachers, after that miracles, then gifts of healings, helps, governments, diversities of tongues. Are all apostles? are all prophets? are all teachers? are all workers of miracles? Have all the gifts of healing? do all speak with tongues? do all interpret?" (verses 28-30).

Today as in ancient times the Spirit of God distributes the gifts as He will. He has not given any one man all of the gifts, nor has He given all men the same gift. So then let not him that speaks with tongues boast against the man who does not, for the same Spirit that gave one man his gift also gave the other his. Furthermore, in listing the gifts in the order of their importance, the gift of tongues is mentioned last. Why have some people put it first and made it the one test of the presence of the Spirit of God in the life? Truly there is but one Bible test of the presence of the Holy Spirit in the heart of man, and that is love. Galatians 5:22 and 23 clearly states this: "But the fruit of the Spirit is love, joy, peace, longsuffering, gentleness, goodness, faith, meekness, temperance: against such there is no law."

"By this shall all men know that ye are my disciples, if ye have love one to another" (John 13:35).

Romans 5:5 says that love is shed abroad in our hearts by the Holy Ghost. It is the love of God that transforms and subdues us. It is His love that melts our hard hearts and gives rise to new purposes and attitudes. It is love that saves the soul, and the Spirit of God is in the soul-saving business. The time has indeed come for all men everywhere to pray for the outpouring of the Spirit of God and for the baptism of fire. It is this that will deliver us from the power of defiling habits. It is the Spirit of God who will develop in us consistent Christian lives. It is He who brings joy to the heart and peace to the soul. He rebukes the barrenness of the sinner's heart, and it is He who can grow an oasis of green on the arid desert of a sin-wasted life. Let the withered soul seek the refreshing waters of the fountain of life. Let him drink deeply until the fruit of the Spirit springs up and ripens for the great harvest yet to come. Let there be a seeking after God such as David described when he said, "As the hart panteth after the water brooks, so panteth my soul after thee, O God" (Psalm 42:1). Then will we realize in our own lives the experience described by the psalmist, "He shall come down like rain upon the mown grass" (chapter 72:6).

This experience we must have before God begins to work His wonders in the earth and in the sky, and the great and dreadful day of our God breaks upon the world.

Shine on me, Lord, shine on me;
Let the light from the lighthouse shine.

"Shine on Me"

WHO IS the Holy Spirit? In the Holy Scriptures the personal pronoun "he" is used in referring to the Holy Spirit. This clearly indicates that the Holy Spirit is a person. He is not a vapor, not an influence, not a disembodied spirit, but a person. This is clearly indicated in the divine commission recorded in Matthew 28:19, 20: "Go ye therefore, and teach all nations, baptizing them in the name of the Father, and of the Son, and of the Holy Ghost: teaching them to observe all things whatsoever I have commanded you: and, lo, I am with you alway, even unto the end of the world."

Here the Holy Spirit is mentioned as the third person of the Trinity. In a previous chapter we discussed the question of the one God we Christians worship. But that one God is in three persons. They are always listed in the Bible in this order: Father, Son, and Holy Spirit. Someone has raised the question: Why in that order? No man on earth can give the complete answer, but we can point out that Jesus Christ was entrusted by God the Father with the heavy responsibility of both creating and redeeming the world. The third person of the Godhead is the only one on earth through whom we may reach heaven now, and that's why this chapter is so important.

Jesus said in John 16:7, "It is expedient for you that I go away: for if I go not away, the Comforter will not come unto you; but if I depart, I will send him unto you." There was a work in heaven that had to be done for us that only the Holy Spirit could do, and there was a work on earth, an enlargement of the kingdom of God, that necessitated a Person who possessed the powers of omnipresence. In other words, the Spirit of God could be everywhere present at once, because He and God the Father are unencumbered by a human body. One of the great sacrifices Christ made for man was that He took on human flesh and localized Himself in a human body, which was glorified at the resurrection.

Needed in this world to circulate the gospel from one end of the globe to the other was a divine Person unhindered by human flesh. The Holy Spirit meets this specification. Several marks of personality attributed in the Bible to the Holy Spirit indicate that He is an intelligent being. According to 1 Corinthians 2: 9-11 He has knowledge. In 1 Corinthians 12:11 we discover that He has a will, and in Romans 8:27, a mind. In Romans 15:30 we find that He loves; and in 2 Corinthians 13:14 He talks. According to Ephesians 4:30 the Holy Ghost can be grieved, and in Hebrews 10:29 we read that He can be insulted. In Acts 5:3, He can be lied to, and in Matthew 12:31, 32, He can be sinned against. These all are marks of personality, clearly indicating that in dealing with the Holy Spirit we are dealing with a Person, a divine Person—the third person of the Godhead, the Holy Spirit.

The Spirit of God is in the earth and has now been on His final mission of sanctification and salvation for some nineteen hundred years. Of course, the Spirit of God was on the earth long before that, but His relationship to the church was different. In Genesis 1 we find that the Spirit of God moved upon the face of the waters. "And God said, Let there be light: and there was light" (Genesis 1:3). So the Holy Spirit was here to work even in the Creation. He worked among God's people in Old Testament times. Centuries later on the day of Pentecost, the Spirit of God descended in power. The room in which the disciples met was filled with His holy presence, and they went forth with a manifestation of spiritual power that converted thousands to Christ. Yes, one of the works of the Spirit of God is to accomplish the work of conversion in human hearts.

Because of the meaningless antics of some people which they attribute to the influence of the Holy Spirit, decent and intelligent men have backed away from Him because they don't want such things to happen to them. According to the Bible, one of the works of the Spirit of God is not to make you shout or fall or foam, but rather to dig deeply into the secret crevices of the human heart, root out sin, create within man a receptive attitude to the Spirit of Christ, to convert, to transform, to ennoble, to empower, to uplift, to change. This is the deep, serious work of the third person of the Godhead, and without Him we dare not live a day.

How does one receive the Spirit of God? This is an important question, and it deserves a truthful answer. In Acts 3:19 we read: "Repent ye therefore, and be converted, that your sins may be blotted out, when the times of refreshing shall come from the presence of the Lord." One prerequisite of the outpouring of the Spirit of God is repentance. We must submit our wills to Christ. We must stop fighting Him and allow His will to become ours. We must permit the principles contained in Holy Scripture to be written in our hearts. We must receive personally the sacrifice of Christ at Calvary for our sins. We must claim the blood of Christ. We must surrender our own selfish, stubborn purposes and plans. We must accept Christ as our personal Saviour and our Companion and Lord. When we do this our hearts are filled with His blessed presence. The Holy Spirit takes charge of the life. He begins to redirect our thinking, to actuate our deeds and to control our words.

This must be with our consent, for in Romans 6:16 we read: "To whom ye yield yourselves servants to obey, his servants ye are to whom ye obey." So when the human will is yielded to Christ the Spirit of God comes in and takes possession of the life and makes of every recipient a new creature. "The path of the just is as the shining light, that shineth more and more unto the perfect day" (Proverbs 4:18). To receive the Holy Spirit there must be a willingness on our part to follow the light even though the light may shine on some very ugly portions of our lives and reveal certain idols, which must be cast out. The light that shines from the Word of God may reveal to us some of our cherished sins, sins we didn't think anybody knew about. When that light comes to us, there must be willingness on our part to walk in the light, to follow the light. We must be willing to pray in the words of the song writer:

> Break down every idol, cast out every foe;
> Now wash me, and I shall be whiter than snow.

It is repentance that brings the third person of

the Godhead—the Holy Spirit—into the life. You may or may not feel His presence, but it is there when you repent. Some people criticize others who have an emotional experience when they accept Christ. When the third person of the Godhead comes into the life He works upon the personality He finds there. Some people are naturally excitable. They are ecstatic over the smallest good thing that happens to them. Naturally, when the Spirit of God visits them with so great a blessing they may say a fervent Amen. Others are calm and collected, and they react to good things by the mere dropping of a tear or a solemnity in their heart. When the Spirit of God comes upon such a person he does not react visibly, but he is nevertheless moved as deeply, if not more so, by the same Spirit who would enable another to cry out Amen.

So we would not confuse man's reaction to the divine Presence with the deeper workings of that Presence. Let us surrender our wills to Christ now. Let us turn to God with all our hearts. Let us plead for the presence of the third person of the Godhead in our lives, and He will come into our lives and guide us. He will reveal to us, according to 1 Corinthians 2:10, the deep things of God. He will spread the love of God abroad in our hearts, according to Romans 5:5. He will aid us in our prayers, according to Romans 8:26. He will fight our battles, according to Isaiah 59:19, and He will continue to strive with us, making us uncomfortable when we go contrary to God's will. What a blessing to have a conscience that is regulated by the Holy Spirit. What a blessing to have that still small voice still speaking to the inner man, saying, "This is the way, walk ye in it."

The Bible uses many symbols to represent the Spirit of God.

12

He is likened to water—cleansing, refreshing, abundantly and freely given. He is likened to fire—purifying, illuminating, and searching. He is likened to wind—independent, powerful, reviving. He is likened to oil—healing, comforting, illuminating, consecrating. He is likened to rain and dew—imperceptible and yet penetrating. He is likened to a dove—gentle, meek, innocent, forgiving. He is likened to a voice—speaking, guiding, warning, and teaching. He is likened to a seal—impressing, securing, and authenticating.

Let us briefly consider the symbol of rain. "Then shall we know, if we follow on to know the Lord: his going forth is prepared as the morning; and he shall come unto us as the rain, as the latter and former rain unto the earth" (Hosea 6:3). The Spirit of God came down with great power on the day of Pentecost, giving the seedling church the power to push its delicate blades above the soil. This visitation of the Spirit of God is known as the early rain. But in nature there follows the latter rain that ripens the grain for the harvest. So in the end of the world we may expect a visitation of the Spirit of God on a scale heretofore unknown, to prepare the church for reaping the harvest and gathering the faithful at the coming of Christ. "Ask ye of the Lord rain in the time of the latter rain; so the Lord shall make bright clouds, and give them showers of rain, to every one grass in the field" (Zechariah 10:1).

It was a custom of Roman emperors at their triumphal entrance to cast new coins among the multitude. So Christ, soon after His triumphal ascension into heaven, sent the Holy Spirit as an evidence of His love and affection.

Sinner, please don't let this harvest pass
And die and lose your soul at last;
For my God is a mighty man of war.

"This Harvest Pass"

MEN HAVE a dozen words with which they describe the predicament man now finds himself in. But the Bible has one simple word for it—sin. Our text brings us face to face with the fact that there is a limit beyond which no man dare go without incurring the wrath of God. The cities of Sodom and Gomorrah, and God's dealing with them, say to us that God will not forever endure the wickedness of man, and that there is a limit beyond which no man dare go. Genesis 13:13 and 19:24, 25 tell the solemn story of these cities.

A few years ago it was my privilege to visit the Dead Sea area where, presumably, these two cities once stood in their glory and pride. But the day came when the cup of their iniquity was full to overflowing, and the God of heaven who is interested in human affairs, who is working on earth today keeping watch over His own, who is not dead, or on sabbatical

179

leave—that great God made His presence felt and His anger known in judgment fires that brought to an end the reign of these proud cities of sin.

Sin is not just breaking rules. It is an insult to God. It is a cause of estrangement between creature and Creator.

Joseph was in trouble. His employer's wife had approached him with an improper proposal. He stated his reason for not succumbing to her wiles in a question: "How then can I do this great wickedness, and sin against God?" You see, all sin is against God. By its very nature, sin is rebellion against God. Man may transgress against his fellow man, but when he turns against God he is in real danger, danger of eternal destruction. Too many of us have trifled with sin. Too many of us have played with it, feeling that it could not harm us. But all sin, like a poisonous snake, is dangerous. Its effect is deadening. There is no such thing as a harmless sin.

At work in the human heart, sin does three things:

1. It weakens the will power. A man who repeatedly transgresses will soon find himself unable to make meaningful decisions, unable to say resolutely, I will not do that again, unable to turn away from that which damns the body, defiles the spirit, and destroys the soul. The weakening of the human will is probably the most serious effect sin has upon the sinner. It immobilizes his capacity to bounce back. It renders him too weak and vacillating to turn to God.

2. Sin destroys hope. This is one of the problems of America's cities today. A large number of our citizens have lost hope, they no longer look forward to bigger and brighter things, and it is this that produces frustration. Many of the violent acts committed are acts of frustration. They are the hope-

less, the forsaken, the downtrodden, calling for attention. Hope has passed, and hope must be restored. And so, in the realm of the spiritual, a man without hope is a man who refuses to look up, to lift up his head, to move forward, or even to try. I come upon many of these wrecks year after year in my work as an evangelist.

3. Sin grieves the Holy Spirit of God. "Grieve not the holy Spirit of God, whereby ye are sealed unto the day of redemption" (Ephesians 4:30). Sin is a source of sorrow and sadness to the Holy Spirit. In Psalm 51:10, 11, David, understanding the seriousness of sin, cried out: "Create in me a clean heart, O God; and renew a right spirit within me. Cast me not away from thy presence; and take not thy holy spirit from me." David realized that sin, persisted in, would result in the departure of the Holy Spirit from the life, and he knew that when the light of life departs there is darkness forever.

Consider the case of Saul, the first king of Israel. God sent him Samuel as a spiritual guide to keep him from making some of the mistakes kings in his day often made, but Saul scorned Samuel's ministry. He called upon the prophet only when the kingdom was in danger. At other times he took Samuel for granted, and indeed ignored the old man. The Spirit of God lingered long with him, but at last came the day when mercy could abide no longer, and silently, like a dove flying away to be at rest, the Spirit of God deserted this unrepentant man and left him to his own devices. The rest of the story of his life is one long nightmare. He committed blunder after blunder, plunging the nation into debt and into servitude to other nations. Finally, in battle he took his own life, falling upon his own sword. There is a song that says,

> How dark and drear my nights and days
> If Jesus' face I could not see,
> To lighten all my weary way.
> I'm overshadowed by His light divine.

Repeated transgression is the same as saying to God, "I don't appreciate Your presence in my life"; "I don't submit to Your discipline"; "I want to run my own life as I like"; "I want to be free of restraint." You know, this is remarkably similar to what Lucifer said back there when he committed the first sin. "I will be like the most High." "I will ascend . . . above the stars." That is what sin is—it is man taking over where God alone legitimately rules. It is man saying to God, "You're welcome here as long as You do what I say, and You're not welcome if you interfere."

God cannot tolerate this forever. A man may go on for years doing this and then suddenly awaken and find himself bereft of God, the Spirit of God having departed, leaving him like "clouds . . . without water," like a tree whose fruit withers.

Was it not this that led David to confess, "I am like a pelican of the wilderness: I am like an owl of the desert. . . . For I have eaten ashes like bread, and mingled my drink with weeping" (Psalm 102:6-9)? This is what led him to cry out, "Restore unto me the joy of thy salvation: and uphold me with thy free spirit" (chapter 51:12).

Sinful habits can be broken. First let us consider the One who can help us overcome sinful habits—the Saviour who "is able to keep you from falling" (Jude 24). "Fear thou not; for I am with thee: be not dismayed; for I am thy God: I will strengthen thee; yea, I will help thee; yea, I will uphold thee with the right hand of my righteousness" (Isaiah 41:10). "Thou shalt call his name Jesus: for he shall save his people from their sins" (Matthew 1:21). "He is able also to save . . . to the uttermost that come unto God by him" (Hebrews 7:25).

There is hope for the sinner. The sinful-habit pattern can be broken. The drunkard can be separated from his liquor, the liar from his lies, the adulterer can be cured of his philandering. Sinful habits can be broken. The dope habit can be shaken. There is no sin too hard for God. "Come ye disconsolate," the song writer wrote. "Where'er ye languish; Come to the mercy seat, fervently kneel; Here bring your wounded hearts, here tell your anguish; Earth has no sorrow that heaven cannot heal."

Under the influence of the cross, under the influence of the Saviour, under the influence of the shed blood of the Lord Jesus Christ, man may prostrate himself before the altar in humble submission to the will of God. "Repent ye therefore, and be converted, that your sins may be blotted out, when the times of refreshing shall come from the presence of the Lord" (Acts 3:19). Persistent refusal to do this is unpardonable. This is the unpardonable sin. Any man who turns his back on the marvelous grace of our loving Lord—how can that man expect pardon? Christ was suspended between heaven and earth on a cross, bore unmentionable shame, was subjected to indescribable torture, wounded for our transgressions, bruised for our iniquities, and the chastisement of our peace was upon him. A man will turn away from that? From the outstretched, inviting arms of Christ? From the pleading voice that calls? This is unpardonable! It will soon become unbearable, and it is this that will bring upon the heads of guilty men the destruction that was formerly meted out upon Sodom and Gomorrah. This is the unpardonable sin.

Some people have the mistaken idea that they can simply get down and pray and God will forgive them, and when they get up they can go right back to what they were doing. They think that as often as they get down and pray they are forgiven even though there is no decision within their hearts to turn from their wickedness. The command of Acts 3:19 would certainly give the lie to this position. Acts 3:19 says, "Repent." The word *repent* means to turn to God. It means to surrender your sins, to change your attitude toward sin. So when the Lord says to repent, He measures with His own searching, all-seeing eye the depths of sincerity of the human heart as it is faced with the claims of the gospel. And if God sees within that heart sincerity; if He sees within that heart a determination to resist the evil that has brought upon man this sorrow, this guilt, this separation; then God does indeed forgive. He does indeed pardon. God cannot resist this type of approach. The sincere, humble, contrite heart always finds a warm spot in the great heart of the Creator, and a sinner, however vile, may come to God with all his heart and find pardon, peace, and power.

But then he must continue to resist. "Resist the devil," says James (James 4:7). The Bible talks about putting away evil, about ceasing to do evil (Isaiah 1:16). Hebrews 12:1 speaks of running the race. 1 Timothy 6:12 talks about fighting the good fight, and Luke 13:24 about striving. There is some *doing* connected with salvation, but all of our doing, all of our putting away, all of our ceasing to do evil, all of our fighting, all of our resistance, is a consequence of our love for God and our faith in Him. It is the natural outworking of divine grace in the human heart. It is the fruitage of a transformed life that says to the world, Here is a captive of Christ.

One day a father said to his son, "Son, remove the log from behind our house."

The son rebelled and said, "I will not."

The father said, "If you're to remain in this home, you'll have to do what I say."

The son said, "All right, I'll leave the house."

The father put his arm around him and said, "All right, son, the day you are ready to remove the log, you are welcome in this home and everything here is yours."

The day came when the young man knocked on the door. He had tasted the apples of Sodom and found them ashes. He found that all the glitter was not gold, and he stood there with a bowed head and a heavy heart and confessed to his father that he was wrong and that he was now ready to remove the log.

God must be obeyed. Sin must be repented of or it will destroy us. Henry Drummond said that the white ants of Africa are the most secretive creatures in the world. Even when they are attacking old forests, they come up under cover, building their dirt tunnels up and down tree trunks to shelter them while they work. One may rise from his chair at night and go to bed, get up in the morning and see it standing there apparently unchanged, but let him take his seat on it and, lo, he and the chair are in a heap on the floor. What is the trouble? The white ants have come in during the night and eaten up the inside of the wooden legs, the rounds, and the frames. Not a nick appears on the surface, but by daylight the chair is a mere shell.

So it is with the inroads of sin in the life. It has to be expunged, put away, repented of, confessed, forsaken. This, and this alone, is acceptable to God. Only this will ensure the presence of God in the life, now and forever. Sin cannot be tampered with. Ora Bolton states it aptly in these words: "If one sin be unrepented of, the man continues still a bond slave of hell. By one little hole a ship will sink into the bottom of the sea. The stab of a penknife to the heart will as well destroy a man as the daggers that killed Caesar in the Roman Senate. The soul will be strangled with one cord of vanity as well as with the cart ropes of iniquity. But to him who lives and dies impenitent, it will be his destruction. One dram of poison will dispatch a man, and one reigning sin will bring him to endless misery."

So then let us "seek . . . the Lord while he may be found, call upon him while he is near: let the wicked forsake his way, and the unrighteous man his thoughts: and let him return unto the Lord, and he will have mercy upon him; and to our God, for he will abundantly pardon."

Ezekiel cried, those dry bones,
Now hear the word of the Lord.

"Hear the Word of the Lord"

IN EZEKIEL 37 the power of the Word of God is clearly demonstrated. A whole nation lies in ruins typified by the dry bones of this particular prophecy. The command is given to the prophet to speak unto the dry bones and to say unto them, "O ye dry bones, hear the word of the Lord" (verse 4). Verse 7 gives the result of this spiritual exercise, "So I prophesied as I was commanded: and as I prophesied, there was a noise, and behold a shaking, and the bones came together, bone to his bone.

"And when I beheld, lo, the sinews and the flesh came up upon them, and the skin covered them above: but there was no breath in them. . . . So I prophesied as he commanded me, and the breath came into them, and they lived, and stood up upon their feet, an exceeding great army" (verses 8-10).

In its immediate application this prophecy refers to the resurrection of a people from their graves (see verse 12). In a

187

broader sense it promises a restoration of the hopes of Israel if, by faith, they lay hold on the mighty arm of God. Such is the power of the Word of God. It is the Word that will bring forth the righteous from their graves in the last day. But presently it is the Word of God that restores our hopes and our dreams of the ultimate righting of all wrongs and the ultimate restoration of God's people to health—physical, mental, spiritual, and social. In short, it is to the Word of God that we turn for our hope for the restoration of the Paradise that once was.

The Bible is the Word of God. No other book can make this exalted claim. This book was inspired by God: "Knowing this first, that no prophecy of the scripture is of any private interpretation. For the prophecy came not in old time by the will of man: but holy men of God spake as they were moved by the Holy Ghost" (2 Peter 1:20, 21).

The writings of Plato, Socrates, Shakespeare, and Milton rank high in the estimate of the educated, but none of them can say, as does the Bible, "Hear the word of the Lord." In past centuries as well as in the present day, critics of the Bible have been legion and vocal, but the good old Book has outlasted them all. Voltaire said, "In less than an hundred years Christianity will have been swept from existence and will have passed into oblivion." He said this during the crass impiety of the French Revolution. Voltaire has passed and his contemporaries are mere names on the pages of history. But the Word of God goes on molding and remolding men, shaping and reshaping destinies. Thomas Paine thought he had demolished the Bible but of him H. L. Hastings says, "After he had crawled despairingly into a dishonored grave in 1809, the Book took such a leap that since that time more than twenty times as many Bibles have been made and scattered throughout the world as ever were made since the creation of man."

Yes, the Bible is a wonderful book. It is wonderful because of its origin. The Bible is in truth the Word of God. Its message was dictated by Heaven. While it is true that the human instrument had to employ the language of the people to whom the messages were sent, these imperfect vehicles called words certainly bore on their wings divinely inspired meaning, and God takes full credit for what the Bible says.

The Bible is wonderful because of its authorship. "It was written by men in exile, in the desert, in shepherds' tents, in green pastures beside still waters. Among its authors we find a tax gatherer, a herdsman, a gatherer of sycamore fruit. We find poor men, rich men, statesmen, preachers, exiles, captains, legislators, judges. Men of every grade and class are represented in this wonderful volume which is in reality a library filled with history, genealogy, ethnology, law, ethics, prophecy, poetry, eloquence, medicine, sanitary science, political economy, and perfect rules for the conduct of personal and social life."— H. L. HASTINGS.

The fact that the Bible, in spite of its varied authorship, has the unique faculty of internal agreement, testifies to its singular origin. Furthermore, the prophecies written thousands of years ago by the prophets either have met or are meeting their fulfillment, some with such remarkable accuracy that we can only conclude that a divine finger traced these pronouncements.

Nothing builds faith in God like reading the Word of God. "So then faith cometh by hearing, and hearing by the word of God" (Romans 10:17).

189

It is when we read of the power of God to redeem a Peter, a Mary Magdalene, or a Thomas that faith grows in our own hearts that we too may be redeemed. It is when we read that in the beginning God created the heavens and the earth that our confidence grows; that He who created us can produce in us His spiritual nature.

"It is the spirit that quickeneth; the flesh profiteth nothing: the words that I speak unto you, they are spirit, and they are life" (John 6:63).

As we read the Word of God the Spirit of God, the divine Author, comes graciously near to us, burning the significance of the words of God into our very consciences, producing in us disciplined behavior born of love for God. In the language of the song we need to

> Dust off the Bible,
> Dust off the Holy Word,
> The words of all the prophets
> And the sayings of our Lord.

And we should claim with the old slave who sang:

> Every promise in this Book is mine;
> Every chapter, every verse, every line.
> I am living by His grace divine,
> For every promise of this Book is mine.

Among the dead on one of the battlefields near Richmond, Virginia, was a rebel soldier who lay unburied several days after the conflict. Already the flesh of his fingers had been eaten by worms, but underneath the skeleton hand lay the open Bible, and the fingers pressed upon those precious words of the twenty-third psalm: "Thy rod and thy staff they comfort me."

Henry Ward Beecher says, "The truths of the Bible are like gold in the soil. Whole generations walk over it and know not what treasures are hidden beneath. So centuries of men pass over the scriptures and know not what riches lie underneath the feet of their interpretation. Sometimes when they discover them they call them 'new truths.' One might as well call gold newly dug 'new gold.'"

A poor soldier in the Crimean War cast himself on the ground, perhaps to die. "One drop, one drop," he cried.

"Not a drop of drink in my canteen," said his comrade. "What can I do for you?"

"Bill, open my knapsack and get it—my Bible—and let me have a drop from that."

Bill obeyed and found the Bible and began to read.

"That's it," said the poor soldier. "It's the blood of Christ that heals our wounds. The blood of Christ makes peace between God and us poor sinners. I shall never get home to England again, but blessed be God, I shall go to a far better country through Christ, the living way. Ah, Bill, if ever the Bible was written for any man, it was written for the soldier."

Nowhere is the power of the Word more clearly stated than in Psalm 33:6-9:

"By the word of the Lord were the heavens made; and all the host of them by the breath of his mouth. He gathereth the waters of the sea together as an heap: he layeth up the depth in storehouses. Let all the earth fear the Lord: let all the inhabitants of the world stand in awe of him. For he spake, and it was *done;* he commanded, and it stood fast."

To a generation brainwashed by fiction through the reading of stimulating novels, TV, and the movies, these words may

13

seem unbelievable, but they are true. The Word of God is the most pleasant book on the face of the earth to read and study.

In the initial stages of recovery from the damage that fictional reading does to the brain, you may find the Bible difficult reading. But continue to force feed yourself, and soon your appetite for spiritual things will increase. At this point you are coming alive. The Bible creates an appetite for itself, but one has to persevere in the initial stages. The Word of God feeds the spirit of man. Temporal food may reach the body and the brain, but only spiritual food can restore man's soul.

Henry Ward Beecher says, "The true Bible is not the dead book but the living reality developed by the Spirit of God in the conscience of mankind. It is not a printed thing. The printed thing is a memorial of it, a souvenir of it, a mere chart, and the chart is not the ocean."

Furthermore, the Bible is an up-to-date book. It talks about man and all that relates to him. It speaks of the issues of our time. It deals with the human problem in all of its complex aspects. There is not a situation into which man may get for which the Bible has no guidance. The Bible is food for young and old. Too bad many people handle it but never read it!

Said Beecher, "The boy holds his ball of twine in his hand and thinks it is not much, he can clasp it so easily; but when he begins to unroll it and his wind-borne kite mounts higher and higher, he is astonished to see how long it is. So there are little texts that look small in your palm but when caught up upon some experience they unroll themselves and stretch out until there is no measuring their length."

The Bible is what it is because it talks about Christ. It is the verbal revelation of the character of God.

A little boy was seen putting the scores of pieces of a difficult puzzle together. Observing him for a little while, his father said, "Sonny, how is it that you are able to do this so easily?"

"Well, Dad," answered the son, "it's not so difficult. You see, on the other side there's the form of a man and as long as I put the pieces of the man in place, I am putting the puzzle together correctly."

And so it is with those who study their Bible diligently. There is a Man inside, and as long as we read the Bible with reference to Him, we cannot read in vain.

A little girl was following her father through the woods. He seemed to be going a little too fast for her, and she could see only the lighted lantern swinging in his hand. "Father, wait a minute. I can't see you," the little girl said.

"Well," asked the father, "can you see the light?"

"Yes," she said, "I see the light, but I don't see you."

"Just follow the light," answered the father, "for if you follow the light, you follow me."

The Bible is the light and as we follow it, we follow Christ.

195

Lord, I want to be a Christian
In my heart, In my heart;
Lord, I want to be a Christian
In my heart.

"Lord, I Want to Be a Christian"

"CREATE IN ME a clean heart, O God; and renew a right spirit within me" (Psalm 51:10). David prays this prayer of his own free will. There is within him a deep desire to be like God. He is tired of the old life. He is desperate for spiritual renewal. He has tasted the apples of Sodom and found them ashes. With his whole being he renounces the old and reaches for the new. "I am like a pelican of the wilderness: I am like an owl of the desert" (Psalm 102:6), he laments. "I have eaten ashes like bread, and mingled my drink with weeping" (verse 9).

These utterances are more than poetry. They mirror deep longings of the soul and disillusionment with the way of the transgressor. "Cast me not away from thy presence; and take not thy holy spirit from me" (Psalm 51:11), David pleaded.

Added to his own desperation is the chronic fear that he will awaken one day, deserted by God and with the door of probation slammed in his face, bereft of God's Spirit, and devoid of conscience. So he prays on, "Create in me a clean heart, O God; and renew a right spirit within me. . . . Restore unto me the joy of thy salvation; and uphold me with thy free spirit" (Psalm 51:10-12).

His prayer was answered. David experienced the truth of the statement later expressed by the apostle, that if any man be in Christ he is a new creature (2 Corinthians 5:17). The newly born child of God is in reality a new creation. By the renewing power of the Spirit he literally becomes another man. The phraseology that describes the creation of the world is appropriate also to the re-creation of man:

"In the beginning God created the heaven and the earth. And the earth was without form, and void; and darkness was upon the face of the deep. And the Spirit of God moved upon the face of the waters. And God said, Let there be light: and there was light" (Genesis 1:1-3).

Our barren souls are like the earth that was without form and void. Then came the Creator, who by the miraculous creative power of the Word transformed the earth into a thing of beauty. It is that same creative Word that makes a saint out of a sinner. Rejoice, O heavens, and be astonished, O earth, at this marvelous transaction between God and man. Let the ocean waves roar their tribute, and let the trees of the forest bend their leaf-covered limbs in acknowledgment of God's creative power. Let the winds whisper their testimony, and flowing streams gurgle their joy at the blessings of a beneficent Lord.

But let it be noted that the recreative act of God is dependent upon the will of man. He does not force this new life on any soul. He has given man an independent will, with which he may choose to do either right or wrong. "If ye be willing and obedient, ye shall eat the good of the land: but if ye refuse and rebel, ye shall be devoured with the sword: for the mouth of the Lord hath spoken it" (Isaiah 1:19, 20). The will of man must be yielded to the will of God. The poet has accurately captured this spirit in the words:

> Have thine own way, Lord! Have Thine own way!
> Thou art the Potter; I am the clay.
> Mold me and make me After Thy will,
> While I am waiting, Yielded and still.

The power of the human will has been underestimated by most of its possessors, and yet, of all our God-given possessions it is the most important. The will of man is like the steering wheel of an automobile. It is by the changing of the will that the direction of the entire life is changed. This is why the great battle between right and wrong is fought at the seat of human activity—the will of man. Men with highly cultivated wills are able to determine their own thoughts and courses of action. Men have been known to break damaging habits by the mere exercise of the will. Christ will never compel the will, and Satan cannot. They can only appeal to it, and what an appeal Christ makes. He appeals to the will of man first on the basis of His sacrifice at Calvary.

The shedding of the blood of Christ should be sufficient to melt the hardest heart, and it merits the supreme devotion of every human being. The poet says,

> When I survey the wondrous cross
> On which the Prince of glory died,
> My richest gain I count but loss,
> And pour contempt on all my pride.

198

The humiliation of Christ is a humbling instrument. That Christ, who was rich, would assume our poverty that through Him we might become rich is a mystery we will study throughout endless ages. Neither the pen of the poet nor the artist's brush can capture the magnitude of this grand event, for "the love of God is greater far Than tongue or pen can ever tell; It goes beyond the highest star, And reaches to the lowest hell." The transforming power of divine love is the saving instrument of grace. The very sight of the Word made flesh brings conviction to the heart, repentance to the soul, and tears to the eyes of man. That the great God would humble Himself even to death on the cross, that we might receive the adoption of sons, should win our wills to the side of Christ for time and for eternity.

At this point it should be made clear that the most faithful human response to the love of God is faulty at best. There is no such thing as an absolutely perfect act performed by man. Our best deeds must be covered by the blood or they would not stand the searching gaze of a sinless God. That is why, according to Jude 9, when Michael the archangel went to resurrect Moses and the devil disputed with him about it, He "durst not bring against him a railing accusation, but said, The Lord rebuke thee." Christ did not argue with the devil about the defects that characterized Moses' most faithful deed. He simply rebuked the devil, resurrected Moses, and took him to glory. For, you see, under the terms of justification, Christ covers our lives with His own righteous garment, and the defects that appear in our most faithful performances are hidden in the blood. "They are underneath the blood of the Lamb of Calvary; as far removed as darkness is from dawn, and I thank

God it's good enough, yes, good enough for me. Praise God, my sins are gone."

But the longer the Christian fellowships with Christ, the more perfect becomes his response to divine love. There is thus a progressive improvement of the Christian's visible performance as he develops his relationship with Christ. There occurs in fellowship with God a strengthening of the spiritual muscles as we lift the bar bells of Christian duty. There is a hardening of the biceps and a strengthening of the spiritual constitution, and a corresponding improvement in the over-all behavior. Thus, progressively, we grow into the likeness of our Lord, while at the same time we are covered by the absolutely perfect life of our Redeemer. This is the good news of the gospel. This is the plan of salvation that excites the wonder of righteous angels and the envy of demons. We may never thoroughly understand it, but we can accept it now and receive its priceless benefits in this world and the world to come.

It is not necessary for us to lose a firm spiritual posture once this stance is achieved. There is always the nagging fear that what we enjoy today we must lose tomorrow. This negative outlook is the special weapon of Satan. He wants us to believe that we can never accept the righteousness of Christ, but once it is received his next step is to lead us to doubt that we can permanently maintain it. We can, however, be "confident of this very thing, that he which hath begun a good work in you will perform it until the day of Jesus Christ" (Philippians 1:6).

We do not initiate our own salvation. It is the Spirit of God who approaches us and draws us to Christ by the instrument of divine love. In short it is He who "hath begun a good work in you." The promise of the Scripture is that He will perform this good work until the day of Christ. This we must believe.

When two young people get married and promise to honor and cherish each other until death parts them, the fact is that they do not know, even as they stand there, that they will be married the next week. But they have two things going for them. They have faith *in* each other and love *for* each other. They may have no money, no assurance for the future, but these two things are considered sufficient for them to unite their interests in holy matrimony. This is, in fact, all that Christ requires of us—faith *in* Him and love *for* Him. With these two Heaven-imparted virtues, we may begin our walk with Him up the highway of life, secure in the knowledge that He will never leave us or forsake us and that what He has begun in us He can and will continue until the day of Christ. In this our faith must not fail.

If religion was a thing that money could buy,
The rich would live and the poor would die.
But I thank God it is not so;
The rich as well as the poor must go.

"If Religion Was a Thing"

WE LIVE in a money-mad age. When I was in Hong Kong a few years ago I heard an interesting story about the people who live on top of the mountains there. It is said that when the Japanese invaded Hong Kong they sent word up and told the people up there to come down. Most of the rich people lived up there. When they didn't come down the soldiers went up to get them, and it was an interesting sight as these people came down the mountainside, tossing their money to the sides of the road. It was worthless because the Japanese would not recognize the British pound.

The Bible says that the day will come when this thing will happen again, not just in Hong Kong, but all over the world. I said this in a certain city where I held a meeting, and a man said to me, "Just tell me where this is going to happen, and I'll be there, and I bet I'll pick some up!"

I have news for that man and for you. Let's go to the Word of God.

In Ecclesiastes 7:12 we read that money is a defense, as indeed it is. It is a defense against mortgage payments, against rental payments, against hunger, against disease, and against ignorance. Money is indeed a blessing. The Bible does not condemn money, neither does it condemn a man for being rich. Jesus did say that it is easier for a camel to get through the eye of a needle than for a rich man to enter the kingdom of God, but here He was not talking about riches themselves, but of rich men who love their money. The needle's eye is supposed to have been a Jerusalem gate that remained open after the other gates were closed. It was a very small gate, and a camel had to kneel and be unloaded, then pushed, pulled, and shoved, and his back bent, in order to get him through the gate. This is true of a rich man who loves money. It is also true of a poor man who loves the little bit that he has.

The Bible does not condemn money itself. In 1 Timothy 6:10 we read that "the *love* of money is the root of all evil." It is a very tempting thing to have money, but one can through prayer and the study of the Word of God cultivate such an attitude toward God that money will never come between him and his Maker.

Covetousness was the great sin committed in the Garden of Eden. Adam and Eve looked upon fruit God had forbidden them to eat, fruit that was not theirs lawfully. They desired it, and they took it. As a result we were all born in sin and shapen in iniquity.

Today men have made a god out of money. They will steal, lie, gamble, or murder to get it. Some people even marry to get it.

The story is told of a Russian czar who was confronted one

203

day by a childhood friend in rags. "Ever since you came to the throne," this friend reminded him, "you've forgotten all about me. I used to play with you as a little boy, and you haven't done anything for me."

"Well," said the czar, "meet me outside the gate tomorrow, and I'll do something good for you."

They met at the time appointed. The czar said to him, "Now look, as much ground as you can encompass and come back to this gate before the sun goes down, all that will belong to you."

The greedy young man began to run. He surrounded a wheat field, and a fruit orchard, and he continued to cover territory, forgetting all about the setting sun. Toward the end of the day, he looked up and sure enough, the sun had almost disappeared behind the mountain, and he wasn't back. He hadn't even started back, so he began to run as fast as his legs could carry him, heading straight for the gate. If he could make it, he would be a wealthy man. The sun began to sink until finally there was but a small crimson gleam above the mountaintop. On and on pressed our greedy young friend, his lungs aching, his muscles aching, his feet hurting; but he ran on and on. I must be rich! I must be rich! was the thought uppermost in his mind. He saw the gate at last and the king waiting, and just as the sun slipped behind the western hills, he fell at the feet of the czar and sighed.

"Stand up, my friend. You've done well, and all the ground you have covered is yours." He reached down and touched his friend, and found him dead.

"What shall it profit a man, if he shall gain the whole world, and lose his own soul? Or what shall a man give in exchange for his soul?" Some men will give anything in exchange for their souls. They do not value their souls as much as they value money.

Proverbs 11:4 says: "Riches profit not in the day of wrath: but righteousness delivereth from death." There will come a time, my friend, when all of the money in the world won't do you a bit of good, and that day is nearer than you think. As a matter of fact, men are going to throw their money into the streets, and no one will pick it up. I'd like to tell you about that day.

In Ezekiel 7:19 we read: "They shall cast their silver in the streets, and their gold shall be removed: their silver and their gold shall not be able to deliver them in the day of the wrath of the Lord: they shall not satisfy their souls, neither fill their bowels: because it is the stumblingblock of their iniquity."

What a day that will be! "They shall go into the holes of the rocks, and into the caves of the earth, for fear of the Lord, and for the glory of his majesty, when he ariseth to shake terribly the earth. In that day a man shall cast his idols of silver, and his idols of gold, which they made each one for himself to worship, to the moles and to the bats; to go into the clefts of the rocks, and into the tops of the ragged rocks, for fear of the Lord, and for the glory of his majesty, when he ariseth to shake terribly the earth" (Isaiah 2:19-21).

This text tells us just when that day is coming. It says it will be when the Lord arises to shake terribly the earth. What a day that will be! It was not the day of Christ's birth, for, according to Matthew 1:21, Christ came to earth the first time to save His people from their sins. Neither is that day the day of the crucifixion, though according to Matthew 27:45-54 there was a great earthquake. Christ was crucified, but He was wounded for our transgressions and bruised for our iniquities. Daniel 9:26 says that He was cut off, but not for Himself. That day witnessed the most selfless sacrifice ever made in history.

> The sun grew dark with mystery,
> The morn was cold and chill
> As the shadow of a cross arose
> Upon a lonely hill.

As the spiritual says, "He never said a mumblin' word; He just hung His head and died." There was a great earthquake. But that was not the day referred to in my text, a day when God will arise to shake terribly the earth; a day when men will run to the rocks and the mountains, saying, "Fall on us, and hide us from the face of him that sitteth on the throne," a day when men will throw their money into the streets, when they will lose their love for gold. They will then understand about these wasted years.

Then there was the day of the resurrection, but it was not that day. Again there was a mighty earthquake, and the angel of the Lord came and rolled back the stone from the door and sat upon it. When Mary appeared, he said, "He is not here: for he is risen" (Matthew 28:6). "Tell his disciples and Peter" (Mark 16:7). What a day that was, a day when faith was vindicated, a day when men could sing with verity and truth and assurance, "I serve a risen Saviour, He's in the world today." Yes, Christ is alive today. He's alive forevermore.

No, the day of my text is the day when Jesus comes back to earth. That will be the day when men run from His presence, when He rises and mightily shakes the earth. Then men will throw their money into the streets and no one will pick it up. Then Christ will fulfill His promise recorded in John 14:1-3: "Let not your heart be troubled: ye believe in God, believe also in me. In my Father's house are many mansions: if it were not so, I would have told you. I go to prepare a place for you. And if I go and prepare a place for you, I will come again, and receive you unto myself; that where I am, there ye may be also." That will be a visible, public appearance, according to Matthew 24:27: "For as the lightning cometh out of the east, and shineth even unto the west; so shall also the coming of the Son of man be."

"Behold, he cometh with clouds; and every eye shall see him" (Revelation 1:7).

"Our God shall come, and shall not keep silence: a fire shall devour before him, and it shall be very tempestuous round about him" (Psalm 50:3).

"The Lord himself shall descend from heaven with a shout, with the voice of the archangel, and with the trump of God: and the dead in Christ shall rise first: then we which are alive and remain shall be caught up together with them in the clouds, to meet the Lord in the air: and so shall we ever be with the Lord. Wherefore comfort one another with these words" (1 Thessalonians 4:16-18).

Yes, when the Lord comes to shake terribly the earth, to strike down the wicked and to receive the righteous into everlasting glory, money will lose its appeal. Men will cast it into the streets for the moles and the bats, and no one will pick it up.

"The earth shall reel to and fro like a drunkard, and shall be removed like a cottage; and the transgression thereof shall be heavy upon it; and it shall fall, and not rise again" (Isaiah 24:20).

This is what the world was to look forward to, and God has mercifully pulled back the veil that we may see what is soon to come to pass in this old world. The time has come when we are wise to accept the invitation of the Master: "And the Spirit and the bride say, Come. And let him that heareth say, Come. And let him that is athirst come. And whosoever will, let him take the water of life freely" (Revelation 22:17). Now is the hour to submit ourselves to Jesus Christ and to make Him our Saviour.

A little boy's mother asked him to get on with a chore. He said, "I don't want to do it."

His mother said, "I'm not asking you if you want to do it; I'm asking you to do it."

"But, Mother," said the little boy, "why should I do it if I don't want to do it? That would make me a hypocrite."

"Well," answered the mother, "if you do it while you don't want to do it, you will get used to doing it, and after a while you will want to do it. So do what I say."

The time has come for us to do what the Lord has told us to do. Someone reading this may say, But I don't want to! The answer comes, Fall on your knees and submit yourself to Him and do it anyhow. After a while the doing will become a pleasure, as you place your hand in the hand of God, for

> If religion was a thing that money could buy,
> The rich would live and the poor would die.
> But I thank God it is not so;
> The rich as well as the poor must go.

Money has been defined as something that buys everything but happiness and takes a man everywhere but heaven. But money used in the right way can bring a great deal of happiness and start many a person on the path to heaven.

When Saladin died he left directions that his empty hands should be placed in full view outside his coffin. By this he meant to teach that, of all his vast wealth and conquests, he could take nothing with him. Naked came we into the world, and naked we will leave this world. Then let us seek first the kingdom of heaven and its righteousness, and all things necessary for our happiness and well-being will be added.

Blessed quietness, holy quietness,
Sweet assurance in my soul.
On the stormy sea, Jesus speaks to me,
And the billows cease to roll.

"Jesus Speaks to Me"

ORIGINALLY GOD communed with man face to face. This was possible in the Garden of Eden before the entrance of sin. Communication is an essential expression of love, and since God loved man they would often talk together, friend to friend and face to face. But sin altered all of this. Face-to-face communication was no longer possible, for man, as a sinner, would have been destroyed by the glory of the divine presence.

Since the entrance of sin, God has used men to communicate His will to their fellow men. The foremost of these earthly communicants we call prophets. "Surely the Lord God will do nothing, but he revealeth his secret unto his servants the prophets" (Amos 3:7). "Believe his prophets, so shall ye prosper" (2 Chronicles 20:20).

For information, guidance, warning, and entreaty, prophets have been God's line of communication between heaven and

14

earth. They are to be believed and obeyed, for their message is from God.

History shows that when these men of God were obeyed, great good came to the people. But when they were disregarded disaster usually followed. Noah prophesied of the Flood, and was ignored. The Flood came, and according to the Bible, "took them all away." Jonah prophesied the destruction of Nineveh. The people believed him and repented. The city was spared. Daniel foretold the fall of Babylon. He lived to see that prophecy come to pass, for the king of Babylon and his drunken lords would not repent.

But as in all other things, the devil has sought to counterfeit this gift of prophecy. History speaks liberally of soothsayers, necromancers, dealers in witchcraft, demon possession, and fortunetelling. These counterfeit prophets, guided by a power from beneath, have sought to duplicate the wisdom of God through the true prophets. But the prophet Isaiah has given this wise counsel: "And when they shall say unto you, Seek unto them that have familiar spirits, and unto wizards that peep, and that mutter: should not a people seek unto their God? for the living to the dead? To the law and to the testimony: if they speak not according to this word, it is because there is no light in them" (Isaiah 8:19, 20).

There is no denial here that evil men allied with devils can, and do, perform some miracles. Revelation 16:14 indicates this also, and according to 2 Corinthians 11:14, 15 it is "no marvel; for Satan himself is transformed into an angel of light. Therefore it is no great thing if his ministers also be transformed as the ministers of righteousness; whose end shall be according to their works."

So false prophets do make predictions, some of which come true. They do touch the sick, who appear to recover. Miracles are no sign of authenticity, for demons can perform them. We must look deeper than miracles for manifest evidences of the divine gift of prophecy in a human being who claims to have that gift, for in these last days many false prophets will arise and deceive many, Christ warned (Matthew 24:5, 23-25).

If some of the dark secrets of the séance room were revealed, thousands would be shocked. It would be surprising to know how many decisions affecting world history and national survival have been made at the counsel of fortunetellers. Through human beings demons impart information of the most secret nature. Lives have been ruined, homes destroyed, and nations torn asunder by the artful, curious work of this demoniacal science. Thus the work of the false prophet has been set up against that of the true. But clear Biblical lines are drawn between the two, so that one need not be confused as to what is a true prophet and what is not.

There are several basic tests that can be applied to a person who claims to be a prophet. The first is the kind of life he lives. It must be in harmony with the will of God. His teachings must be in harmony with the teachings of the Scriptures. Certainly the Spirit of God is not at war with Himself, and any prophet claiming divine inspiration must authenticate and confirm the Word of God. A true prophet will confirm the Creation story of the origin of the earth. He will also support the teachings of the Bible on the origin of sin and death, and teach the divine plan of redemption. He will teach that the Holy Spirit, on earth, makes salvation effectual and that the blood of Jesus Christ cleanses from all sin. He will exalt the law of God.

He will teach that grace is the basis of salvation, and that right-eousness is a gift of God. His teaching must harmonize with already revealed truth. He must strengthen and encourage men and women to believe in Christ.

Many make the mistake of judging a prophet by his gifts, but the Bible makes it clear that he is to be judged by the fruit of the gospel in his life—the fruit of "love, joy, peace, longsuf-fering, gentleness, goodness, faith, meekness, temperance" (Ga-latians 5:22, 23).

There is really but one fruit of the Spirit, and that is love. The other eight words describe love in action. Love is joyful, love is peaceful, love is long-suffering, love is gentle, love is good, love believes, love is meek, love is temperate; and against love there is no law. So we judge the gifts of a prophet by the fruit of the Spirit, and if the fruit is not there, then the source of the gift is alien to the love of Christ.

Messages from nearly forty prophets can be found in the Bible. These prophets have been classified as major and minor prophets, but in all honesty the only difference between the two is that some wrote longer books than others. The so-called minor prophets were no less inspired than the major ones. Whether major or minor, "believe his prophets, so shall ye prosper" (2 Chronicles 20:20). Some, upon reading prophecies of which some detail may not have been fulfilled, have con-cluded that the prophets were false. But all prophecies are con-ditional. Take Nineveh, for instance, whose people repented of their sins in sackcloth, and as a result God stayed His heavy hand of judgment. If men meet the conditions set by the proph-ets and repent of their sins, the hand of judgment may be stayed. The God of heaven reserves the right to exercise mercy as well as judgment. For this we should be eternally thankful.

In all ages God has made His will known to His people. He has not left them unprotected, nor will He in these last days. "And it shall come to pass afterward, that I will pour out my spirit upon all flesh: and your sons and your daughters shall prophesy, your old men shall dream dreams, your young men shall see visions: and also upon the servants and upon the handmaids in those days will I pour out my spirit" (Joel 2: 28, 29).

In our day we can expect a revival of the prophetic gift. I have seen evidences of this gift in the writings of Ellen G. White, who died in 1915. Records of her life indicate she met every test that would authenticate her gift—from piety of life through the manifestations of the will of God in visions and dreams. For a detailed study of this remarkable woman, I refer you to the book, *A Prophet Among You,* by T. H. Jemison, published by the Pacific Press, in Mountain View, California.

Had the Israelites studied more closely the words of the prophets they would have recognized Christ as their long-hoped-for Messiah. The prophet Isaiah recorded enough evidence in advance to correctly identify the hoped-for Deliverer of Israel. Isaiah spoke of Him as growing up like a root out of dry ground, having no form nor comeliness that men would desire Him, and that He would be wounded for our transgressions and bruised for our iniquities.

The following is but a small list of Old Testament predictions that met their fulfillment in the New Testament record:

Matthew 1:23 refers to Isaiah 7:14

Matthew 2:6 refers to Micah 5:2

Matthew 2:17, 18 refers to Jeremiah 31:15

Matthew 3:3 refers to Isaiah 40:3
Matthew 4:14-16 refers to Isaiah 9:1, 2
Matthew 8:17 refers to Isaiah 53:4
Matthew 11:10 refers to Malachi 3:1
Matthew 12:18 refers to Isaiah 42:1
Matthew 13:14 refers to Isaiah 6:9
Matthew 13:35 refers to Psalm 78:2
Matthew 21:4, 5 refers to Zechariah 9:9

Yes, the prophet predicted the coming of the greatest of all the prophets, for some of the most accurate predictions covering our time were made by our Lord Himself when as the Word made flesh He dwelt among men.

In Luke 21:25 Christ made predictions that were fulfilled as recently as May 19, 1780, and November 13, 1833. In Luke 21:20, 21, He predicted the destruction of Jerusalem, which took place thirty-nine years later. In this same passage He predicts that He will come again to this earth. "And then shall they see the Son of man coming in a cloud with power and great glory" (Luke 21:27). We are living in the shadow of the fulfillment of that important prophecy. We have not been left in darkness to fumble our way into the future.

"We have also a more sure word of prophecy; whereunto ye do well that ye take heed, as unto a light that shineth in a dark place, until the day dawn, and the day star arise in your hearts: knowing this first, that no prophecy of the scripture is of any private interpretation. For the prophecy came not in old time by the will of man: but holy men of God spake as they were moved by the Holy Ghost" (2 Peter 1:19-21).

I'm so glad Jesus lifted me,
Singing glory hallelujah, Jesus lifted me.

"I'm So Glad"

CHRISTIANITY IS a religion of joy; the long face and heavy heart are not its natural products. God has been pictured to this world as a stern judge who frowns on those who smile. The Christian way of life has been represented as the path of the stern stoic, and those who tread its way are characterized by drooping lids, sad eyes, and tear-stained cheeks. Nothing could be further from the truth.

The Bible speaks again and again of the gladness of heart that should characterize the Christian experience of all practitioners. "Rejoice evermore" (1 Thessalonians 5:16). "Delight thyself also in the Lord; and he shall give thee the desires of thine heart" (Psalm 37:4). "This day is holy unto our Lord: neither be ye sorry; for the joy of the Lord is your strength" (Nehemiah 8:10).

Christians are commanded to be joyful even under the fierc-

215

est persecution: "Blessed are ye, when men shall hate you, and when they shall separate you from their company, and shall reproach you, and cast out your name as evil, for the Son of man's sake. Rejoice ye in that day, and leap for joy: for, behold, your reward is great in heaven: for in the like manner did their fathers unto the prophets" (Luke 6:22, 23).

But it is difficult to be happy with a guilty conscience. I would suggest, then, the confession of our sins to Him as the number one prerequisite for receiving the joy of the Lord: "He that covereth his sins shall not prosper: but whoso confesseth and forsaketh them shall have mercy" (Proverbs 28:13).

The removal of guilt from the human heart is like the lifting of a heavy block of lead from a wagon bed. The soul becomes as light as a feather, and joy literally sparkles through the countenance. Another happiness aid is singing, and there is something infectious about it. One may begin a cheerful song in a state of depression, but if he sings long enough he will snap out of his depression. There is power in music to lift the spirits.

Unselfish service for others has a way of bringing deep satisfaction to the soul. A food basket carried to the needy, or a visit to the hospital for instance. Yes, the road of Christian service, paved with the asphalt of self-sacrifice, leads inevitably to green pastures beside still waters.

Cultivate a pleasant manner. Some people are miserable because they have cultivated a miserable outlook on life. They seldom smile, and a negative point of view and an unpleasant tone of voice have become a habit. This wilts the spirit and dampens the internal ardor. Conversely, the adoption of a pleasant manner, even when one's spirits are sagging, tends to build morale. The cheerful practice breeds the cheerful attitude.

216

Good health is usually conducive to a good spirit; it is difficult to smile with a headache. Proper care of the body exerts a wholesome influence on the attitude. Normally mild-mannered men have been turned into raging maniacs by drinking alcoholic beverages. Body-destroying, debilitating habits that depress should be broken forthwith. People who stay up late at night usually find their dispositions suffering from the practice. Good health will help develop good humor.

Expose the mind to character-building influences. Depressing fiction and certain types of movies do little to buoy the spirits. In fact, some of them are actual depressants. One patient went to the doctor, complaining of chronic depression. Skillful questioning revealed that she was participating too fully in an emotional way in the problems of a fictional heroine. Wholesome reading and recreation are like a fresh breath of air to the soul.

Read your Bible. It is full of spiritual nourishment for the inner man. Inward renewal is infinitely easier with help from the Bible. Christianity is the only path to genuine happiness. The apostle Peter speaks of "joy unspeakable and full of glory" (1 Peter 1:8) in his description of the experience of the born-again Christian.

Jesus expressed the desire that "your joy may be full" (John 16:24). Certainly we who follow Him have every reason in the world to be happy. Consider this: When Adam sinned a mysterious pall, referred to in the Bible as spiritual darkness, descended over the earth as a consequence of man's transgression. For four thousand years thereafter the darkness was occasionally illumined by men and women who cherished the hope of the coming Messiah. He would dispel the darkness and bring salvation to His people. So through the long night of waiting, faith often grew dim and footsteps strayed into forbidden paths, only to be called back to the worship of the true God by the stern voice of Heaven-sent prophets. Then came the day when shepherds, tending their flocks by night, saw the skies illumined and heard angels' voices singing and the announcement: "Unto you is born this day in the city of David a Saviour, which is Christ the Lord" (Luke 2:11).

The next thirty years were uneventful as far as the record is concerned. Not even Jesus' own brothers recognized His true identity, and His mother, after all the evidences surrounding His birth, seemed not to understand His mission. Little did those who rubbed shoulders with Him then understand that "the hopes and fears of all the years" met in Bethlehem that night. Upon Him would devolve the heavy responsibility of solving the sin problem, of pardoning all those who lived before the cross, and laying a foundation for pardon for all who should come after. Those who lived before and those who lived after the cross were equally dependent upon Christ for salvation from sin. When we think of His goodness to us, our joy is full.

The song writer says: "When waves of affliction sweep over the soul And sunlight is hidden from view; Whenever you are tempted to doubt or complain, Think of His goodness to you."

To the human family the coming of the Saviour was the one ray of light in an endless tunnel of darkness. It was like the sight of a rescue ship to those lost at sea, like a beacon light flashing in the dense darkness of the jungle guiding the lost to safety. Our joy at the coming of the Lord into the world is fitting, and with the children we can sing, "I've got the joy, joy, joy, joy, down in my heart, down in my heart to stay."

Henry Ward Beecher put it this way: "Christian, it is your duty not only to be good but to shine, and of all the lights which you kindle on the face, joy will reach farthest out to sea where troubled mariners are seeking the shore. Even in your deepest griefs rejoice in God. As waves of phosphorescence, let joy flash from the swing of the sorrows of your souls."

Dean Farrar, speaking of the joy of the Christians who were forced to worship underground in the catacombs, makes this statement: "Joy, blithe serenity, which received death with no alarm or self-abasement were their marked characteristics. St. Luke throws a flood of light on the tone of their society; drunken but not with wine, intoxicated so to speak with the rushing influences of Pentecost. They did take their food with exultation and singleness of heart. The words indicate their bounding gladness, their simplicity and smoothness of feeling as of a plain without stones or a field without furrows."

Edwin Markham has captured this spirit in his poem:

> At the heart of the cyclone tearing the sky
> And flinging the clouds and the towers by,
> Is a place of central calm;
> So here in the roar of mortal things,
> I find a place where my spirit sings,
> In the hollow of God's palm.

It is said that an old Comanche man told a girl who had just been baptized, "You make me happy today, giving your heart to Jesus while you are in the springtime of life. Keep close to Christ, and your whole life will be a springtime." On his conversion another young man said: "Today Jesus unlocked my heart and let the Father's Spirit in. Now my heart is like a new silver dollar just made, new and bright."

Finally, let us cherish the promise of life in the hereafter. Of course, the gospel does much more than create within us this blessed hope, but it does nothing more important than this. What can better lift the sights than to be pointed to "the other side of Jordan near the sweet fields of Eden where the tree of life is blooming; where there's rest for me," or to the vision of the song writer: "On the margin of the river, Washing up its silver spray, We will walk and worship ever, All the happy golden day."

This view of the hereafter makes more bearable the here. Then "Walk on; walk on with hope in your heart, And you'll never walk alone."

On my journey now, Mount Zion;
On my journey now, Mount Zion.
I wouldn't take nothing for Mount Zion,
On my journey now, Mount Zion.

"On My Journey Now"

"TO EVERY THING there is a season, and a time to every purpose under the heaven: a time to be born, and a time to die; a time to plant, and a time to pluck up that which is planted" (Ecclesiastes 3:1, 2).

Some have read this passage and felt that somehow every detail of a man's life is planned in advance, and that when he is born he is simply acting out a preplanned program for his life. Is that really true? Are some born to be saved and others born to be lost? Are some good and some bad by the decision of the great God in heaven? Has man no control at all over his own fate? Let us admit to begin with that there is a time to die, but it is within our power to lengthen or shorten our days.

"Ye shall walk in all the ways which the Lord your God hath commanded you, that ye may live, and that it may be well with you, and that ye may prolong your days in the land which ye shall possess" (Deuteronomy 5:33). "The fear of the Lord prolongeth days: but the years of the wicked shall be shortened" (Proverbs 10:27).

These passages make it clear that walking in harmony with the will of God and cooperating with the King of the universe lengthens one's days, whereas fighting against Him and following the paths of transgression literally shortens a man's days. It is therefore evident that man is able to shorten or lengthen his own life and has a controlling effect over his own destiny.

"Be not over much wicked, neither be thou foolish: why shouldest thou die before thy time?" (Ecclesiastes 7:17).

The one thing about man that God does not control is the free will He gave man. He could easily have kept Adam and Eve from sinning in the Garden of Eden and prevented the development of sin, but for the fact that He had chosen to make man a free moral agent. Both the Old and the New Testaments strongly assert man's power to make his own choices and thus to influence his own destiny.

"Come now, and let us reason together, saith the Lord: though your sins be as scarlet, they shall be as white as snow; though they be red like crimson, they shall be as wool. If ye be willing and obedient, ye shall eat the good of the land: but if ye refuse and rebel, ye shall be devoured with the sword: for the mouth of the Lord hath spoken it" (Isaiah 1:18-20).

If man did not have a free will and the power of choice, why would God address him thus? There would then be no place for such expressions as, "if ye be willing," or "if ye refuse and rebel." If man were but a helpless robot propelled by remote control he could neither refuse or choose.

"I call heaven and earth to record this day against you,

that I have set before you life and death, blessing and cursing: therefore choose life, that both thou and thy seed may live" (Deuteronomy 30:19). Note again that interesting word, "choose." "And if it seem evil unto you to serve the Lord, choose you this day whom ye will serve" (Joshua 24:15).

Hebrews 11:25 and 26 makes it clear that Moses had the power to choose and refuse. This passage of Scripture says that man is a free moral agent, that he can make his own choices and make them stick. Once he has made his decision, man is likely to find that the consequences are already established. God preordains results, not choices. There are certain consequences that go with certain decisions. We may know this in advance.

Galatians 6:7 says, "Be not deceived; God is not mocked: for whatsoever a man soweth, that shall he also reap." It is the reaping that is predestined, not the choices that we make. When a man is going to take a journey, he has a choice as to the highway he wants to follow. Once on that road, however, there are certain things along that road he must pass, and certain experiences through which he must go. It is predetermined that anyone traveling that road must meet these experiences.

Now, life has only two great highways, and while we make thousands of decisions each day with reference to these paths, basically there are only two decisions a man makes in his whole life—a decision for right or for wrong, for good or for evil, for life or for death. Everything we have ever done or attempted to do tends in one of these two directions. The song writer says,

> There are two ways for trav'lers, only two ways:
> One's the hill pathway of battle and praise;
> The other leads downward: tho' flow'ry it seem,
> Its joy is a phantom, its love is a dream. . . .

223

There are two guides for trav'lers, only two guides:
One's the Good Shepherd, e'en thro' the death tides;
The other,—the serpent, beguiling with sin
Whose beauty external hides poison within. . . .

Quickly enter the strait way, leading to life;
Shun the wide pathway of folly and strife.
The Spirit invites you this moment to come;
The Saviour is waiting to welcome you home.

If a man has made a decision to go the wrong way, he should know that it is within his power to make a change. It doesn't matter how long a man has traveled the wrong path, or how deeply involved he is with some of the experiences that are consequent to his wrong decision. He may be sure that change is not only possible, but the power to change is likewise within his grasp. His will must be changed. In short, the man himself must decide that he is tired of the path he is following, and, God giving him grace, he is willing to be changed. Once that decision is made, the promise of Isaiah 41:10 will be fulfilled in his life: "Fear thou not; for I am with thee: be not dismayed; for I am thy God: I will strengthen thee; yea, I will help thee; yea, I will uphold thee with the right hand of my righteousness."

Yes, the power to decide is within us, but the power to change lies with God, and He has offered all the resources of heaven when we deeply and sincerely desire the better way of life.

"For the grace of God that bringeth salvation hath appeared to all men, teaching us that, denying ungodliness and worldly lusts, we should live soberly, righteously, and godly, in this present world; looking for that blessed hope, and the glorious appearing of the great God and our Saviour Jesus Christ; who gave himself for us, that he might redeem us from all iniquity, and purify unto himself a peculiar people, zealous of good works" (Titus 2:11-14).

But Christ will not do it all Himself. Having begun a good work in us through an act of grace born of love, He expects a constant exercise of the will in His favor. In short, living the Christlike life is not automatic. You do not set a dial and goodness naturally flows from the life. There must be conscious effort on the part of the practitioner in response to the divine operation of grace.

"Stand therefore, having your loins girt about with truth, and having on the breastplate of righteousness" (Ephesians 6:14). The word "stand" is an active verb. It requires will power and stamina. When the will is on the side of Christ, the power will come.

"Strive to enter in at the strait gate: for many, I say unto you, will seek to enter in, and shall not be able" (Luke 13:24). Grace does not take the striving out of human experience. As a matter of fact, it is grace that inspires our striving and that makes it possible.

"Submit yourselves therefore to God. Resist the devil, and he will flee from you" (James 4:7). Both submission and resistance are active experiences. It takes the supreme exercise of the will to submit to the will of God.

"Humble yourselves therefore under the mighty hand of God, that he may exalt you in due time" (1 Peter 5:6). "I therefore so run, not as uncertainly; so fight I, not as one that beateth the air: but I keep under my body, and bring it into subjection: lest that by any means, when I have preached to

15

others, I myself should be a castaway" (1 Corinthians 9:26, 27).

Just look at the action verbs in these words of Paul: "run," "fight," "keep under my body," "bring it into subjection." Habits long cherished will not depart from human experience without human effort. There must be an exercise of the will in response to the transforming power of divine grace and love. Many have a perverted idea of grace. They think of it as something done for man by God which does not involve human effort. This is spurious grace. First of all, God does not perform the operation of grace on an unwilling heart. Man must accept. Man must submit. Man must believe. Man must claim by faith the promises of God; and this involves effort. While it is true that God does all the work, it is equally true that man is not passive in salvation. He literally comes alive.

We conclude, therefore, that the fate of man lies not with the stars or the planets, as the astrologer falsely assumes. It matters little under what sign of the Zodiac you were born. What is important is that you have a free will, and that you are not condemned by predetermination, environmental circumstances, or hereditary tendencies to be anything other than what you choose to be. When, by our own free will and volition, we invite Christ into the heart, we have exercised the highest freedom. The slave is the man who gives in to sin and accepts it as his inevitable lot. There is a better life to be lived in this present world—the life of Christ, and by your simple acknowledgment of His lordship in the universe and in your life, you bring that priceless gift into your own experience. Thus you become a new creation.

PART III

Prophecy

I hear the trumpet sound
To wake the nations underground.
Look in my God's right hand
When the sun refuse to shine;
My Lord, what a morning!

"What a Morning!"

THE LAND of Egypt grew cool under the shimmering rays of a silver moon. Pharaoh and his people cringed in the hopelessness of their tenth confrontation with the God of Israel. Moses was urgently summoned and given the good news that his people could now go free. The long night of slavery was past. The morning of deliverance had come, and freedom's cadence found its rhythm in the irregular swish of sandals on the desert sands. The grim specter of the desert journey could not dampen their ardor or blight their hopes. They were free. Oh, what a day!

But Titus 2:13 points to an even brighter day for all who love the Lord: "Looking for that blessed hope, and the glorious appearing of the great God and our Saviour Jesus Christ." "The night is far spent, the day is at hand: let us therefore cast off the works of darkness, and let us put on the armour of light" (Romans 13:12).

228

Yes, "the golden morning is fast approaching; Jesus soon will come To take His happy and faithful children To their promised home. O, we see the gleams of the golden morning, piercing thro' this night of gloom! O, we see the gleams of the golden morning That will burst the tomb."

Jesus Christ came to earth nineteen hundred years ago in the quietness of a manger. A thousand singing angels heralded His birth, but the great masses of humanity were unaware that the God of heaven had come to tabernacle with man. Not even Herod, the ruler of the region, with his elaborate spy system, knew of the birth of Christ. He had to be told by the Wise Men from the East. Such was the secrecy that surrounded the birth of our Lord, and such was the widespread ignorance of the prophecies that so clearly predicted the coming of the Messiah. But when Jesus comes back to the earth, it will be different. His coming will be heralded by the great sounds of a trumpet, the voice of the archangel, and the summons from the Lord Himself that will call the dead from their graves.

"For the Lord himself shall descend from heaven with a shout, with the voice of the archangel, and with the trump of God: and the dead in Christ shall rise first: then we which are alive and remain shall be caught up together with them in the clouds, to meet the Lord in the air: and so shall we ever be with the Lord" (1 Thessalonians 4:16, 17).

This will be no secret rapture, but a public, earth-shaking event. All men will know of the coming of the Lord. "And then shall appear the sign of the Son of man in heaven: and then shall all the tribes of the earth mourn, and they shall see the Son of man coming in the clouds of heaven with power and great glory" (Matthew 24:30). "Behold, he cometh with clouds;

and every eye shall see him, and they also which pierced him: and all kindreds of the earth shall wail because of him. Even so, Amen" (Revelation 1:7).

This wailing will be the expression of dismay from those who have neglected their great opportunity to be saved. They were too busy with other things to give their hearts to Christ and surrender their lives to His beneficent control. To them the coming of Christ will not be a welcome sight. Men who deliberately transgress God's law are not eager to face the Almighty. They literally spend their lives running away from Him, as did our first parents.

After Adam and Eve sinned, God came walking in the Garden in the cool of the evening. "And the Lord God called unto Adam, and said unto him, Where art thou? And he said, I heard thy voice in the garden, and I was afraid, because I was naked; and I hid myself" (Genesis 3:9, 10).

It is significant that at the very beginning of human history when man sinned, he ran from God. So will it be when Jesus comes to this earth the second time:

"And the heaven departed as a scroll when it is rolled together; and every mountain and island were moved out of their places. And the kings of the earth, and the great men, and the rich men, and the chief captains, and the mighty men, and every bondman, and every free man, hid themselves in the dens and in the rocks of the mountains; and said to the mountains and rocks, Fall on us, and hide us from the face of him that sitteth on the throne, and from the wrath of the Lamb: for the great day of his wrath is come; and who shall be able to stand?" (Revelation 6:14-17).

For the righteous this will be a joyous occasion. For them it will mean glorious immortality. It will mean their exodus from the presence of sin. It will mean an eternity with Christ. And so with shouts of unmingled joy, they will welcome our Lord's glorious appearing in the clouds. The Lord Jesus is coming soon.

One day Jesus said to the people, "When ye see a cloud rise out of the west, straightway ye say, There cometh a shower; and so it is. And when ye see the south wind blow, ye say, There will be heat; and it cometh to pass. Ye hypocrites, ye can discern the face of the sky and of the earth; but how is it that ye do not discern this time?" (Luke 12:54-56).

It is unfortunate, but true, that man gauges temporal things more accurately than spiritual things. As a result, to the vast majority of earth's inhabitants the coming of the Lord will be a great surprise. But this need not be so. The Word of God is replete with warnings and evidences of the nearness of His coming. What are some of these?

Luke 21:8 warns of false christs and messiahs appearing on the earth, duplicating in part many of His great miracles. "Go ye not therefore after them," is the Master's admonition. Verse nine speaks of wars and commotions. "Be not terrified," He counsels. Verse eleven speaks of earthquakes, famines, pestilences, and fearful sights, and verse twelve of persecution and governmental investigations. But Christ promises, "I will give you a mouth and wisdom, which all your adversaries shall not be able to gainsay nor resist" (verse 15). Verse 16 speaks of betrayal by one's closest kin, and verse 17 about hatred being directed at all commandment-keeping sons of God. But Christ counsels, "In your patience possess ye your souls" (verse 19).

Verse twenty-five speaks of signs in the sun and the moon, and the stars, distress of nations, and great tidal waves. But counsels Jesus, "And when these things begin to come to pass, then look up, and lift up your heads; for your redemption draweth nigh" (verse 28).

In spite of all these manifest evidences of the nearness of the end of the age, Christ could say, "For as a snare shall it come on all them that dwell on the face of the whole earth" (verse 35). Why this mysterious lack of awareness? How could it come as a snare when prophets have traced in painful detail the events that would usher in the coming of our Lord? Few people are reading the signs. Few are even concerned about the return of our Lord. But to those who are, Christ admonishes: "Watch ye therefore, and pray always, that ye may be accounted worthy to escape all these things that shall come to pass, and to stand before the Son of man" (verse 36).

On a hot August afternoon in 1619 a Dutch ship appeared off the coast of Virginia bearing twenty African slaves. They were exchanged for New England rum and silver, and put to work as the first of a cargo of millions who were subjected to cruel bondage. Their plaintive cries for deliverance could be heard in the night as they poured into the ears of the Lord their pitiful desire for freedom. Over the long weary years there was born in them the hope that one day a messiah would come to set them free. Toward the end of the Civil War word circulated among the slaves that Abraham Lincoln was about to sign the Emancipation Proclamation. Hope, thrice dead, rose again and kindled the flame of faith in millions of human hearts. Black men across the nation united in prayer that God would deliver them from bondage and grant them the privileges of free men. The day came, and the hand that held the pen trembled as the emancipator affixed his signature to the documents that meant freedom to millions of men and women who yearned for freedom.

From a thousand plantations all over the South, as thousands of bonfires lent their glow to the slow dawn of freedom's day, the voice of the slave, hoarse with shouting, phrased words worthy of his dreams, "My Lord, what a morning!"

Tell me who is that writing;
John the revelator,
Writing Revelation. Writing in
The book, of the seven seals.

"The Seven Seals"

THOSE WHO READ Bible prophecy are often mystified by the prophets' frequent use of symbols to convey their messages. The book of Revelation employs this method more than any other book in the Bible. In our study of the seven seals of the book of Revelation, we are dealing with the history of the Christian church from the date of its establishment in the earth until the day that Christ comes to take it out of the earth. Perhaps John employed symbols to veil the true meaning of his prophecies from the offices of the Roman state, while making them abundantly clear to the church to whom and for whom the messages were intended. This served the dual purpose of preserving the prophet's life, while at the same time sending the Word of God to the churches. The study of these seven seals covering the history and the future of the church is fascinating, because of the strange symbols and the information they impart.

In the book of Revelation, the sixth chapter and the first two verses, we read, "And I saw when the Lamb opened one of the seals, and I heard, as it were the noise of thunder, one of the four beasts saying, Come and see. And I saw, and behold a white horse: and he that sat on him had a bow; and a crown was given unto him: and he went forth conquering, and to conquer."

This first seal symbolizes the church in its infancy. The rider of the white horse, with a crown upon His head, is none other than Jesus Christ, the Founder of the church. That Christ went forth conquering and to conquer tells of the rapid growth of the infant church in the early apostolic age.

Christ had made a wonderful promise to His disciples: "But ye shall receive power, after that the Holy Ghost is come upon you: and ye shall be witnesses unto me both in Jerusalem, and in all Judaea, and in Samaria, and unto the uttermost part of the earth" (Acts 1:8).

The first seal may be thought of as covering the years from the inception of the church until the death of the last of the twelve apostles, about A.D. 100.

Revelation 6:3, 4 says: "And when he had opened the second seal, I heard the second beast say, Come and see. And there went out another horse that was red: and power was given to him that sat thereon to take peace from the earth, and that they should kill one another: and there was given unto him a great sword."

This undoubtedly refers to the pagan persecutions that plagued the church from about A.D. 100 to 313. From the start the Roman emperors resented the existence of a church within their domain that taught of a God other than Caesar. Under

Nero, Caligula, Diocletian, Justinian, and others—some of them half madmen—the Christians endured unspeakable horrors. They were fed to the lions, burned at the stake, and driven underground to the catacombs for their worship. The church was under extreme pressure from the state. But, as someone has said, "The blood of the martyrs is the seed of the church." It is a fact that under persecution the church and its influence spread more rapidly than in times of peace. Persecution, though a curse in itself, has proved a blessing to the cause of God on the earth.

"And when he had opened the third seal, I heard the third beast say, Come and see. And I beheld, and lo a black ·horse; and he that sat on him had a pair of balances in his hand" (verse 5).

The third seal covers church history from about A.D. 313 to 538. During this time a union of church and state developed. The church fathers reached a compromise with the state, the terms of which called for the state to execute the will of the church in return for certain ecclesiastical favors. The rider on the black horse had a pair of balances in his hand, indicating, perhaps, that men would assume powers of judgment due alone to God. During those years the church increasingly assumed prerogatives that belong to God alone.

"And when he had opened the fourth seal, I heard the voice of the fourth beast say, Come and see. And I looked, and behold a pale horse: and his name that sat on him was Death, and Hell followed with him. And power was given unto them over the fourth part of the earth, to kill with sword, and with hunger, and with death, and with the beasts of the earth" (verses 7, 8).

This may be thought of as applying to the church between

about A.D. 538 and 1517 when the church became a persecuting power. Happily, there were dissenters living in the hills who clung to the original teachings of Christ and the apostles—the Waldenses and the Albigenses, for instance. But in the large cities the established religion hunted out the dissenters and persecuted them for such simple "sins" as possessing a Bible and reading it in their home.

In the fourteenth century Wycliffe translated the Bible into English. The anger of the established church was so great against him that they dug up his bones and had them burned in a public square. The persecution of the church against dissenters within its ranks was equaled only by the fury of the state persecutions of the church in its early years.

"And when he had opened the fifth seal, I saw under the altar the souls of them that were slain for the word of God, and for the testimony which they held: and they cried with a loud voice, saying, How long, O Lord, holy and true, dost thou not judge and avenge our blood on them that dwell on the earth? And white robes were given unto every one of them; and it was said unto them, that they should rest yet for a little season, until their fellow-servants also and their brethren, that should be killed as they were, should be fulfilled" (verses 9-11).

We may think of the fifth seal as lasting from about A.D. 1517 to 1755. During these years persecution by the established church flared again, and—figuratively speaking—the blood of the saints cried out for vengeance. These people were guilty of nothing but obeying God. The age-old question rings out, How long will the wicked flourish and the righteous be oppressed?

The answer comes in the eleventh verse: "And white robes were given unto every one of them." As far as the state and the established church were concerned, these thousands died in shame and disgrace. But with the Reformation world opinion about this persecution slowly began to change. White robes of respectability were given the martyred saints, and they are now looked upon as benefactors of mankind for having died for what they felt was right. By the shedding of their blood they established the right of dissent and broke the power of a huge, monolithic church which dominated not only religion but science, art, and politics, thereby creating an atmosphere so repressive that thousands fled to discover a new world where they might worship God according to the dictates of their own conscience.

"And I beheld when he had opened the sixth seal, and, lo, there was a great earthquake; and the sun became black as sackcloth of hair, and the moon became as blood. And the stars of heaven fell unto the earth, even as a fig tree casteth her untimely figs, when she is shaken of a mighty wind" (verses 12, 13).

The most widespread earthquake in history goes by the name of the great Lisbon (Portugal) earthquake. It occurred on November 1, 1755, and was felt over more than 1.5 million square miles of earth's surface. At least thirty thousand people (estimates vary) lost their lives when a whole section of Lisbon simply fell into the sea. The prophet talks also about the sun becoming black as sackcloth made of hair, and the moon becoming as blood. On May 19, 1780, at noonday, the sun was darkened. It was not an eclipse, for the sun and moon were not in the right position for an eclipse. Men were working and doing business as usual when, it seemed, every light in the universe went out. These fearful signs pointed forward to the great climactic event of the ages, the coming of Christ (Matthew 24:3, 7, 29, 30).

PAINTING BY VERNON NYE   © BY REVIEW AND HERALD →

As a boy, Frederick Douglass saw the stars fall on November 13, 1833, and recognized it as a sign that Christ would soon return.

"And the heaven departed as a scroll when it is rolled together; and every mountain and island were moved out of their places. And the kings of the earth, and the great men, and the rich men, and the chief captains, and the mighty men, and every bondman, and every free man, hid themselves in the dens and in the rocks of the mountains; and said to the mountains and rocks, Fall on us, and hide us from the face of him that sitteth on the throne, and from the wrath of the Lamb: for the great day of his wrath is come: and who shall be able to stand?" (Revelation 6:14-17).

The sixth seal carries us forward to the second coming of Christ to this earth, to the end of the world. It speaks of the redemption of the righteous and the terror of the wicked. They will run to the rocks and the mountains to hide from His presence.

Under the seventh seal there is silence in heaven for half an hour. In prophetic time this may refer to the time that it takes the great heavenly entourage to leave heaven, pick up the saints on earth, and transport them back to the great City of God. When that takes place the church of God, which was established on the earth nineteen hundred years ago, will be safe at last in the kingdom of Him who is the Author and Finisher of our faith.

Daniel saw the stone
That was hewed out of the mountain;
Daniel saw the stone
That came rolling through Babylon,
Coming down to redeem a mighty world.

"Daniel Saw the Stone"

MEN PEER INTO the future with anxious hearts for signs that are evident before our very eyes and which clearly indicate that man does not have a bright future on this earth. We turn to the Bible for the answer to calm our nerves, for the Word of God alone can give us the key to the future.

In Daniel 2 the God of heaven revealed many things that would take place on this earth, to a heathen king. That king was Nebuchadnezzar. While he was asleep, God gave him a dream and then took it from him. The next morning when the king awakened he was vaguely aware that he had had a disturbing dream, but couldn't recall just what it was. The Bible says that he called his magicians and sorcerers and fortunetellers and asked them not only to tell him what he had dreamed but to give the interpretation. When the fortunetellers could not reconstruct the dream, they freely confessed that his dream had come from the gods of whom they had no knowledge. Then the king, in his anger, commanded that all the wise men of Babylon be slain.

There was in Nebuchadnezzar's kingdom a Hebrew named Daniel. He called a prayer meeting with some of his friends, and to him God revealed not only the dream but its interpretation also. This dream claims our attention now because it relates to our own day and to events that are still in the future.

Daniel testified before the king: "Blessed be the name of God for ever and ever: for wisdom and might are his: and he changeth the times and the seasons: he removeth kings, and setteth up kings: he giveth wisdom unto the wise, and knowledge to them that know understanding: he revealeth the deep and secret things: he knoweth what is in the darkness, and the light dwelleth with him" (Daniel 2:20-22).

Daniel then proceeded to reveal the dream that Nebuchadnezzar had seen and forgotten. A peculiar dream it was! The king had seen the image of a man with a head of gold, breast and arms of silver, belly and thighs of brass, legs of iron, and feet partly iron and partly clay. "Thou sawest till that a stone was cut out without hands," Daniel told the king, "which smote the image upon his feet that were of iron and clay, and brake them to pieces" (verse 34).

What does this strange dream mean? A man with a head of gold, breast and arms of silver, belly and thighs of brass, legs of iron, and feet of iron and clay! What does he mean when he says that he saw a stone cut out without hands that smites the image in the feet and breaks it in pieces?

The Bible is clear in its interpretation of this God-given dream. Guided by God, Daniel said to Nebuchadnezzar, king of Babylon, "Thou art this head of gold." The head of this strange dream-image represented the king of Babylon and his empire. But Babylon would pass away, for the head of gold was followed by the breast and arms of silver. We who live this side of the prophecy are fortunate in that we know the kingdoms that succeeded Babylon. We know that Medo-Persia followed the kingdom of Babylon, that the Grecian kingdom, represented by the belly and thighs of brass, followed Medo-Persia, and that Rome followed the Grecian kingdom. This is the historical sequence in which the nations followed one another. But as Daniel stood in front of the king, all of this was yet future.

Babylon ruled the world from 626 to 539 B.C. Interesting things happened during those years that should claim our attention, for we are studying the rise and fall of nations. The Bible says that "righteousness exalteth a nation: but sin is a reproach to any people" (Proverbs 14:34). Can it be that in our own nation and in the other nations of the earth today the seeds of dissolution are making their appearance? Read the story of Belshazzar's feast (Daniel 5), and you will discover four things that caused the downfall of Babylon. The king and his lords were drunk with wine and strong drink; there was a multiplicity of wives and concubines; the people praised gods of gold and silver, and they had no respect for holy things. These four sins are present with us now on a worldwide basis.

But let us examine the prophecy more closely. It was under the Babylonian government that the three Hebrew youth of Daniel 3 made a gallant stand for their faith. The king had issued an order that everybody was to bow down to the golden image he had erected on the Plain of Dura. As you remember, after Nebuchadnezzar heard Daniel's description of the image and his prediction that another kingdom would replace Babylon, Nebuchadnezzar was angry and built an image completely of gold—signifying that he did not believe his kingdom would ever pass away. But there were three young men—Shadrach, Meshach, and Abednego—who refused to bow down to his image. As a result they were cast into a burning, fiery furnace from which the God of heaven delivered them.

We see here one of the failings of an absolute government. Only God is truly absolute, and He claims the total allegiance of man—physical, mental, and spiritual. When a dictatorial earthly government makes the same claim, inevitably there will be a clash of loyalties, and men who obey the God of heaven are caught in the middle.

It was the same under the Medes and the Persians. The king issued an order that no one was to bow down to any god other than himself for thirty days. Daniel, who worshiped the God of heaven, disobeyed the order and was cast into a den of lions, from which he was delivered by the God he served.

The Greeks multiplied gods. During the rule of Rome the influence of the Greeks was still felt, and when the apostle Paul came to preach the gospel in Athens, he even found an inscription to an "unknown god." He told the people he had come to tell them about the God they knew not, the God of heaven.

The Romans ruled the world with an iron hand. It was under Rome that Jesus Christ was crucified at Calvary. Under Rome thousands of Christians paid with their lives for their faith in Jesus.

But Daniel described all these nations hundreds of years before they existed. What a precious book is the Bible! We need to read it more. It has outlined well in advance the course of human history. The four great world empires were foretold in

Daniel 2. We have the advantage of reading history, and we can attest that the prophecy proved true. Medo-Persia did follow Babylon, Greece did follow Medo-Persia, and Rome did follow Greece. The feet of iron and clay refer to the division of the world into many separate kingdoms.

Since Rome fell no other kingdom has ruled the known world. "And whereas thou sawest iron mixed with miry clay, they shall mingle themselves with the seed of men: but they shall not cleave one to another, even as iron is not mixed with clay" (verse 43). Following Rome, even down to our own day, the kingdoms of earth have been partly strong and partly broken. We read that in verse 42. Some will have in them the strength of iron, and others will have the weakness of clay. Doesn't this aptly describe the world as it is today? Some nations are strong, rich, and powerful; others are weak and dependent. Before our very eyes we see the iron and the clay.

But, thank God, the prophecy does not end on this dismal note, for Daniel looks away to the stone cut out without hands that will smite the image on its feet and break them in pieces. Under this figure he describes the second coming of Jesus Christ in the clouds of heaven.

When He went away Christ said, "Let not your heart be troubled: ye believe in God, believe also in me. In my Father's house are many mansions: if it were not so, I would have told you. I go to prepare a place for you. And if I go and prepare a place for you, I will come again" (John 14:1-3).

Daniel 2:44 refers to that second coming: "And in the days of these kings [the partly strong and the partly weak kingdoms] shall the God of heaven set up a kingdom, which shall never be destroyed: and the kingdom shall not be left to other peo-

ple, but it shall break in pieces and consume all these king-doms, and it shall stand for ever."

Sooner or later every kingdom established by man falls into decay or is destroyed. Archeologists dig into the soil and uncover layer after layer of buried cities, of past civilizations that once flourished but are now extinct. But the kingdom of God, Daniel says, will never be destroyed. It will be permanent, it will be lasting, it will be forever. And it shall not be left to other people. When God made this world He placed Adam in charge of it. But Adam sinned, and a succession of sinful Adams have been in control of the affairs of the earth ever since. During his six-thousand-year reign man has failed to solve any of his most pressing problems. Thank God, when the kingdoms of this world become the kingdom of our Lord and of His Christ, He shall reign forever and ever, and He will not leave the kingdom to other people. That is what has caused trouble before—the kingdom has been left to other people.

> But when Christ reigns
> Where'er the sun doth
> Its successive journeys run,
> Of His righteousness and peace and justice,
> There will be no end.
> And it is in that day
> That justice will run down like water
> And righteousness like a mighty stream.

In Luke 20:18 we read, "Whosoever shall fall upon that stone shall be broken; but on whomsoever it shall fall, it will grind him to powder."

The citizens of this world cannot afford to wait until the Stone, hewed out of the mountain, strikes the earth. We must fall upon that Stone and have our hard hearts broken. The state-

Nebuchadnezzar's amazing dream of an image of gold, silver, brass, iron, and clay foretold the future history of our world.

ment, "fall upon that Stone," is a reference to faith, repentance, conversion, baptism, and obedience. This is how we cast ourselves upon the mercies of the Lord, and we may be assured that He will sustain us. The vision of the stone smiting the image in the feet and grinding them to powder, and the wind blowing the powder away as it would the chaff from a summer's threshing floor, points to the transitory nature of life on this earth. The Bible predicts the utter obliteration of everything that man has constructed with his own hands.

Describing the end of the world John wrote: "And the great city was divided into three parts, and the cities of the nations fell. . . . And every island fled away, and the mountains were not found" (Revelation 16:19, 20).

But we cannot close this chapter on a negative note, for according to Daniel's prophecy, the stone begins to grow until it finally fills the whole earth. This is the establishment of the kingdom of our Lord and of His Christ. Then God will wipe away all tears from our eyes, and there will be no more sorrow nor death nor crying, for the former things are passed away.

There's a hand writing on the wall;
O, my Lord, it writes on the wall.

"There's a Hand Writing"

BELSHAZZAR'S FEAST has been the subject of the artist's brush and the poet's pen. Within this simple story lies the secret of the decline of one of the greatest world empires the world has ever known. Golden Babylon ruled the world from 626 to 539 B.C. Her kings were the envy of the known world. Their word was law throughout the empire. Their rule was absolute. Their warriors were feared. Unconquered nations paid them tribute. The future of the Babylonian Empire seemed assured for a thousand years, but a Hebrew poet with the prophetic gift had already predicted the fall of this empire.

Under King Nebuchadnezzar, the prophet Daniel enjoyed privileged status because of his wisdom. Under King Belshazzar, Daniel was relegated to obscurity because his prophecies did not please the ear of the young monarch. So it was, one murky Chaldean evening, that "Belshazzar the king made a great feast

249

to a thousand of his lords, and drank wine before the thousand" (Daniel 5:1).

"In the same hour came forth fingers of a man's hand and wrote over against the candlestick upon the plaister of the wall of the king's palace: and the king saw the part of the hand that wrote. Then the king's countenance was changed, and his thoughts troubled him, so that the joints of his loins were loosed, and his knees smote one against another" in terror (verses 5, 6).

Within the first six verses of Daniel 5, we discover not only the cause of the decline of ancient Babylon but of every civilization that has ever existed in the history of the world. These signs, incidentally, are highly visible in our own age. And why did that great nation fall? Her leaders "drank wine before the thousand" (verse 1). The people of Babylon had been softened by the use of alcoholic beverages. Liquor had robbed them of their self-respect and decency. The Bible says, "Wine is a mocker, strong drink is raging: and whosoever is deceived thereby is not wise" (Proverbs 20:1). "Nor thieves, nor covetous, nor drunkards, nor revilers, nor extortioners, shall inherit the kingdom of God" (1 Corinthians 6:10).

"Who hath woe? who hath sorrow? who hath contentions? who hath babbling? who hath wounds without cause? who hath redness of eyes? They that tarry long at the wine; they that go to seek mixed wine. Look not thou upon the wine when it is red, when it giveth his colour in the cup, when it moveth itself aright. . . . At the last it biteth like a serpent, and stingeth like an adder" (Proverbs 23:29-32).

That night the Babylonians felt the serpent's sting. As a matter of fact, the guards who were supposed to be watching over the safety of the city were drunk that night, and it was relatively easy for the Medo-Persian soldiers to come into the city and accomplish its destruction. They were fighting drunk soldiers.

The effect of alcohol upon the body has been clearly demonstrated scientifically. It destroys taste, overworks the heart, dilates the blood vessels, paralyzes the brain, and affects the vision. It also destroys the delicate tissues and membranes of the stomach. Alcohol benumbs the highest sensibilities, and converts a gentleman into a brute. We've come to a time in America when you can buy liquor as easily as food. This is true, in fact, all over the world. This sign of civilization's decay is very much in evidence. Once again the mysterious hand writes on the wall. Can you read the writing?

Daniel 5:2 says that the king commanded that the servants should "bring the golden and silver vessels which his father Nebuchadnezzar had taken out of the temple which was in Jerusalem; that the king, and his princes, his wives, and his concubines, might drink therein."

Now these golden vessels were sacred to the Temple, dedicated and consecrated to the true God. Thus to profane these holy Temple furnishings revealed that the king had no respect for holy things. By this one act he desecrated the holy Temple of the Lord. This act, which demonstrated the king's utter contempt for God, brought the hand of divine justice down upon his head. Is there not evident around us today a similar lack of respect for holy things? The Bible, the church, prayer, and Christian virtues are all sneered at in a thousand places, a thousand times a day. Christ, no longer regarded as the Son of God, is spoken of as a good teacher and a man whose moral and ethical

teachings are worthy of emulation. What blasphemy that the Son of God Himself should be reduced to the position of a man and the thinking of man!

Once again the hand of God writes on the wall. Can you read the writing? Twice this narrative refers to the king's wives and concubines (verses 2 and 3). Aside from his many marriages, the king had ladies in waiting to satisfy his lustful desires. A similar form of iniquity is widespread today. Men act as if there were no God to whom they must give account, and throw off the yoke of moral law, denying that it is binding on human behavior. This leaves them free to roam far and wide, venting their lust wherever they desire. To some men, the brothel is as common as the grocery, and human nature, undisciplined, gallops the earth, leaving broken hearts and homes in its wake. Like the pale horse of the Revelation, death and hell follow. Statistics tell their own sorry tale. One small nation reports more than one hundred thousand illegitimate babies are born each year. The number of abortions is not known. Thousands of young people disappear into prostitution yearly. Dope addiction and alcohol consumption add to their misery as they live the life of the damned. One day begins to merge into another, until time becomes an endless stream of yielding that which cannot be recaptured, and a burgeoning burden of guilt crushes the soul.

But there is help. "Fear thou not; for I am with thee: be not dismayed; for I am thy God: I will strengthen thee; yea, I will help thee; yea, I will uphold thee with the right hand of my righteousness" (Isaiah 41:10).

One day a young man came to me in confidence, and after explaining a moral problem asked the question: "Is there any help for me?" I was happy to be able to answer him: "There is balm in Gilead; there is a physician there." There is no incurable sin. "If we walk in the light, as he is in the light, . . . the blood of Jesus Christ his Son cleanseth us from all sin. . . . If we confess our sins, he is faithful and just to forgive us our sins, and to cleanse us from all unrighteousness" (1 John 1:7-9).

As we kneel in prayer before our Maker there must be in us a repentant heart. We must be sincerely willing to part with our sins. There must be no vacillation here, no holding back. "All to Jesus I surrender, All to Him I freely give," must be the spirit of our hearts. There must be a yielding of our selfish desires, a merging of our purposes with His. We must cease to resist the molding of divine grace. We must cooperate with God. A transforming power of love must work unhindered in our souls. There must be no preservation of long-cherished idols; no off-limits signs must greet the eyes of the Hunter for souls. He must find us as yielding as clay in the hands of the potter. The brittle, crusty heart must be replaced. The heart of stone must be removed, and He will give us a heart of flesh. He will heal our weak vacillation, and that which was our downfall will become the anchor point of our strength. The hand of God still writes on the walls of men's hearts. Can you read the writing?

"They drank wine, and praised the gods of gold, and of silver, of brass, of iron, of wood, and of stone" (Daniel 5:4). Yes, they became materialists, worshipers of things. That which could be seen was placed in the position of the unseen. The transitory assumed the status of the eternal and that which corrupts received honor due to the incorruptible God. Humanity stands again at that same point. Materialism has become the god of this age. One philosopher put it this way: "We have a new trinity now: God the Father, God the Son, and god the almighty dollar." But, thank God, there are a few souls who have not bowed the knee to Baal. Jehovah, the Creator of heaven and earth, the Redeemer of all mankind, still takes first place in their lives.

A little boy was in the habit of praying often to the Lord and, like Enoch, became so familiar with Him that he addressed the Master in familiar terms. He would begin his prayer by saying: "Hello, Jesus, this is Johnny." So, day after day he would approach his Master, present his needs, and always introduce it with: "Hello, Jesus, this is Johnny." Came the day that little Johnny was afflicted with an incurable disease, and he received the bad news that he had to die. But he continued that familiar little prayer: "Hello, Jesus, this is Johnny." On the day of his death, it is said he heard a voice speaking to him, saying, "Hello, Johnny, this is Jesus."

All who make Christ first will find that He will be with them to the end.

Going to lay down my sword and shield,
Down by the river side; to study war no more.

"Study War No More"

THE WORLD is tired of war, and yet the nations rush into it again and again. Geographical boundaries, economic advantages, positions of power are the lures that beckon madmen into conflict with their fellow men. With the oppressed souls of the Revelation, I cry out, "How long, O Lord?" (Revelation 6:10).

The Bible prophecy speaks of a war to end wars. It tells of an end to the carnage that has so long afflicted the human family, an end to the rattling of muskets, the belching of cannon, the metallic crunch of moving tanks, exploding bombs, and the deadly whine of fighter planes. The Bible tells of a day when men will study war no more, and this planet will be at peace. This cheering prophecy is found in Revelation 16:14: "For they are the spirits of devils, working miracles, which go forth unto the kings of the earth and of the whole world, to gather them to the battle of that great day of God Almighty."

255

The encouragement in this text is found in the last phrase of the verse: "that great day of God Almighty." Today is not His day on this planet. The dragon, the beast, and the false prophet are having their day now. These are the three contrary forces mentioned in our text. They are arrayed against God, they are at war with His purposes and plans, they seek the destruction of His people, they seek to wreck the great plan of salvation.

According to Revelation 12:7-9, the dragon is the devil himself, and through the agency of spiritualism he is working to bring ruin to men and nations. It is significant that many of the great statesmen of history have had spirit mediums as their closest advisers. In Nebuchadnezzar's court they constituted his privy council, and the king based his state policy on their recommendations. But we need not go back to Nebuchadnezzar's day to find examples of this. Adolph Hitler followed their advice when he plunged Europe into World War II. Many generals have consulted with demons before making great decisions involving thousands of lives.

Spiritualism, which is the old practice of the black arts, has assumed new respectability. The prophet John points this out as one of the factors leading men to the great confrontation with the Almighty. This is the day of the dragon. It is also the day of the beast. The beast referred to in Revelation 16:14, 15, is the same as the one described in detail in chapter 13—the Papacy, that mysterious union of church and state that had its supreme manifestation in the Middle Ages. It dominated religion, politics, and economics for hundreds of years. This Roman power made changes in religious thought and practice that have influenced hundreds of millions of people. This subversion of the plain teaching of the Scriptures has led to the grossest apostasy, and in our own day we are seeing a resurgence of the influence of the beast of Revelation 13. This is the day of the dragon and the beast.

But it is also the day of the false prophet. The false prophet was not always false. The Protestant Reformation offered the world great hope. Its founders were men of God, especially raised up by Him to strike at the power of the beast and to check his influence on the religious thought and practice of the world. This the early founders of the Protestant movement did, but in recent years strange things are being heard in Protestant circles also: "God is dead," and "His law does not have to be observed," "A whole commandment—the fourth one—has been nailed to the cross," and "Right and wrong are relative and entirely dependent upon the approval of a conscience, not necessarily regulated by external moral law." Thus the apostasy deepens, and man's estrangement from his Maker widens like rampaging waters, spilling over to inundate the countryside. These three influences will accomplish the ruin of the world, for they strike at the very heart of man's being, his spiritual nature. They have to do with religion. They have to do with the spirit of man. They have to do with the relationship between man and his Maker. They will serve to sever the connection between God and man, and it is this that will bring man face to face with God at Armageddon. "And he gathered them together into a place called in the Hebrew tongue Armageddon" (Revelation 16:16).

The name Armageddon probably refers to the mountains of Megiddo in Palestine. The valley of Megiddo (the Plain of Esdraelon) was anciently a famous battleground, where some of the decisive battles of the world have been fought. Nevertheless, let it be clearly understood that the battle of the great day of God Almighty will be far more widespread than that. It is because Armageddon stood for the decisive defeat of Israel's enemies that John employs Armageddon as a name for God's great confrontation with the nations of earth.

The Bible teaches that Armageddon will be a three-phase conflict:

1. It will be a conflict between man and man. "And the sixth angel poured out his vial upon the great river Euphrates; and the water thereof was dried up, that the way of the kings of the east might be prepared" (verse 12). As we near the end of the world, and the Spirit of God is withdrawn from the earth, men will become more belligerent one toward the other. There is evidence that conflict between nations and individuals will increase until the great day of God.

2. It will be a conflict between Christ and Satan. "And the devil that deceived them was cast into the lake of fire and brimstone, where the beast and the false prophet are, and shall be tormented day and night for ever and ever" (chapter 20:10). In the final phase of Armageddon, Satan and his angels will be fully and finally dealt with. The battle begins at the second coming of Christ. It will be interrupted by the millennium. It will end at the close of the millennium, when the destructive fires of Jehovah finally purge the earth of all wickedness.

3. More important to us, Armageddon will be a confrontation between man and his Maker, in fact, the final one. Armageddon marks the end of the world. A battle foretold by the prophet Joel aptly describes what will take place at the end of the world: "Let the heathen be wakened, and come up to the valley of

Jehoshaphat: for there will I sit to judge all the heathen round about. . . . . Multitudes, multitudes in the valley of decision: for the day of the Lord is near in the valley of decision. The sun and the moon shall be darkened, and the stars shall withdraw their shining. The Lord also shall roar out of Zion, and utter his voice from Jerusalem; and the heavens and the earth shall shake; but the Lord will be the hope of his people, and the strength of the children of Israel" (Joel 3:12-16).

The human race is traveling a one-way street with breath-taking speed toward its destiny—a date with God in Armageddon. From Fiji to Finland and from Bombay to Los Angeles, men will keep this date with God. It will not be necessary for God to herd the billions of human beings into one geographical location to do His work, "his strange work; and bring to pass his act, his strange act." His voice pronouncing judgment upon the wicked will be heard to the ends of the earth, and wherever men walk they will meet their end, their Armageddon.

But for the righteous this will be a day of triumph. "And they shall be mine, saith the Lord of hosts, in that day when I make up my jewels; and I will spare them, as a man spareth his own son that serveth him" (Malachi 3:17). Just as Armageddon will mean the total destruction of the wicked, so it will mean the total triumph of the saints. Affliction will not rise again a second time, because the very source of iniquity will be destroyed: "For behold, the day cometh, that shall burn as an oven; and all the proud, yea, and all that do wickedly, shall be stubble: and the day that cometh shall burn them up, saith the Lord of hosts, that it shall leave them neither root nor branch" (chapter 4:1).

The root of the rebellion against God was Satan himself. He

started it all. His branches are those men and angels foolish enough to follow him, blind enough to accept his orders. Of such people Jesus said while on earth, "Ye are of your father the devil." The sad story is one of the blind leading the blind. The Bible says that both will fall into the ditch. That ditch is Armageddon. It marks the end of the world, the end of the wicked, the end of the rebellion. But it is more than that. It vindicates God, and everyone who serves God. The entire universe will acclaim the justice and the righteousness of God's motives, purposes, and plans. Even His archenemy, Satan, will be forced to kneel and acknowledge His goodness: "At the name of Jesus every knee should bow, . . . every tongue should confess that Jesus Christ is Lord, to the glory of God the Father" (Philippians 2:10, 11). Then and then only will men lay down their swords and shields, down by the riverside, to study war no more.

"*Trouble in the Air*"

WHEN WE SPEAK of the anger of God, we're not speaking in a human sense. When we talk about human anger, we speak of a man losing his temper, a man threatening violence, or a man who has lost self-control. This is not what we're talking about when we talk about God. When we use the phrase, "when God gets angry," we're referring to that part of the character of God that is basic to His nature—His justice. You see, there are two parts to the character of God—His justice and His mercy, His grace and His law.

Concerning the love of God we read: "That Christ may dwell in your hearts by faith; that ye, being rooted and grounded in love may be able to comprehend with all saints what is the breadth, and length, and depth, and height; and to know the love of Christ which passeth knowledge, that ye might be filled with all the fulness of God" (Ephesians 3:17-19).

261

The love of God for man passes knowledge; furthermore, it never runs out. Some people will love you today and hate you tomorrow, but this isn't true of God. His love is eternal, it is everlasting, it is beyond all human comprehension. According to 2 Corinthians 12:9, His grace, or love, is sufficient for us. It is sufficient for our peace, it is sufficient for our sustenance, it is sufficient for our family relationships, it is sufficient for our international relationships, it is sufficient for our community relationships. The love of God is the solution to all our problems. The problem is with man. Does he accept this love? Does he believe that God loves him? This is the big question.

There is a method by which we express our love for God. He has already expressed His love for us. For thirty-three years He walked the earth as a man. "The Word was made flesh and dwelt among us" (John 1:14). Romans 2:13 makes it clear that those who love God will obey Him: "For not the hearers of the law are just before God, but the doers of the law shall be justified." Or take John 14:15: "If ye love me, keep my commandments." Or Luke 6:46: "Why call ye me, Lord, Lord, and do not the things which I say?"

There was a woman whose husband wandered away one weekend. When he came back Monday morning he said to his wife, "Darling, I have three little words for you."

She said, "What are they?"

He answered, "I love you."

But the next week he disappeared again, and Monday morning when he came back the same conversation took place. After this happened the third time she said to him, "Well, I have two little words for you."

"What are they?" he asked.

"Show me," she said.

I love you. Yes. If you love me, then show me. These are the words God has for us. It's one thing to love in our hearts and another thing to love with our lives. God wants us to put our love for Him on the line just as He has put His love and His life on the line for us.

God has done many things to try to save us from the fate that will overtake the wicked. In Matthew 23:34 Jesus says that He sent us the prophets, but we stoned them. According to Psalm 119:158, God gave us His Word but we rejected that. God gave us Jesus, and we crucified Him. When Jesus returned to heaven He sent the Holy Spirit, and you know that men have insulted the Spirit of grace (Hebrews 10:29). God has sent messenger after messenger who has faithfully proclaimed the Word of the living God, yet the Word of truth is despised today as it always has been.

And so God's anger is not without reason. Hosea 4:6 gives one of the reasons for God's mounting anger with His creatures. "My people are destroyed for lack of knowledge: because thou hast rejected knowledge, I will also reject thee, that thou shalt be no priest to me: seeing thou hast forgotten the law of thy God, I will also forget thy children." One reason for God's anger with man is that man has turned his back on the knowledge of God. He is full of knowledge about other things. Knowledge of sin covers the earth. Men have turned away from the knowledge of God, essential though it is. There is good reason for God's anger to mount by the hour.

Psalm 119:126 tells us about another root cause for the anger of God. "It is time for thee, Lord, to work: for they have made void thy law." Men have declared themselves outside the range, outside the jurisdiction, outside the prerogatives of the law of God. Man has put his own reasoning in the place of God and made his own conscience the court of last appeal. He proceeds as though he had the power to decide what is right and what is wrong. This is the second reason why the anger of God mounts against the human family.

The third reason is found in Proverbs 1:22-33: "How long, ye simple ones, will ye love simplicity? and the scorners delight in their scorning, and fools hate knowledge? Turn you at my reproof: behold, I will pour out my spirit unto you, I will make known my words unto you. Because I have called, and ye refused; I have stretched out my hand, and no man regarded; but ye have set at nought all my counsel, and would none of my reproof: I also will laugh at your calamity; I will mock when your fear cometh; when your fear cometh as desolation, and your destruction cometh as a whirlwind; when distress and anguish cometh upon you. Then shall they call upon me, but I will not answer; they shall seek me early, but they shall not find me: for that they hated knowledge, and did not choose the fear of the Lord: they would none of my counsel: they despised all my reproof. Therefore shall they eat of the fruit of their own way, and be filled with their own devices. For the turning away of the simple shall slay them, and the prosperity of fools shall destroy them. But whoso hearkeneth unto me shall dwell safely, and shall be quiet from fear of evil."

Even when God punishes man for his wickedness there is a mixture of mercy with justice. "Whoso hearkeneth unto me shall dwell safely, and shall be quiet from fear of evil." But "the soul that sinneth, it shall die" (Ezekiel 18:4). That death is described vividly in Jeremiah 25:30, 31: "Therefore prophesy thou against them all these words, and say unto them, The Lord shall roar from on high, and utter his voice from his holy habitation; he shall mightily roar upon his habitation; he shall give a shout, as they that tread the grapes, against all the inhabitants of the earth. A noise shall come even to the ends of the earth; for the Lord hath a controversy with the nations, he will plead with all flesh; he will give them that are wicked to the sword, saith the Lord."

Let's face it. That day will come. What will take place then makes an ugly picture, but it's an ugly picture now—men turning their backs on God, men despising the knowledge of God, men turning their backs on God's Word, men doing despite to the Spirit of grace, men neglecting the Bible, men turning their backs on the messages of the prophets, men scorning God's messengers, and ministers. The crucifixion of Christ was an ugly picture. It will be another ugly picture when the anger of the Lord is felt in the land and the flames of hell begin to lap at the carcasses of the wicked. "Be not deceived; God is not mocked. Whatsoever a man soweth, that shall he also reap"—and he will reap it in full.

We read in Ezekiel 39:17 and 19: "And, thou son of man, thus saith the Lord God; speak unto every feathered fowl, and to every beast of the field. . . . And ye shall eat fat till ye be full, and drink blood till ye be drunken, of my sacrifice which I have sacrificed for you."

Somebody who was interested in what preachers think about hell-fire these days sent out a questionnaire. One of the answers that came back will interest you—hell is when you're unhappy, and heaven is when you're happy. If it were that easy, there would be no need to serve God, and certainly no need to fear the hell the Bible talks about. Some men have existentialized hell out of existence!

The hell the Bible tells us about is not the one this minister was talking about, for Ezekiel 39:17 says, "And, thou son of man, thus saith the Lord God; Speak unto every feathered fowl, and to every beast of the field, Assemble yourselves, and come; gather yourselves on every side to my sacrifice that I do sacrifice for you, even a great sacrifice upon the mountains of Israel, that ye may eat flesh, and drink blood."

On the last great day the Lord will issue this order to the birds and the beasts: "Ye shall eat the flesh of the mighty, and drink the blood of princes of the earth, of rams, of lambs, and of goats, of bullocks, all of them fatlings of Bashan. And ye shall eat fat till ye be full, and drink blood till ye be drunken, of my sacrifice which I have sacrificed for you" (verse 18). A sad fate that will be!

And so the anger of God mounts. It will soon be felt in the land on an overwhelming scale.

We read in Acts 3:19: "Repent ye therefore, and be converted, that your sins may be blotted out, when the times of refreshing shall come from the presence of the Lord." This is the age of repentance, this is the time when we may turn to God with all our hearts. This is the day when we should seek Him until we find Him when we shall search for Him with all our hearts.

"The Lord is not slack concerning his promise, as some men count slackness; but is longsuffering to us-ward, not willing that any should perish, but that all should come to repentance" (2 Peter 3:9).

The mercy of God is offered to us in verse nine, but a

solemn promise is made in verse ten. If we don't repent, if we don't turn from our sins, if we don't seek the Lord with all our hearts, if we don't grasp by faith the promises of the Almighty, if we don't give Him our love and our lives, if we don't renounce the world, if we don't turn our back on that which damages the body and defiles the soul—then "the day of the Lord will come as a thief in the night; in the which the heavens shall pass away with a great noise, and the elements shall melt with fervent heat, the earth also and the works that are therein shall be burned up.

"Seeing then that all these things shall be dissolved, what manner of persons ought ye to be in all holy conversation and godliness, looking for and hasting unto the coming of the day of God, wherein the heavens being on fire shall be dissolved, and the elements shall melt with fervent heat? Nevertheless we, according to his promise, look for new heavens and a new earth, wherein dwelleth righteousness" (verses 11-13).

In the book, *The Silence of Dean Maitland,* the author tells how the dean fell into sin and then committed one misdeed after another to cover up his first sin. Worst of all, he permitted an innocent man to be punished and imprisoned in his stead. All kinds of temporal adversities broke over him. He lost his wife and children, yet he would not repent. He said, "I cannot, I will not, I dare not, I must not repent." But at length the man who had spent part of his own life in prison for the other man's crime wrote, forgiving him. That letter broke Maitland's heart and brought him to repentance. "God called to me," he said, "through many years, by many judgments, but I repented not until I was forgiven."

Yes, Christ is willing to forgive us all, no matter what the transgressions, if in sincere repentance we turn to Him too with all our hearts. Why wait until the angry breakers of divine retribution dash against the soul, leaving us helpless to serve our new Master, even if we did repent? Let us turn to God with all our hearts here and now, and spare ourselves the pain of procrastination.

Go down, Moses, way down in Egypt's land;
Tell old Pharaoh to let my people go.

"Go Down, Moses"

"PRINCES SHALL COME out of Egypt; Ethiopia shall soon stretch out her hands unto God" (Psalm 68:31).

That there was a time when black African nations were both wealthy and powerful, possessing cultures and civilizations of their own, is a fact of history. There were, for instance, the Ghana empire, the Mali empire, the Songhai empire; and recent excavations in northern Rhodesia indicate that many ruins formerly attributed to outside influences are in truth relics of past black African glory.

When the explorer John Speke went to Uganda he found an organized society, people wearing clothes (the most famous was known as barcloth), and a government complete with a judicial system. That a great people can fall from a position of eminence in world affairs is a fact of history not peculiar to the African continent. Europe and Asia have also known their years of mys-

269

terious slumber, during which people performed their tasks in primitive ways and worshiped pagan gods. Black Africa is only now beginning to emerge from its prolonged stupor. But during the time of David and as late as the prophet Ezekiel, the black nations of Africa were recognized as powers in the world.

Even the most powerful nations of earth have never been known to worship the God of heaven for prolonged periods of time. In Africa, worshiping gods that were products of men's hands, or members of the brute creation, the nations declined in power and influence. But the words of the prophecy indicated that this would not be forever so. "Ethiopia shall soon stretch out her hands unto God." No nation ever does so without enjoying a corresponding resurgence of culture, enlightenment, and power. When the Bible came to Africa it awakened in the African a new sense of his worth and dignity as a human being. The earliest training in Western culture was brought to Africa by missionaries who opened church schools and began to develop the cultural and spiritual nature of the people.

Karl Marx characterized religion as "the opium of the people." Exactly the opposite is true, for wherever the Christian religion goes, men mysteriously come alive. The fires of ambition are rekindled in their hearts, and the passing years testify to an awakening of every facet of human interest and progress on all levels of human endeavor.

At the root of the emergence of the independent nations of Africa lies the zealous inculcation of the principles of the Bible in the classrooms of the early missionaries who went into Africa. Many prominent African leaders trace their introduction to the progressive culture and thought of the twentieth century to the faithful efforts of missionaries in church-sponsored, church-supported, and church-operated schools. Further, churches built the first hospitals on the continent for the care of the physically ill.

While a few members of the church have misrepresented their organizations and missions, by and large the over-all influence of the missionary program in Africa and the world has been a positive factor in the development of nations. All over the continent obscure mounds cover the remains of its true heroes. History will pay tribute to Cecil Rhodes and the great warriors who conquered as they went, but the true heroes of our day are the selfless and often unknown men and women of all races who have gone into the vastness of Africa and carved out a monument to God's glory.

The Bible says, "Righteousness exalteth a nation: but sin is a reproach to any people" (Proverbs 14:34). So the dissemination of the knowledge of the saving grace of the Lord Jesus Christ and the teaching of the moral and ethical principles of Christ alone can elevate and ennoble those who are the beneficiaries of this priceless service.

Africans have sometimes said: "Before the coming of the European, he had the Bible and we had the land. Now he has the land, and we have the Bible." History does not bear out this contention. The record shows that the land was seized from the African, not with the Bible, but with guns and bullets. The enslavement of the continent was accomplished by overwhelming force. The missionaries and the Bible followed the soldiers, but far from serving as instruments of pacification, they taught the Fatherhood of God and the brotherhood of man, and awakened in the African an awareness of his dignity in spite of his condition. He may therefore credit Christ with his arouse-

271

ment, and with the hope that flickered in his heart during the long years of colonial oppression. The Bible and its promises comforted him in moments of frustration and helplessness. The Word of God brought him promise of a brighter day to come. Because Israel found her Moses, the African could hope that one day he would find his—and he did.

Today on that vast continent, well-trained, distinguished statesmen lead their nations. Freedom and independence have swept the continent with what one great statesman called the winds of change. Significantly, it is in Africa today that the largest number of converts to Christ are being added to the church, and in America the per capita accessions of black people to the faith far exceed those of other races. In this broad sense, Ethiopia is indeed stretching forth her hands to God, and enjoying corresponding blessings in cultural awareness, spiritual fervor, and intellectual development. Today the black man is finding his place in the sun, but he can thank God for it.

But there are dangers ahead. There is the danger of arrogance and pride. What blessing will come to the world if the black man imitates the worst in other races, in terms of arrogance and pride and self-superiority? Black supremacy is no more desirable than white supremacy, and black prejudice is no less cruel than white prejudice. We will fail in our quest for equality, and if we get it we will not be able to maintain it if, in the process, we become calloused and inhuman. Pride still goes before destruction and a haughty spirit before a fall.

There is also the question of worship, honor, and adoration, which are due to the God of heaven alone. Recognition must be given Him for the miracle of our exodus and emergence, but what if we turn again to idols? What if the pagan rituals of the past reclaim their adherents? We can only point to the sad case of the children of Israel as an example. When they entered their Promised Land and became rich and affluent, they succumbed to the lure of pagan ritual and heathen forms of worship. They debased themselves more than the heathen, because of their superior knowledge, and as a result the Jews were scattered abroad among the nations of the earth. Persecutions unparalleled in the history of the world have plagued the steps of the Hebrew people.

We cannot become guilty of the excesses that have caused the collapse of other nations without witnessing in our own race the sure decay that results from them. Deterioration and ultimate subjugation always await the undisciplined; violence, destruction, and bloodshed ultimately return upon the head of their perpetrator. The record of history gives no surer lesson than this. Then let us turn back to the Word of God as our guide. This Book and its laws form the foundation of all civilized governments in our world today. There is no culture superior to it and no spiritual provisions equal to it.

God is the God of the individual; He is also the God of races and nations. Ultimately, when this world is redeemed, thank God there will follow Him men from every nation and kindred and tongue and people. "And they sung a new song, saying, Thou art worthy to take the book, and to open the seals thereof: for thou wast slain, and hast redeemed us to God by thy blood out of every kindred, and tongue, and people, and nation" (Revelation 5:9).

18

273

Where shall I be when that
first trumpet sounds?
When it sounds so loud that
it wakes up the dead?
Where shall I be when it sounds?

"Where Shall I Be?"

LET'S THINK ABOUT the two resurrections. What happens to the soul after death? When a man dies, his breath goeth forth, he returneth to his earth, and that very day his thoughts perish. We find this in Psalm 146:4. According to Ecclesiastes 3:20, the dead go to the grave. They return to the dust. In Job 7:10 we discover that when a man dies he does not come back to haunt the living. You know, there's a great fear among a lot of people about staying overnight in the same room with a casket. They are afraid that somehow the dead might rise and harm them. But the tenth verse of Job seven says that he shall return no more to his house, "neither shall his place know him any more." So we need not worry about dead people. We have more problems with the living than we do with the dead.

But are there any such things as haunted houses? Are there any such things as rattling dishes when there is no one there?

Can astrologers, crystal gazers, or spirit mediums tell the future? Can they communicate with the dead or bring them back?

Mysterious manifestations, moving pianos, furniture being slung around rooms by invisible hands? Is there any substance at all to all the stories we hear about such things?

The Bible says that there are influences in this world that do these mysterious things in the name of the dead, but the Bible also makes very clear that it is not the dead that do these things. The dead "know not any thing," according to Ecclesiastes 9:5, 6. Then who are these impersonators who would have us believe that the dead are not really dead?

For a clue to this question we go to Genesis 3:4. The first lie ever told on earth was told by the devil, and it was about dead people. The devil had asked Eve what God had said to her about eating the forbidden fruit. Eve told him that God said the day she ate of it she would surely die. To this the devil replied, "Ye shall not surely die." This first lie laid the foundation for spiritism, for the impersonation of the dead by evil spirits and demons. The world is full of them. Revelation 12:7-9 makes this clear! "And there was war in heaven: Michael and his angels fought against the dragon; and the dragon fought and his angels, and prevailed not; neither was their place found any more in heaven." The devil was cast out. His angels were cast out with him.

Yes, there are invisible creatures in this world. We have company here, and they are not interested in having us believe in Jesus Christ. They don't want anyone to believe in the Bible or to be saved. So, they try to give the lie to the Bible and everything God has said. "Ye shall not surely die," the devil said. Strangely enough most people, even some Christians, have chosen to believe this satanic lie. They believe that when a man dies he is not really dead, but that some part of him goes away

276

to glory, or to purgatory or hell. The Bible clearly reveals, however, that this is not a Christian teaching. Actually, it was of pagan origin, and was introduced into the church during the second, third, and fourth centuries by so-called Christian philosophers who sought to fuse paganism with Christianity. Plato and Aristotle adopted this old Egyptian theory, and these Christians got it from them. Today the pagan notion that a man is not really dead when he dies is accepted by many as if it were Bible doctrine. But the Bible is clear on this subject. A man who isn't really dead will not need a resurrection. If the dead are in heaven, why bring them out of the ground? These are interesting questions no one has yet answered.

2 Corinthians 11:14, 15 makes it clear that these evil spirits impersonate human beings. Some people have actually seen beings that look like their relatives and speak like them and manifest the same mannerisms. These are evil spirits impersonating the dead. They do more than that. They tell fortunes, they engage in sorcery, they manifest themselves through ouija boards and in a thousand other ways. Their purpose is to inspire doubt in the Word of God, and to lead men to traffic with demons, to venerate dead people, to pray to the dead, to doubt that God is God and that man is sinful.

These devils contradict the Bible teaching that the wages of sin is death. They say the wages of sin is a higher plane of life. Isn't that what the devil said to Eve? "Ye shall be as gods, knowing good and evil" (Genesis 3:5). Devils give false comfort. They feed the fatal hope of a second chance, saying that if you don't make it in this life, it's all right anyway because God will give you another chance.

Where are the dead, then? The answer is: They are dead,

and all impersonations to the contrary are perpetrated by that father of lies, the creator of all fraud—the devil himself, whose purpose is to make man doubt the Word of God.

But the dead will not be forever dead. Thank God, there will be two resurrections of the dead. Of the first resurrection we read in John 5:28, 29: "Marvel not at this: for the hour is coming, in the which all that are in the graves shall hear his voice, and shall come forth; they that have done good unto the resurrection of life; and they that have done evil, unto the resurrection of damnation."

So, then, there will be two resurrections, and furthermore, *all* who are in their graves will hear His voice and come forth. The Bible makes it clear that the righteous will come forth first: "For the Lord himself shall descend from heaven with a shout, with the voice of the archangel, and with the trump of God: and the dead in Christ shall rise first: then we which are alive and remain shall be caught up together with them in the clouds, to meet the Lord in the air: and so shall we ever be with the Lord. Wherefore comfort one another with these words" (1 Thessalonians 4:16-18).

True comfort must come from the truth, and the truth is that when a man dies he is dead—stone-cold dead. But the day will come when the dead—all that are in their graves—will hear the Life-giver's voice and will come forth. The dead in Christ, all Christians—that is, those who have accepted the sacrifice of Christ at Calvary for their sins, repented of their sins, and surrendered their lives to Him—will rise first. Some Christians will be alive on this earth when Jesus comes again and interrupts the cycle of history. We who live and remain shall be caught up together with the resurrected dead to meet the Lord in the air, and "so shall we ever be with the Lord." We shall never be separated from Him again.

Thank God "affliction shall not rise up the second time." Man will never again transgress the law of God. So, throughout endless ages, we will have the blessed fellowship of the presence of the Son of God in person with us. We will walk in the shadow of His presence and bask in the sunlight of His love.

Then there will be a second resurrection, and I don't think anyone will want to be in on this one. But the Bible clearly teaches it, and we might as well examine it. After those who have done good come forth from the grave, there is to be another resurrection: "The rest of the dead lived not again until the thousand years were finished. This is the first resurrection" (Revelation 20:5). So the unrighteous, you see—those who denied Christ and turned their backs on Him—will just sleep on while the righteous are resurrected and transported to heaven. The wicked dead will sleep on. The rest of the dead will not come forth until a thousand years later. So a thousand years will separate the resurrection of the righteous from the resurrection of the wicked. But it will be the same voice of God that brings them forth.

What a sad day that will be when the resurrected wicked look into the great, beautiful City of God and see the resurrected righteous gloriously immortalized. It will be a sad day for them to realize that they could have been there too, but they are a thousand years too late. They will be called from their graves to see what they missed, and it is then that hellfire will consume the wicked.

"Behold, I shew you a mystery; We shall not all sleep, but we shall all be changed" (1 Corinthians 15:51). This ties in very well with the words of 1 Thessalonians 4:17: "we which are alive and remain." You see, Christ is not going to allow the atom bomb to decimate the human family. He's not going to allow war to destroy everybody. Someone will be alive and remain when Jesus comes back to the earth. He promised to do that: "Let not your heart be troubled: ye believe in God, believe also in me. In my Father's house are many mansions: if it were not so, I would have told you. I go to prepare a place for you. And if I go and prepare a place for you, I will come again, and receive you unto myself; that where I am, there ye may be also" (John 14:1-3).

It is at Christ's second coming that He will resurrect the righteous, and some will be living on this earth when He comes. We shall not all sleep, but we shall all be changed. Thank God for that. Nobody is going to heaven without being changed, about which we read in verses 51 and 52 of 1 Corinthians 15: "We shall all be changed, in a moment, in the twinkling of an eye, at the last trump." It's not going to take Jesus long to do it. These old death-prone bodies will be gloriously changed. These bodies that were laid in the grave, victims of sickness, will be gloriously immortalized.

"For this corruptible must put on incorruption, and this mortal must put on immortality" (verse 53). Thank God, I'm not going to be somebody else; I'm going to be me. I'm going to be "this mortal," except that I'm going to put on immortality. I am not immortal now. I will become immortal then. I am subject to death now, but then I will not be subject to death. Sorrow and sighing will flee away. This corruptible shall put on incorruption and this mortal must put on immortality, so when this corruptible shall have put on incorruption and this mortal

280

shall have put on immortality, "then shall be brought to pass the saying that is written, Death is swallowed up in victory" (verse 54). Death is not swallowed up in victory until then. Man is not immortal now. No men are immortal now. Man is subject to death now, and when he dies he is entirely dead.

But in that day when, gloriously, the great Son of God who now transforms our hearts, then transforms our bodies, death will be swallowed up in victory, and the cry will go forth, "O death, where is thy sting? O grave, where is thy victory?" (verse 55). And I give you the answer: Death's victory will be swallowed up, for the power that destroys sin will destroy death. Then those who have served the Lord in spirit and in truth will at last defy the law of gravity and, not in man-made rockets, but on newly fitted wings be transported beyond the sun, moon, and stars. Past the first, or atmospheric heaven, and the second, or stormy heaven, they will fly to the very heaven—that city that hath foundation whose builder and maker is God.

It is said of Attila, the Hun, that he gave orders before his death that he should be sealed in three caskets and then placed in the bottom of the river. Upon his death this was done. It is believed that Attila did not want to be resurrected and sought to ensure himself against it by this means. But He who broke the seal of His own tomb will find it easy to handle three caskets and put together the man that was Attila that he might stand before the judgment bar of God. Job made it clear when he said, "Though after my skin worms destroy this body, yet in my flesh shall I see God" (Job 19:26).

God gave Noah the rainbow sign;
It won't be water, but fire next time.

"Fire Next Time"

"FOR THE TIME is come that judgment must begin at the house of God: and if it first begin at us, what shall the end be of them that obey not the gospel of God?" (1 Peter 4:17).

The subject of hell-fire answers that question. Hell will be the end of those who obey not the gospel of Jesus Christ. In the Bible several different Hebrew and Greek words are all translated into English by the word *hell*. Because those different words had different meanings, it is sometimes confusing. Thus, *hades* in the original actually means "grave," *tartaros* means "the abyss of space," and *gehenna* means "a place of burning." Yet all three are translated "hell."

Where is hell? What is it? Will it be universal, or is it a hole in the ground where the devil stokes the fire, turning sinners over every thousand years, and seeing that everyone is well roasted? Or is hell what one man described as a state of mind?

282

Some politicians give their opposition what they call hell. But what really is hell?

"The Lord is not slack concerning his promise, as some men count slackness; but is longsuffering to us-ward, not willing that any should perish, but that all should come to repentance" (2 Peter 3:9).

Thank God, it is not His will that any man should perish. Hell was not originally conceived for human beings anyway. God doesn't want us to perish, and He proved it by giving His Son to live for thirty-three years on earth, fellowshiping with men who rejected and despised Him. God's Son suffered, bled, and died on Calvary for our sins. The love of God is not in question here. We know God loves us. Furthermore, He is not slack concerning His promises to us, and He has promised never to leave us or forsake us. Some of us forsake Him. He has promised to help us in the hour of temptation, but most people don't ask Him. The Bible says, "Ask, and it shall be given you; seek, and ye shall find; knock, and it shall be opened unto you" (Luke 11:9). These are the promises of God, and the Lord is not slack concerning His promises. We're the slackers. God doesn't neglect us; we neglect Him. God is long-suffering toward us, not willing that any should perish but that all—every man, every reader of these words—should come to repentance. This is God's will for man—for you.

But because all men will not repent, the next verse (2 Peter 3:10) says, "But the day of the Lord will come. . . ." You see, now is man's day; at least man thinks it is his day. He has taken over God's place. He believes his own brain is capable of getting him out of any emergency. In spite of the lessons of history man goes on believing in himself and worshiping himself, and when he doesn't worship himself he worships things he makes with his own hands. This is man's day, according to man.

Thank God for the promise, "But the day of the Lord will come . . ." It will come "as a thief in the night, in the which the heavens shall pass away with a great noise, and the elements shall melt with fervent heat, the earth also and the works that are therein shall be burned up. Seeing then that all these things shall be dissolved, what manner of persons ought ye to be in all holy conversation and godliness, looking for and hasting unto the coming of the day of God, wherein the heavens being on fire shall be dissolved, and the elements shall melt with fervent heat?" (2 Peter 3:10-12).

So, hell is not burning now. It is yet future. When it does burn, it will be the whole earth that burns, from one end to the other, from Moscow to Washington, from Hammerfest to Santo Domingo, wherever men walk the earth. Wherever there is earth there will be fire. It is not a local condition. Even the heavens will be on fire, the atmospheric heavens that is. I am told that the gasses comprising the air we breathe are all combustible—nitrogen, hydrogen, oxygen—all of this. Yes, the atmospheric heavens will be on fire.

An old slave who understood this sang this song:

> What are you going to do when the world's on fire?
> Don't you want God's bosom to be your pillow?

Another spiritual he sang, said:

> You run to the rocks to hide your face;
> The rocks cry out, "No hiding place!"
> You run to the caves, saying, "What will we do?"
> The caves shout back, "We're burning too;
> There's no hiding place down here."

When hell burns, there will be no hiding place. There will be no escape. Thank God, now there is a hiding place; there is a way of escape. It is in the great heart of God—His love extended to man in the person of His Son.

But what will be the end of those who obey not the gospel? "For, behold, the day cometh, that shall burn as an oven; and all the proud, yea, and all that do wickedly, shall be stubble: and the day that cometh shall burn them up, saith the Lord of hosts; that it shall leave them neither root nor branch" (Malachi 4:1).

Hell is not only going to burn wherever men walk the earth, but it's going to burn them up, and it is going to leave them neither root nor branch. This is somewhat different from what we sometimes hear about hell. We hear that saints go to heaven at death and live forever. We have learned that this isn't true, but that they go to the grave, and then in the resurrection morning they will go to heaven and live forever. We hear that sinners go to hell and burn forever. But we've just seen that that isn't true either. Hell isn't even burning now, and when it does burn sinners won't go to it, it will come to them. Furthermore, the Bible says that it will burn them *up*. Hell is going to burn *up*. It won't burn on and on.

You read in Jude 7 about eternal fire burning Sodom and Gomorrha. But that fire is not still burning. It went out long ago. It was eternal in the sense that its effects were, and are, eternal. Those cities were never rebuilt. When you read about the world being burned with unquenchable fire, remember that Jerusalem was burned with that kind of fire. It was unquenchable because nobody could quench it. It couldn't be put out. The city burned until everything that could burn was burned up. When you read about the smoke of their torment ascending forever and ever (Revelation 14:9-11), John does not mean that the smoke keeps rising up forever, but that it goes up once and for all and never comes back down. The wicked will *stay* burned up. As Jonah 2:6 indicates, the word *forever* does not always mean on and on endlessly. Jonah says that he was in the belly of the whale "forever," but Jonah is not still there. The whale coughed him out in three days.

So this burning will be forever in that it will be lasting in its effect. It will be unquenchable. Nothing will put it out. It will burn until it burns out. It will burn until it burns up everything man has built on the earth, and it will burn until it burns up every rebellious man who has walked the earth. It will burn until every rebellious angel has been consumed out of the universe. This will be the end of those who obey not the gospel. Hell-fire is for real.

When will hell burn? "Let both grow together until the harvest: and in the time of harvest I will say to the reapers, Gather ye together first the tares, and bind them in bundles to burn them: but gather the wheat into my barn" (Matthew 13: 30).

"The enemy that sowed them is the devil; the harvest is the end of the world; and the reapers are the angels. As therefore the tares are gathered and burned in the fire; so shall it be in the end of this world" (verses 39, 40).

So hell is going to burn at the end of this world. It isn't burning now. Furthermore, the Bible makes it clear that the tares are the wicked ones—wicked men and wicked angels. They will be gathered and burned in the fire. Even the devil is going to be destroyed then: "And the devil that deceived them was cast into the lake of fire and brimstone, where the beast and the false prophet are, and shall be tormented day and night for ever and ever" (Revelation 20:10).

But why must it burn? In the first place, God's authority is at stake. It has been at stake ever since Satan challenged His authority in heaven. "In the days of these kings shall the God of heaven set up a kingdom, which shall never be destroyed: and the kingdom shall not be left to other people, but it shall break in pieces and consume all these kingdoms, and it shall stand for ever" (Daniel 2:44).

God left this old earth to other people, and men have ruled it for centuries. Rather, they have misruled it, and have come to the point where they challenge God's very existence as well as His authority. His authority is still at stake in this old world. Thank God it will all be settled when He burns this earth with fire.

In the second place, hell has to burn because, if it didn't, man would export his rebellion to other planets. He's already building rockets that will take him to the planets and, maybe someday, beyond. Where would man go if God didn't put a stop to it all?

In the third place, sin's cruelty to man makes hell-fire necessary. God can't stand to watch man deface his body, destroy his soul, and so one day He is going to put an end to it all—physical disease, war, famine, mental debasement and derangement, the spiritual death. God is going to stop it all. Sin separates man from God, and God can't hear the sinner pray unless that sinner is repentant of his sins. So sin will be destroyed. The destruction of the devil will be accomplished. Lucifer cannot be allowed to live on and on. He has to be destroyed, and hell will do this.

287

According to 2 Peter 3:13 paradise will be restored, but paradise can't be restored as long as there is a sinner in the universe. Hell-fire will rid the earth of sin and sinners, and make possible the restoration of the earth to its former beauty.

In the fourth place, sin's destruction must be permanent and everlasting, and it will be. God purified the earth with water during the time of Noah, and that failed. Sin bounced back alive and strong. He tried to purify the earth with blood by the shedding of His own blood, but men have ignored that magnanimous sacrifice. It won't be blood, and it won't be water the next time. It will be fire. The old slave knew it, and he sang:

> God gave Noah the rainbow sign;
> It won't be water, but fire next time.

Thank God, Christ's blood is still offered. It is still efficacious. It is still sufficient. Men may still turn to God with all their heart. Men may still repent of their sins and find full and complete absolution, complete remission, complete pardon, complete cleansing, complete power.

When will hell burn? "And I saw an angel come down from heaven, having the key of the bottomless pit and a great chain in his hand. And he laid hold on the dragon, that old serpent, which is the Devil, and Satan, and bound him a thousand years. . . . And after that he must be loosed a little season. . . . And when the thousand years are expired, Satan shall be loosed out of his prison, and shall go out to deceive the nations which are in the four quarters of the earth, Gog and Magog, to gather them together to battle: the number of whom is as the sand of the sea.

"And they went up on the breadth of the earth, and compassed the camp of the saints about, and the beloved city: and fire came down from God out of heaven, and devoured them. And the devil that deceived them was cast into the lake of fire and brimstone. . . .

"And I saw a great white throne, and him that sat on it, from whose face the earth and the heaven fled away; and there was found no place for them. And I saw the dead, small and great, stand before God; and the books were opened: and another book was opened, which is the book of life: and the dead were judged out of those things which were written in the books, according to their works. . . . And death and hell were cast into the lake of fire. This is the second death. And whosoever was not found written in the book of life was cast into the lake of fire" (Revelation 20:1-15).

This passage of Scripture clearly pinpoints the worst event that will ever happen to our world—the burning of the earth by fire. This will take place at the end of the millennium, or thousand years. You see, the next great event that we expect on this earth is the coming of Christ.

When Jesus went away He said, "Let not your heart be troubled: ye believe in God, believe also in me. In my Father's house are many mansions: if it were not so, I would have told you. I go to prepare a place for you. And if I go and prepare a place for you, I will come again, and receive you unto myself; that where I am, there ye may be also" (John 14:1-3).

Christ will come back to this earth a second time, and when He comes He will take the righteous out of this world (1 Thessalonians 4:16, 17). But those who are wicked and still alive at the coming of the Lord will be struck dead by the brightness of His coming (2 Thessalonians 1:7, 8). This combination of circumstances will bind Satan for a thousand years, for the right-

19

eous will be out of his reach because they are in heaven. The wicked will be out of his reach too, for they will be dead. So this old earth will become a prison for Satan for a thousand years.

At the end of the thousand years will be the resurrection of the wicked. "The rest of the dead lived not again until the thousand years were finished" (Revelation 20:5). Satan will assemble the resurrected wicked and deceive them into thinking they can do battle with the saints of God in the City of God. The Bible says they surround the camp of the saints, the beloved city. Then it is that fire will come down from God out of heaven and devour them. This is hell-fire. The whole earth will be converted into a lake that burns with fire and brimstone. This is the second death.

> God gave Noah the rainbow sign;
> It won't be water, but fire next time.

PAINTING BY WILLIAM HEASLIP   © BY REVIEW AND HERALD

Walk together, children,
Don't you get weary.
There's a great camp meeting
In the promised land.

"The Promised Land"

THE BIBLE FILLS the long gap in human experience from promise to fulfillment. In many a lonely hour after Adam and Eve sinned their hearts must have ached for reassurance of a Redeemer and Saviour. The Word of the living God carries us down the broad sweep of time to the restoration of all things. The plan of salvation includes not only man, but the complete restoration of the planet on which he lives. Sin has defiled everything, including the atmosphere. The earth on which we work and walk has been cursed by the blight of man's misconduct. "The earth also is defiled under the inhabitants thereof; because they have transgressed the laws, changed the ordinance, broken the everlasting covenant" (Isaiah 24:5). But we can look forward to a complete restoration of all things to their Edenic beauty. The gospel not only restores man but promises the complete restoration of the Edenic paradise that Adam and Eve once enjoyed.

291

I have visited many of the scenic spots of the earth and marveled at the natural beauty that remains. God in His mercy has not allowed sin to completely deface the earth, but has left many evidences of what the earth must have been like before the reign of sin. It is a testimony to His love and infinite thoughtfulness that He will restore man's home and re-establish him in it.

In a previous study we established that Christ will take His children out of this earth, and that the fires of hell will purify this planet of all man-made things. This chapter answers the question: What will happen after hell burns? "For, behold, I create new heavens and a new earth: and the former shall not be remembered, nor come into mind. But be ye glad and rejoice for ever in that which I create: for, behold, I create Jerusalem a rejoicing, and her people a joy. And I will rejoice in Jerusalem, and joy in my people: and the voice of weeping shall be no more heard in her, nor the voice of crying" (chapter 65:17-19). "For as the new heavens and the new earth, which I will make, shall remain before me, saith the Lord, so shall your seed and your name remain" (chapter 66:22).

Once again this planet will shine like a pearl as it comes from the hand of a loving Creator. And the new Jerusalem, the City of God, will be implanted on this earth and will become the great capital of the universe. "And I saw a new heaven and a new earth: for the first heaven and the first earth were passed away; and there was no more sea. And I John saw the holy city, new Jerusalem, coming down from God out of heaven, prepared as a bride adorned for her husband" (Revelation 21:1, 2).

And where will this great city be located? Let us consider the events that will occur at the end of the millennium just before Christ destroys the wicked.

"Behold, the day of the Lord cometh, and thy spoil shall be divided in the midst of thee. For I will gather all nations against Jerusalem to battle; and the city shall be taken, and the houses rifled, and the women ravished; and half of the city shall go forth into captivity, and the residue of the people shall not be cut off from the city. Then shall the Lord go forth, and fight against those nations, as when he fought in the day of battle. And his feet shall stand in that day upon the mount of Olives, which is before Jerusalem on the east, and the mount of Olives shall cleave in the midst thereof toward the east and toward the west, and there shall be a very great valley; and half of the mountain shall remove toward the north, and half of it toward the south. . . . And the Lord shall be king over all the earth: in that day shall there be one Lord, and his name one" (Zechariah 14:1-9).

"Blessed are the meek: for they shall inherit the earth," said Jesus (Matthew 5:5). After a stay in heaven of a thousand years—a millennium—the righteous will return to the earth and inhabit it.

"And they shall build houses, and inhabit them. . . . They shall not plant and another eat: for as the days of a tree are the days of my people, and mine elect shall long enjoy the work of their hands. They shall not labour in vain, nor bring forth for trouble; for they are the seed of the blessed of the Lord, and their offspring with them. And it shall come to pass, that before they call, I will answer; and while they are speaking, I will hear. The wolf and the lamb shall feed together, and the lion shall eat straw like the bullock: and dust shall be the serpent's meat. They shall not hurt nor destroy in all my holy mountain, saith the Lord" (Isa. 65:21-25).

"Strengthen ye the weak hands, and confirm the feeble knees.

293

Say to them that are of a fearful heart, Be strong, fear not: behold, your God will come with vengeance, even God with a recompence; he will come and save you. Then the eyes of the blind shall be opened, and the ears of the deaf shall be unstopped. Then shall the lame man leap as an hart, and the tongue of the dumb sing: for in the wilderness shall waters break out, and streams in the desert. And the parched ground shall become a pool, and the thirsty land springs of water: in the habitation of dragons, where each lay, shall be grass with reeds and rushes. . . . And the ransomed of the Lord shall return, and come to Zion with songs and everlasting joy upon their heads: they shall obtain joy and gladness, and sorrow and sighing shall flee away" (Isaiah 35:3-10).

Henry Ward Beecher said of that glorious state: "I could hardly wish to enter heaven did I believe its inhabitants were idly to sit by pearling streams, fanned by balmy airs. Heaven, to be a place of happiness, must be a place of activity. Heaven is a place of restless activity, the abode of never-tiring thought. David and Isaiah will sweep nobler and loftier strains in eternity, and the minds of the saints, unclogged by cumbersome clay, will forever feast on the banquet of the rich and glorious thought. My young friends, go on then, you will never get through. An eternity of untiring action is before you, and the universe of thought is your field."

This paradise of which I write is not—and should never seem to us—a remote and unattainable dream. It is real, and because the vision is certain and the words of the prophets will surely come to pass, we should embrace these promises by faith. Like pilgrims of old, we should be guided by them as a seaman navigates by the stars.

In the twilight of a summer evening a pastor called at the

residence of one of his parishioners, where he found a little boy seated in the doorway, both hands extended upward, holding a string. "What are you doing, my little friend?" inquired the minister.

"Flying my kite, sir," was the reply.

"I can see no kite, and you can see none," said the minister.

"I know it, sir," responded the little boy. "I cannot see it, but I know it is there, for I feel its pull."

So the promise of a glorious future in Christ lures us, and we can feel the pull. According to Beecher, "One should go to sleep at night as homesick passengers do, saying, 'Perhaps in the morning we shall see the shore.' To us who are Christians it is not a solemn but delightful thought that perhaps nothing but the opaque bodily eye prevents us from beholding the gate that is open just before us, and nothing but the dull ear prevents us from hearing those bells of joy which will welcome us to the heavenly land."

PAINTING BY HARRY BAERG

© BY REVIEW AND HERALD

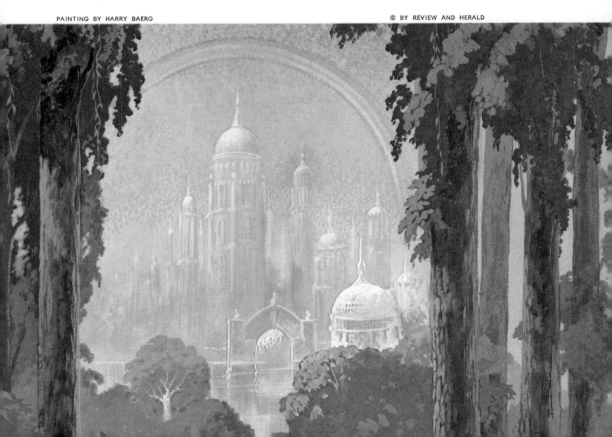

"Standing at the Judgment"

"SO THEN," wrote the apostle Paul in the long ago, "every one of us shall give account of himself to God" (Romans 14:12).

This rebel world hates the doctrine of individual accountability. The guilty do not want to face either the fact of their own guilt or its consequences. To avoid the consequences of their deeds, men and angels have asserted themselves and exalted themselves to the status of gods. They would make their own determinations as to what is right and what is wrong. They would deny that there is anyone anywhere in the universe to whom they are answerable.

This rebellion against divine authority began in heaven, interestingly enough. There, the most beautiful and powerful of all the angels became restive under the benevolent rulership of the Almighty. He contested the authority of God, and for a time seemed to prosper. Sooner or later, of course, the rebel must face

296

his Master and make a final decision. This happened to Lucifer, and the results are recorded in the Holy Scriptures:

"Son of man, say unto the prince of Tyrus, Thus saith the Lord God; Because thine heart is lifted up, and thou hast said, I am a God, I sit in the seat of God, in the midst of the seas; yet thou art a man, and not God, though thou set thine heart as the heart of God." "Thou art the anointed cherub that covereth; and I have set thee so: thou wast upon the holy mountain of God; thou hast walked up and down in the midst of the stones of fire. Thou wast perfect in thy ways from the day that thou wast created, till iniquity was found in thee. . . . Thine heart was lifted up because of thy beauty, thou hast corrupted thy wisdom by reason of thy brightness: I will cast thee to the ground, I will lay thee before kings, that they may behold thee" (Ezekiel 28:2, 14-17).

In this conversation with Lucifer, God reminded him that He was Lucifer's creator, and reasoned with him concerning the folly of this rebellion. But all in vain. God gave this mighty angel ample opportunity to repent, but divine wisdom fell on deaf angelic ears. Then came the inevitable confrontation.

"And there was war in heaven: Michael and his angels fought against the dragon; and the dragon fought and his angels, and prevailed not; neither was their place found any more in heaven. And the great dragon was cast out, that old serpent, called the Devil, and Satan, which deceiveth the whole world: he was cast out into the earth, and his angels were cast out with him" (Revelation 12:7-9).

O the folly of resisting the authority of God! The human family need not have learned this lesson the hard way, for we had the example of Lucifer before us. But did we really learn?

The scene now shifts to the Garden of Eden. Here were the man and woman whom God had created perfect and put in a perfect environment. He gave them every advantage—spiritual, mental, and physical. Then to this happy couple came the evil one with his subtle suggestions of rebellion: "And the serpent said unto the woman, Ye shall not surely die" (Genesis 3:4).

In this he flatly contradicted a divine command. The Lord had told Adam and Eve that in the day they ate of the fruit of the forbidden tree they would surely die. In the very next verse the tempter insinuates that God has been withholding from man and woman something that was for their best good. What an insult to divine love! Adam and Eve became party to the rebellion. They defied God by eating the fruit. Then came the inevitable confrontation: "And they heard the voice of the Lord God walking in the garden in the cool of the day: and Adam and his wife hid themselves from the presence of the Lord God amongst the trees of the garden. And the Lord God called unto Adam, and said unto him, Where art thou?" (verses 8, 9).

Now Adam discovered anew his accountability. He was not God. He could not pit his reasoning powers against those of God. He could not exalt his power over the power of God. Adam and Eve learned to their sorrow that no creature can win the battle against his Creator. "So he drove out the man; and he placed at the east of the garden of Eden Cherubims, and a flaming sword which turned every way, to keep the way of the tree of life" (verse 24).

For every action there is a judgment, and men and angels are subject to the decisions of the great Judge of all the earth. Knowing this should sober our actions and regulate our behavior. We cannot behave like runaway automobiles, colliding with other cars and finally wrapping ourselves around life's destructive posts. We must act responsibly, for we are responsible, we are accountable, and we must answer for what we think and what we do, before the great Judge of all the earth.

For about two thousand years men lived in rebellion while the God of heaven looked on. Because sentence against their evil was not executed speedily, they descended from one level of brute immorality to another, and then God sent a man— Noah by name—who for one hundred and twenty years warned of the coming judgments, defined the nature of human iniquity, pleaded for men to forsake their sins; and for one hundred and twenty years he was ignored. These years of grace were frittered away, although every opportunity was given for repentance and reconciliation. The words of the man of God fell on deaf ears, while human philosophy was exalted, and men were reduced morally to the level of beasts. Violence filled the earth. While men were intellectual giants, they were moral infants.

"And God said unto Noah, The end of all flesh is come before me; for the earth is filled with violence through them; and, behold, I will destroy them with the earth" (chapter 6:13).

At last Noah came face to face with the fact of accountability. The antediluvian world was to find out that man does have to answer, that there is a God who rules over men and nations, and that we just can't live ignoring the fact of our relationship to Him.

"And every living substance was destroyed which was upon the face of the ground, both man, and cattle, and the creeping things, and the fowl of the heaven; and they were destroyed from the earth: and Noah only remained alive, and they that were with him in the ark" (chapter 7:23).

With these examples before us, why do men persist in their rebellion? Because it is easier than to reform, and men—like water—take the path of least resistance.

The Bible also speaks of the twin cities of Sodom and Gomorrah. These cities were shining examples of architectural splendor, but they were rotten to the core. Their inhabitants had long since cast aside the knowledge of God, denied His authority in the earth. They sneered at anyone's suggesting that man was in any way responsible to an invisible God for his actions. So corrupt had the men of these cities become that they were prepared to attack two angels who were guests in the home of Lot. Righteous Abraham went again and again to the cities of Sodom and Gomorrah, pleading with men to turn to Christ, but to no avail. Lot himself, in the closing moments of their probation, pleaded with his own sons and daughters, but to no avail.

"And there came two angels to Sodom at even" (chapter 19:1). Indulging in their customary revelry, the people were unaware that the two agents who would accomplish their destruction had just entered the city gates. The verses that follow are a sad chronicle of the actions of men who are totally bereft of conscience. They were so debased mentally that they could not perceive the celestial character of two visitors from out of this world. A few hours later the angels literally dragged Lot and his immediate family out of the city, and then kindled the fire that totally destroyed Sodom and Gomorrah.

"And Abraham gat up early in the morning to the place where he stood before the Lord: and he looked toward Sodom and Gomorrah, and toward all the land of the plain, and beheld, and, lo, the smoke of the country went up as the smoke of a furnace. And it came to pass, when God destroyed the cities of the plain, that God remembered Abraham, and sent Lot out of the midst of the overthrow, when he overthrew the cities in which Lot dwelt" (verses 27-29).

But what of the city of Jerusalem? This great symbol of the Hebrew nation was especially honored, for the Son of God Himself had walked its streets, extending the hand of mercy to all who sought His help. But it was in Jerusalem that He met the most severe persecution. Jerusalem rejected Him. Nothing He did or said seemed to make an impression on its vested interests. The established religion and the government leaders were all bent on His destruction. Jesus looked on this fair city one day and wept as He said, "O Jerusalem, Jerusalem, thou that killest the prophets, and stonest them which are sent unto thee, how often would I have gathered thy children together, even as a hen gathereth her chickens under her wings, and ye would not!" (Matthew 23:37).

All of the original disciples ministered in the city of Jerusalem, but the more powerfully they preached, the harder grew the hearts of the opponents of their message. Eventually the Jewish nation came face to face with the fact of its accountability. In the year A.D. 70 the great Roman general Titus sacked the city and burned it. For seven years an unnamed man is said to have walked up and down the city, crying, "A voice from the east, a voice from the west: woe is Jerusalem, woe, woe, woe." This he did day after day, only to perish in the flames that consumed the city.

With these examples before us, twentieth-century man stands before God today a confirmed rebel. He has exalted his knowledge above the knowledge of God. Indeed, he denies that there is a God and worships science and technology. He considers himself a product of evolution, the son of a one-celled amoeba, and declares that his redemption will be the result of his own brain and his own hands. Here man is, planning his own escape from this doomed planet through the science of rocketry. Instead of turning this world into an oasis of joy, man has converted it into a hell of unbridled passion, and inevitably he inches toward that great confrontation with his Creator. Man is waltzing toward his inevitable end, and the madness of his music has quickened the tempo of his pace. The human race has nearly severed all connection with its Creator, and is busy blotting out the knowledge of Him from the earth. Little wonder that the Bible speaks of the end of the world. This corrupt civilization of ours cannot go on and on. Inevitably we will have to face our Maker, and the Bible vividly describes that confrontation.

"As the days of Noe were, so shall also the coming of the Son of man be" (chapter 24:37). Those ancient days are a reflection of what will happen at the end of the world. In Luke 17:29, 30 Jesus sets forth the destruction of Jerusalem as an object lesson of what the end of the world will be like: "But the same day that Lot went out of Sodom it rained fire and brimstone from heaven, and destroyed them all. Even thus shall it be in the day when the Son of man is revealed." Once again man will come face to face with God, to give an account of the deeds done in the body, "for God shall bring every work into judgment, with every secret thing, whether it be good, or whether it be evil" (Ecclesiastes 12:14).

"And I saw a great white throne, and him that sat on it, from whose face the earth and the heaven fled away: and there was found no place for them. And I saw the dead, small and great, stand before God; and the books were opened: and another book was opened, which is the book of life: and the dead were judged out of those things which were written in the books, according to their works. And the sea gave up the dead which were in it; and death and hell delivered up the dead which were in them: and they were judged every man according to their works" (Revelation 20:11-13).

PAINTING BY VERNON NYE   © BY SOUTHERN PUBLISHING ASSOCIATION

Ride on King, ride on, King Jesus,
Ride on, conquering King,
I want to go to heaven in the morning.

"Conquering King"

"I BEHELD till the thrones were cast down, and the Ancient of days did sit, whose garment was white as snow, and the hair of his head like the pure wool: his throne was like the fiery flame, and his wheels as burning fire. A fiery stream issued and came forth from before him: thousand thousands ministered unto him, and ten thousand times ten thousand stood before him: the judgment was set, and the books were opened" (Daniel 7:9, 10).

The prophet Daniel gives us a glimpse into the solemn scenes transpiring in the great sanctuary in heaven. He points to the temple of God, where the greatest issues of man are now being settled. Of course, Daniel sees this in vision. To him it is a prophecy, but by the time of the writing of the book of Hebrews, Christ had already entered upon His priestly ministry in that tabernacle, and Paul was able to write, "Now of the things which we have spoken this is the sum: We have such an high priest, who is set on

304

the right hand of the throne of the Majesty in the heavens; a minister of the sanctuary, and of the true tabernacle, which the Lord pitched, and not man" (Hebrews 8:1).

When Christ ascended to heaven after His thirty-three years of earthly ministry, He went into the presence of the Father to settle forever some of the greatest issues of our time. That heavenly temple, or sanctuary, should therefore claim our most earnest attention, in view of the fact that the decisions being made there will determine forever the destiny of this planet and every human being who has ever lived on it.

Frequently the heads of nations will call a summit conference. Often these conferences are held at crucial times in world history, and the attention of the world is focused on these meetings and their outcome. But in the great tabernacle in the skies events of even greater importance are being decided, and we who know this await with solemn anticipation their outcome.

First of all, the question of lordship is being decided there.

"I saw in the night visions, and, behold, one like the Son of man came with the clouds of heaven, and came to the Ancient of days, and they brought him near before him. And there was given him dominion, and glory, and a kingdom, that all people, nations, and languages, should serve him: his dominion is an everlasting dominion, which shall not pass away, and his kingdom that which shall not be destroyed" (Daniel 7:13, 14).

Satan's original challenge in heaven was a power grab for the throne itself, and when the controversy was transferred to the earth, the true nature of Lucifer's struggle came to light. He wasn't satisfied with God's being God. He felt that he could be a better sovereign. Thus challenged, the Creator must, of course, answer. That answer will come from the sanctuary: All people, all nations must serve Christ. This judgment is final; from it there will be no appeal. The devil understands this; do we?

The sin problem is also being resolved in the sanctuary in heaven. "For there is one God, and one mediator between God and men, the man Christ Jesus; who gave himself a ransom for all, to be testified in due time" (1 Timothy 2:5, 6). "Let us therefore come boldly unto the throne of grace, that we may obtain mercy, and find grace to help in time of need" (Hebrews 4:16).

It is our privilege to converse with our heavenly Priest, Jesus Christ our Lord, with reference to our sins. It is to Him that we should bring them for resolution. He it is who can absolve us of our guilt. Christ, and Christ alone, can pardon iniquity. It is in heaven that sin is canceled and forgiven, and it is from Heaven that we receive strength to rise above the weaknesses of the flesh.

The question of human destiny is being determined in the skies: "Every one of us shall give account of himself to God" (Romans 14:12). "And, behold, I come quickly; and my reward is with me, to give every man according as his work shall be" (Revelation 22:12).

According to this passage, when Jesus Christ comes back to the earth, destiny will already be settled. His reward will be with Him. Accordingly, our destiny has already been determined before He comes. Will it be life or death? Will you be saved or lost? These are the vital, soul-searching questions that are finding their answer even now in the great temple of God in the skies. Thank God, I can do something about this by living a faith-filled, repentant life on this earth. I can thwart those negative environmental pressures that pull me downward, and by the grace of God I can subdue those inner tendencies that war against the soul.

The question of territory must also be forever settled. Lucifer has claimed this earth as his own. When the sons of God came to meet before God, as recorded by Job, Satan presented himself as the constitutional monarch of this planet. He went there, presumably, to speak for us. He considers himself rightful ruler here. But our allegiance is not to the god of this world, but to Him who made heaven and earth, the seas, and the fountains of waters. This world is *His,* and He will reclaim it.

"But be ye glad and rejoice for ever in that which I create: for, behold, I create Jerusalem a rejoicing, and her people a joy" (Isaiah 65:18). "For, behold, I create new heavens and a new earth: and the former shall not be remembered, nor come into mind" (verse 17).

Christ is establishing His authority with His own blood. The sin problem, His Lordship, human destiny, and the reclamation of the universe—all hang on His blood. The death of Christ at Calvary was more than an act for saving man. It was an act of benefit for God and the universe as well, and the message of the gospel encompasses the total restoration of all things. The gospel applies to the whole man—body, mind, and spirit. And when the Son lay sleeping in the tomb for three days, the gospel envisioned His resurrection and His reunion with the Father and the Holy Spirit. The gospel envisions the complete restoration of the entire universe. Sin is to be eradicated from the whole of God's creation. Thus, Creator and created will stand at last in perfect harmony, as before. All of this is being settled now in the sanctuary of God, where Christ sits at the right hand of the Majesty in the heavens.

Also being decided in the sanctuary above is the judgment of earthly kingdoms. In Daniel 7 the four great empires of the

Bible are presented symbolically as four great beasts. It is not unusual to symbolize nations, for even today we follow this custom. America is symbolized by an eagle, Russia by a bear, and Great Britain by a lion. The rise and fall of the four great empires—Babylon, Medo-Persia, Greece, and Rome—is depicted in Daniel 7. Each of these nations considered itself permanent. But God had other plans: "And the kingdom and dominion, and the greatness of the kingdom under the whole heaven, shall be given to the people of the saints of the most High, whose kingdom is an everlasting kingdom, and all dominions shall serve and obey him" (verse 27).

What a great day this will be for the saints! In all of human history those who have followed God have not had it easy. They have often been persecuted and put to death by earthly governments. Thank God for the promise, "But the judgment shall sit, and they shall take away his dominion, to consume and to destroy it unto the end" (verse 26).

Persecuting nations will come to an end. The children of God will one day be beyond the reach of wicked men, and will stand revealed for what they really are—the salt of the earth. The world has never shown proper appreciation for the children of God. Noah was derided, Jeremiah ignored, Paul stoned, and Peter crucified, like his Master. Perhaps this is what the Lord had in mind when He advised His followers: "Blessed are ye, when men shall hate you, and when they shall separate you from their company, and shall reproach you, and cast out your name as evil, for the Son of man's sake. Rejoice ye in that day, and leap for joy: for, behold, your reward is great in heaven: for in the like manner did their fathers unto the prophets" (Luke 6:22, 23).

But all of this will change. The enemies of God and His children will be subdued. The rebellion will be stamped out. The honest in heart will be exalted, and the wicked put to flight. How cheering is this view of the ultimate exaltation of the saints. Dear reader, it pays to be on the winning side. I know it may not look that way now, but God's side is the winning side. Men have mistreated Him, abused Him, misrepresented Him, stoned His prophets, despised His Word, and blasphemed His Spirit. All of this God has in mercy borne, that the honest in heart might see the light and be saved. The patience of the Almighty is almost at an end because man's cup of iniquity is full to running over. The rebellion against God has reached its peak in our century. We can boast of the unenviable accomplishment of outsinning all previous sinners, and for this our generation will pay in full. For God is going to move this wicked race and set up a nation that will obey.

As we catch the apocalyptic vision of John, of a rider on a white horse—with a crown upon his head, our own hearts catch the spirit and these lips of clay breathe a fervent Amen.

I'm a pilgrim and a stranger,
Traveling through this barren land.
I have a home in yonder city
That was not made by hand.

"I'm a Pilgrim"

THE CHRISTIAN has double citizenship—in heaven and on earth. This is true because he has been born twice. He was born to citizenship on the earth by being the child of his earthly mother, but when he submits to the new birth described in John 3, he becomes a citizen of the world to come. His dual citizenship imposes important choices on him, for often there is a sharp conflict of interest between the two worlds.

The apostle exhorts us not to be conformed to this world, not to allow our lives to be shaped by its customs and traditions and concepts, inasmuch as this is an apostate world, a runaway, a rebellious planet, a planet doomed to destruction. To be shaped by it is to court disaster. The hidden nature of this present world is aptly described in Galatians 5:19-21:

"Now the works of the flesh are manifest, which are these; adultery, fornication, uncleanness, lasciviousness, idolatry,

310

witchcraft, hatred, variance, emulations, wrath, strife, seditions, heresies, envyings, murders, drunkenness, revellings, and such like: of the which I tell you before, as I have also told you in time past, that they which do such things shall not inherit the kingdom of God."

This is the nature of a man born physically into this present world. This is why Jesus said, "Marvel not that I said unto thee, Ye must be born again" (John 3:7).

The man to whom these words were spoken did not understand. Was Christ speaking again of physical birth?

"Jesus answered, Verily, verily, I say unto thee, Except a man be born of water and of the Spirit, he cannot enter into the kingdom of God" (verse 5).

This is spiritual birth. This is the necessary requisite for entrance into the kingdom of grace, and grace is that state of fitness for the kingdom of glory. Those who enter into the new birth testify that they are but pilgrims here.

"These all died in faith, not having received the promises, but having seen them afar off, and were persuaded of them, and embraced them, and confessed that they were strangers and pilgrims on the earth. For they that say such things declare plainly that they seek a country" (Hebrews 11:13, 14).

Those who, in these latter days, declare themselves pilgrims in this world and seekers of a better one are in good company, for Hebrews 11 gives a list of men and women of similar persuasion. Verse four speaks of righteous Abel, to whom the word of God was sufficient. He did what God told him to do and made a righteous offering before the Lord; whereas Cain his brother followed his own stubborn will and set his intellect up as in the place of God as the final arbiter of right and wrong. God accepted Abel's sacrifice, and a flash of fire from His throne room devoured it, as a token of His favor. Abel was obedient, for he sought a better world. He was but a pilgrim here.

Verse 5 speaks of righteous Enoch, who refused to become entangled with this present world, but who, through a life of prayerfulness so grew in the likeness of Christ that he was translated to heaven without bodily seeing death. But he pleased God while here on earth. He was human, but he was different. He learned the true value of prayer, and literally breathed the atmosphere of heaven, for prayer is the breath of the soul.

Verse 7 of Hebrews 11 talks about Noah, who was warned by God about things that were yet to come, and who believed God and acted on his faith. Noah built an ark according to divine instructions, and preached the message God gave him for more than a hundred years. He refused to become entangled with the allurements of the antediluvian world. Setting his face resolutely to be a servant of God while on the earth, he condemned this world and became an heir of righteousness by faith. He endured ridicule, scorn, and ostracism for his faith but nevertheless remained steadfast, and in the day of God's wrath he was sheltered from the storm. Noah was a pilgrim here, headed for a better world.

Verse 8 speaks of Abraham, to whom the word of God was especially dear. The word of God came to Abraham while he was in Ur of the Chaldees, telling him to leave home and go to a place to which he would afterward be directed. Most people don't like to move, even when they know where they are going. This man didn't know where he was going yet took God at His word. The Bible says he sojourned in tabernacles among a strange people in the land of promise. "For he looked for a city which hath foundations, whose builder and maker is God" (verse 10). What a miracle the heavenly vision performs on the human heart. It enables a man to rise above the problems of this present world, for he knows there is a better one to come. It does not make him insensitive to the issues of this life, but in his vision of the future he finds courage to tackle the problems of the present. Such a man was Abraham.

In Hebrews 11:21 Jacob is mentioned. What a courageous son of God this man became! We see him by the Brook Jabbok, wrestling with God all night for a blessing, and when the blessing of conversion came he went forth boldly to meet his brother who was leading an army of hundreds of men. God wrought mightily for him, and Jacob became the father of the men who would found the twelve tribes of Israel. Through prevailing prayer and faithfulness to God, Jacob declared to the world that he was a pilgrim, seeking a better country.

Verse twenty-four speaks of Moses and states, "By faith Moses, when he was come to years, refused to be called the son of Pharaoh's daughter." You see, Moses was faced with the age-old problem of choosing between this world and the world to come. He had been trained in the arts of warfare, schooled in the highest cultural schools of Egypt. He was heir to the throne of Egypt, but he had a choice to make. Would it be this world or the world to come? He could have wound up a mummy in a museum somewhere, looked upon and marveled at for his shriveled age, or he could one day walk on streets of gold in the city of God by choosing the better world. Thank God for his choice—"to suffer affliction with the people of God" rather "than to enjoy the pleasures of sin for a season." "Esteeming the reproach of Christ greater riches than the treasures in Egypt," he "had respect unto the recompence of the reward" (verses 25, 26).

Yes, Moses looked forward to the greater reward that would come hereafter, and turned his back on the riches of Egypt. How many of us join Moses in making this choice? The truly born again would. Only those whose hand is in God's hand, and who live by faith in Christ, can make decisions like this. See this man of God as he returns to Egypt and leads Israel through the Red Sea, up to the very borders of Canaan.

Hebrews 11 also mentions Rahab, a woman of ill repute, who when she came in contact with representatives of Jehovah rose above the slavery of human nature and became a child of God by faith. The chapter talks also about Gideon, Barak, Samson, Jephtha, David, and Samuel. The faith of each of these people gave him superhuman fortitude in hardship. Faith in Jesus Christ and in the world to come imparts bravery. The religion of Jesus Christ does not transform a man into a vegetable, disinterested in the problems of this present world. The faith of Jesus Christ imparts the sterling qualities of Christian character that makes a man a better person here and now, for the Bible says that through faith they "subdued kingdoms, wrought righteousness, obtained promises, stopped the mouths of lions, quenched the violence of fire, escaped the edge of the sword, out of weakness were made strong, waxed valiant in fight, turned to flight the armies of the aliens. Women received their dead raised to life again: and others were tortured, not accepting deliverance; that they might obtain a better resurrection: and others had trial of cruel mockings and scourgings, yea, moreover of bonds and imprisonment: they were stoned, they were sawn asunder, were tempted, were slain with the sword: they wandered about in sheepskins and goatskins; being destitute, afflicted, tormented; . . . they wandered in deserts, and in mountains, and in dens and caves of the earth. And these all, having obtained a good report through faith, received not the promise" (Hebrews 11:33-39).

You see, they looked for a better day ahead; they fought, lived, and suffered for it. They made their contribution to this world by living for the world to come. Religion is not the opium of the people. Christianity makes giants of pygmies and converts weaklings into men of strength.

In my work of delivering the gospel, how often I have seen men perverted in mind, their bodies weakened by destructive habits, suddenly respond to the gospel of the Lord Jesus Christ. I have seen great changes take place in their hearts. They may have been enslaved by the tight grip of vice, but the chains have been broken by the power of divine love. Christ claims another captive, and what happens to the man? He suddenly becomes alive and aware and awake to his own possibilities in Christ, while on this earth he becomes a joy to the heart of God and a marvel to his fellow men. At first his new life is incredible, unbelievable; but he persists, and as word of the genuineness of his experience spreads, others are led to hope because of the change in his life.

"And be not conformed to this world" (Romans 12:2). "Set your affection on things above, not on things on the earth" (Colossians 3:2).

The time has come when a discernible difference should be evident in the lives of Christians. Men should know from your manner of dress, speech, and action that you have been with Christ and learned of Him. When Peter, in a state of backslidden apostasy rashly denied his Lord with cursing and swearing, it was uncharacteristic of him, for he had been too long with his Lord, and those who heard him exclaimed, "Thy speech betrayeth thee!" The pilgrim cannot play a dual role. He has a choice to make. Like Moses he must choose and refuse; he must, in the language of the little chorus, "Turn your eyes upon Jesus, Look full in His wonderful face; And the things of earth will grow strangely dim In the light of His glory and grace."

PART IV

The Obedience of Faith

You've got to stand your test in judgment,
You've got to stand there by yourself.
There's nobody here to stand it for you;
You've got to stand there by yourself.

"By Yourself"

A MAN who had committed a crime but escaped conviction because of a legal technicality, was lectured thus by the judge:

"I know that you are guilty, and you know it, and I wish you to remember that one day you will stand before a better and wiser Judge, and there you will be dealt with according to justice."

And so shall we all. The world stands arraigned at the judgment bar of Christ. Who shall be able to stand?

In Daniel 8:14 we read, "And he said unto me, Unto two thousand and three hundred days; then shall the sanctuary be cleansed." This vision of the eighth chapter of Daniel is important to us, for it talks about the great judgment day. The phrase "then shall the sanctuary be cleansed" speaks of the judging of the people. This phrase was borrowed from an earthly service in an earthly temple that occurred once a year. Under the old earthly sanctuary system, the tenth day of the seventh month of

319

Faith rode in the hearts of the astronauts as they took off for the trip to the moon. Faith will lift our lives heavenward, too.

the year was a day of judgment, when people were to afflict their souls because of their sins, or they would be cut off from among God's people. This solemn event, called the cleansing of the sanctuary, was thus a day of judgment.

Let us turn to the book of the prophet Daniel. Daniel was concerned with the captivity of his people. He wanted to know when God would set the Israelites free from Babylonian bondage. Daniel thought the time of exile was almost over, and when God told him that the sanctuary would be cleansed after 2300 days, Daniel thought this implied that their release from Babylon was being postponed. Daniel was disappointed, and under the influence of this great disappointment he "fainted, and was sick certain days" (Daniel 8:27). Later, in chapter 9, the angel returned and continued his explanation of the vision, beginning where he had left off in chapter 8.

The cleansing of the sanctuary referred to in Daniel 8:14 is the same as the sitting of the Ancient of days in judgment over the people mentioned in chapter 7, verses 9 and 10. The ancient cleansing of the sanctuary on the day of atonement is highly significant to us who live in the gospel age, for the ancient sacrifices typified the body of Christ that would one day be offered for the sins of man. According to Hebrews 8:5; 9:9; and 9:23, all of these ancient sacrifices served as an example of heavenly things, and represented the ministry of Christ as our great High Priest in the heavenly sanctuary. As we study the coming of the great future day of judgment, we must be aware that the ancient Jewish ritualistic practices pointed forward to the things that are taking place today.

Numbers 14:34 and Ezekiel 4:6 give us the scale for measuring prophetic time—one day in prophecy represents a year of actual time. Many students of prophecy through the years have accepted this time scale. So when we read in Daniel 8:14 that the sanctuary would be cleansed after 2300 days, we are actually dealing with 2300 literal years. If we knew when the 2300 days began, we could know also when the judgment is to begin in heaven.

Daniel 9:25 gives us this answer. When the angel returned after Daniel's illness he indicated the going forth of the commandment to restore and rebuild Jerusalem as the beginning point of this period of time. The decree for the restoration of the Jewish city went forth in 457 B.C. Counting 2300 years from that date, we come to the date of 1844. Daniel thus predicts the beginning of the judgment, or the cleansing of the heavenly sanctuary, at the end of that 2300-year period. We may say, then, that the judgment has been in session since 1844. There is Biblical proof that it is going on even now. In Revelation 11:18 we read, "And the nations were angry, and thy wrath is come, and the time of the dead, that they should be judged, and that thou shouldest give reward unto thy servants the prophets, and to the saints, and them that fear thy name, small and great; and shouldest destroy them which destroy the earth." According to this scripture, the nations are angry at the same time the judgment is going on in heaven. When we see the nations at each other's throats we may know that we are not only in the end of the age but that we have come to the time when the dead should be judged. We've also come to the time when the retributive fires of Jehovah will destroy those who would destroy the earth, if left to their own devices.

In Revelation 22:12 Christ says, "My reward is with me," clearly indicating that when Christ returns to this earth it will be too late to repent, too late to reform, too late to turn to God —for His reward will be with Him! That reward, then, must be in the process of being made up now.

The Bible tells us that God keeps a record of all that we think, do, and say. Malachi 3:16 indicates that there is a book of remembrance, in which the good things we say about Christ are recorded. Revelation 3:5 makes it clear that there is a book of life there, in which our names are written when we accept Christ. The song writer asks:

> Is my name written there,
> On the page white and fair?
> In the book of Thy kingdom,
> Is my name written there?

We may be sure today that our names are written there if we repent of our sins, turn to Christ with all our hearts, accept Him as our Saviour, and by faith make Him Lord of our lives from that time forward.

According to Psalm 139:16 and Matthew 10:30 there is also a record containing a personal description of each of us. Even the hairs of our heads are numbered. Every move we make, every deed we commit is written there. Finally, there is what we may call a book of death containing the names of men and women who have not lived according to the light they had, but who acted as though God was not on His throne, and as though they could decide for themselves what is right and what is wrong (Revelation 20:12). They have declared that God is dead or on sabbatical leave, that He isn't interested in what we think, do, and say, that He is too busy running the great big universe to be bothered about what we are doing as individuals—all 3.5

billion of us. Those who take this attitude are candidates for the book of death.

The Bible also says in Revelation 21:8 that the fearful, the unbelieving, whoremongers, idolaters, and all liars will have their part in the lake that burns with fire and brimstone, which is the second death. Their names are listed in the book of death. It is sobering to think of one's name being in this book. But if it is there, you still have time to get it transferred to the book of life simply by repenting of your sins, turning to God with all your heart, and believing on the Lord Jesus Christ.

Some will say, "I don't have faith in anything or anybody. Where can I get it?" Well, the Bible says that faith cometh by hearing and hearing by the Word of God. Matthew 7:7 says, "Ask, and it shall be given you; seek, and ye shall find." Through prayer, through the study of the Word of God, we can enter into the believing experience. Love for God will spring up in our hearts, and we will turn to Him as naturally as a flower turns to the sun.

A few years ago as I stood preaching the Word of God a man staggered up to my desk and took my hand. He was under the influence of liquor and narcotics. He said, "Preacher, help me. You're my last step between here and hell. What can you do for me?" I got him on his knees and prayed for him. There was no evidence of a miracle then, but later there was, for that man had been instantly cured of dope addiction and of his love for alcohol. Today he is a sober, refined, disciplined Christian, rejoicing in the goodness of God and the power of His grace.

Yes, the grace of God is real; His power effectual. But just as real is the fact of His judgment, and of our accountability to Him for all we think, do, and say.

Daniel Webster, when secretary of state, once had dinner with twenty men at the Astor House in New York. Someone turned and asked him the question, "Mr. Webster, tell me, what is the most important thought that ever occupied your mind?" Mr. Webster replied, "The most important thought that ever occupied my mind was that of my individual responsibility to God."

It is a most solemn thought that we will have to answer before the supreme Judge of all the earth for the deeds done in the body. Finally, it is comforting to know that, even as we read these pages, we have an advocate with the Father, Jesus Christ the righteous, a high priest who can be touched with the feeling of our infirmities. May we turn to Him with all our hearts, surrendering our lives and our wills to Him. Let us walk with Him day by day until, like Enoch, we are caught away ever to be with the Lord.

Upon the mountain, my God spoke;
Out of His mouth came fire and smoke.
I looked around me; all was fine,
I asked my Lord if all was mine.

"My God Spoke"

"THE MIGHTY GOD, even the Lord, hath spoken, and called the earth from the rising of the sun unto the going down thereof" (Psalm 50:1).

It is said today that God isn't talking to man anymore in a way modern man can understand Him. Some claim He isn't even trying to communicate with man. But God does speak to modern man. The words of my text would seem to make that clear. Furthermore, He is speaking in a language that man can understand. "The mighty God, even the Lord hath spoken, and called to the earth from the rising of the sun to the going down thereof." God is not only talking continually, but universally—as the latter part of the verse makes clear.

In this, the fiftieth psalm, God makes a fourfold declaration to man. He wants man to know four things, and these four things are essential to his security and happiness. The first of these four great facts is this: "Hear, O my people, and I will speak; O Israel, and I will testify against thee: I am God, even thy God" (verse 7).

If man would accept this declaration, it would save him from idolatry—of persons, of places, and of things. As you know, men do worship persons, persons of wealth, of power, or advanced training. These are the gods of the twentieth century. They also worship places, and by this I mean positions of power and authority. They also worship material things—things man makes with his hands. But this is an old form of idolatry. The declaration, "I am God," is understandable, for the great God made this earth. He recognizes that there is a competition down here for supremacy, that men have made other gods, and that these gods are coming between the Creator and His creatures. The declaration, "I am God," assumes deeper significance with the passage of time, for increasingly men are turning from the true and living God to worship idols.

Now the second great declaration God makes in the fiftieth psalm is found in verses ten through twelve: "For every beast of the forest is mine, and the cattle upon a thousand hills. I know all the fowls of the mountains: and the wild beasts of the field are mine. If I were hungry, I would not tell thee: for the world is mine, and the fulness thereof."

What God says here is, "I own everything." He further makes it clear that He is sufficient, that every beast of the forest is His, the cattle upon a thousand hills—all of this belongs to God. Sometimes we think that the few things we have in our possession belong to us, and we treat God's goods as if they were our own. We mishandle them, we appropriate them for our own selfish purposes. It is important that man understand that he is but a steward here and that whatever is under his jurisdiction

326

is lent him by God. It is actually God's goods. This should make a man liberal with his less-fortunate fellow man. This should make us sensitive to the needs of the poor. This should make us share what we have with those who have not, knowing God is our Father and He does indeed own all things.

God's third declaration is in Psalm 50:15. It says, "Call upon me in the day of trouble: I will deliver thee, and thou shalt glorify me." What a blessed promise! In moments of trial and stress there is One to whom we may turn. "God is our refuge and strength, a very present help in trouble" (Psalm 46:1). It is good to know when death strikes a member of our family, it's good to know when the bills are high and the money is low, it's good to know when we're being mistreated and persecuted by enemies, it's good to know when warfare strikes and the enemy is at the gate—that we can call upon the Lord in the day of trouble, and He will deliver us. It's good to know when disease strikes and we're laid low on a hospital bed, that the great God said through His Son, "I will never leave thee, nor forsake thee." He makes this blanket promise, "Call upon me in the day of trouble: I will deliver thee, and thou shalt glorify me."

The problem is with us. There are times when, in trouble, we do call upon God and He does deliver us. Then we go back to living the old hypocritical, sinful lives we were living before we got into trouble. We forget about the God who delivered us until we are laid low again. So the promise is made, "Call upon me in the day of trouble: I will deliver thee," and God would add, With thy delivered strength, "thou shalt glorify me."

The fourth declaration is in Psalm 50:21: "These things hast thou done, and I kept silence; thou thoughtest that I was alto-

327

gether such an one as thyself: but I will reprove thee, and set them in order before thine eyes."

God says here that you are not getting away with anything. He makes it clear that He's not only a Saviour, but a Judge, and that man is accountable for what he does. He warns men here not to think, when He may be silent, that they are getting away with something, not to think that He is like them. Fortunately for our sakes God doesn't strike the sinner down immediately. But God's patience with us is no reason why we should become bold in transgression. The sinner says, "Oh, God's just like I am. He can't do anything to me." But God declares: "I will reprove. I will call you to the judgment bar. I will require of you an accounting of your stewardship. I will judge you." What does this do for me? It makes me cautious about the things I do, the things I say, and the things I think. It should make every Christian repent of his sins, knowing that for everything he thinks, does, and says he will have to give an account in the day of judgment. "I will reprove," God says.

What right does God have to tell man what he can do and what he cannot do? He has all authority, for all power in heaven and in earth is His, and that authority is based on the fact that He created man. According to Isaiah 45:18, God made man, and is responsible for him: "For thus saith the Lord that created the heavens; God himself that formed the earth and made it; he hath established it, he created it not in vain, he formed it to be inhabited: I am the Lord; and there is none else." Yes, the Bible is clear on this fact. God does not shift responsibility. We read in Isaiah 45:22, 23: "Look unto me, and be ye saved, all the ends of the earth: for I am God, and there is none else. I have sworn by myself, the word is gone out of my mouth in

328

righteousness, and shall not return, That unto me every knee shall bow, every tongue shall swear." So God does have authority, and that authority is, in the first place, based on the fact that He made us. But His authority is also based on the fact that He has redeemed us.

> On a hill far away stood an old rugged cross,
> The emblem of suffering and shame.

Do we love that old cross on which the dearest and best was slain for a world of lost sinners? When He died on that cross God assumed additional authority to deal with man, for He paid the penalty for man's transgression. He was wounded for our transgressions and bruised for our iniquities; the chastisement of our peace was upon Him, and by His stripes we are healed (Isaiah 53:5). In 1 Corinthians 6:19, 20 He asks, "What? know ye not that your body is the temple of the Holy Ghost which is in you, which ye have of God, and ye are not your own?" Then He answers, "For ye are bought with a price: therefore glorify God in your body, and in your spirit, which are God's."

God speaks to us through the Scriptures. God does speak to modern man. The Bible is the word of God—the Old Testament and the New. Why don't you read it? God is speaking; man just isn't listening. He also speaks to us in nature: "The heavens declare the glory of God; and the firmament sheweth his handywork" (Psalm 19:1). He speaks to men through prayer. When we get on our knees and talk to Him, He talks back to us. Yes,

> He speaks, and the sound of His voice
> Is so sweet the birds hush their singing;
> And the melody That He gave to me,
> Within my heart is ringing.

And He walks with me, and He talks with me,
And He tells me I am His own,
And the joy we share as we tarry there,
None other has ever known.

He speaks to us through the experiences of life,

Joys are flowing like a river,
Since the Comforter has come;
He abides with us forever,
Makes the trusting heart his home.
Blessed quietness, holy quietness,
Sweet assurance in my soul;
On the stormy sea, Jesus speaks to me,
And the billows cease to roll.

Out on the Sea of Galilee one day a great storm arose and
the boat in which Jesus rode was tempest-tossed. The disciples,
fearful of going to the bottom of the sea, turned to the Saviour
and cried out in the language of the song writer:

Master, the tempest is raging!
The billows are tossing high!
The sky is o'er-shadowed with blackness;
No shelter or help is nigh;
Carest Thou not that we perish?
How canst Thou lie asleep,
When each moment so madly is threatening
A grave in the angry deep?

"The winds and the waves shall obey My will,
Peace, be still!
Whether the wrath of the storm-tossed sea,
Or demons, or men, or whatever it be,
No water can swallow the ship where lies
The Master of ocean, and earth and skies."

Jesus stood up in that boat, spoke to the winds, and they ceased, and to the waves, and the sea was calm. Yes, God speaks to modern man. He has a message to old and young, rich and poor. There is no problem that plagues the human family to which God has not addressed Himself.

The Bible is full of counsel for all men everywhere, under all circumstances. We just can't read Him out of His own universe, nor can we exist independently of Him. We cannot continue to ignore His voice or to deny that He is speaking. Open His Book, study His Word, and you will discover to your own satisfaction and peace of mind that there is light, precious light, on every area of human experience, and that a thoughtful, all-wise God has addressed himself to man's deepest needs and to the most earnest yearnings of the human heart. There you will find satisfaction, in the ever-flowing fountain of eternal wisdom.

Ezekiel saw the wheel,
Way in the middle of the air.
Little wheel runs by faith,
Big wheel runs by the grace of God.
A wheel in a wheel,
Way in the middle of the air.

"A Wheel in a Wheel"

LIKE THE WHEELS in Ezekiel's vision, those of the marriage relationship should move in harmony. Certainly harmony is the key to any union, and that is just what marriage is: "Therefore shall a man leave his father and mother, and shall cleave unto his wife: and they shall be one flesh" (Genesis 2:24).

Marriage is a union of two individuals, spiritually, physically, and mentally. God Himself performed the first ceremony: "And the rib, which the Lord God had taken from man, made he a woman, and brought her unto the man" (verse 22). In marriage a man is entitled to only one wife, and a wife to one husband. This was evident in the most ideal situation—the Garden of Eden —God gave Adam one Eve, and He gave Eve one Adam.

"Yet ye say, Wherefore? Because the Lord hath been witness between thee and the wife of thy youth, against whom thou hast dealt treacherously: yet is she thy companion, and the wife

The principles God has given to protect marriage make the difference between hell on earth and a little heaven on earth.

of thy covenant. And did not he make one? Yet had he the residue of the spirit. And wherefore one? That he might seek a godly seed. Therefore take heed to your spirit, and let none deal treacherously against the wife of his youth" (Malachi 2: 14, 15).

There are certain laws, or principles, that safeguard the marriage institution, and when they are obeyed marriage is a happy, blissful estate. When they are disobeyed, it can be a little hell on earth. What are these laws of marriage?

1. *The law of moral faithfulness.* In the marriage vow each party to the covenant is specifically asked, "Will you remain true to him or her as long as you both shall live?" This is not an arbitrary law. It is tailored to the mental, spiritual, and physical make-up of the man and the woman. One cannot violate this law without serious damage. "Can a man take fire in his bosom, and his clothes not be burned? Can one go upon hot coals, and his feet not be burned? . . . But whoso committeth adultery with a woman lacketh understanding: he that doeth it destroyeth his own soul" (Proverbs 6:27-32).

2. *The law of difference.* No home can have two heads, and the Bible has clearly indicated who the head of the home is. "For the husband is the head of the wife, even as Christ is the head of the church: and he is the saviour of the body" (Ephesians 5:23). In every organization, whether it be home, or school, or government, someone must bear the ultimate responsibility for the conduct of affairs. In the home that someone is the man, the husband. Violation of this law has contributed heavily to the mounting divorce statistics. The woman who does not recognize this is not likely to have a marriage for very long. The world has little respect for a hen-pecked man or a domineering

woman. Being head of the home implies spiritual leadership. A man is the priest in the home. He should lead out in the devotional services of the home and should lead his family to church at worship time. Further, the husband is responsible for the financial prosperity of the home. "If any provide not for his own, and specially for those of his own house, he hath denied the faith, and is worse than an infidel" (1 Timothy 5:8). This does not give the husband the license to beat his wife and to be domineering. "Husbands, love your wives, even as Christ also loved the church, and gave himself for it. . . . So ought men to love their wives as their own bodies. He that loveth his wife loveth himself. For no man ever yet hated his own flesh; but nourisheth and cherisheth it, even as the Lord the church" (Ephesians 5:25-29). A husband is to deal kindly with his wife, and the wife with her husband. Husbands should not beat their wives, nor should wives beat their husbands.

3. *The law of adaptability.* Being human, we might as well expect to find some traits within every personality that are not pleasing. This is a fact of human nature. Marriage brings two people together twenty-four hours a day, three hundred sixty-five days of the year, for the rest of their lives. They are bound to discover these objectionable traits in each other. They must adapt to them rather than allow them to become focal points of controversy. Love covers a multitude of ills, and therefore each mate should be prepared to make allowances for the other.

4. *Each party to the marriage vow should deliberately seek to make the other happy.* During courtship each tries to discover what cheers the other up. After marriage, concentrate on these things.

5. *Instant forgiveness.* Either one of the parties to the mar-

riage contract who holds a grudge is jeopardizing the love of his mate and the success of his marriage. Christ's advice to His disciples to forgive seventy times seven surely applies here.

6. *Resistance to outside influences.* This certainly includes the proverbial mother-in-law problem. The daughter or son must understand that marriage is personal between him and his mate, and that he cannot afford to permit any outside influence to jeopardize that union.

7. *A proper balance between attention given to the children of the home and to one's mate.* Many a marriage has gone on the rocks because one of the two parties to the contract gave too much attention to the child in the home and too little to the mate.

8. *Money must not be allowed to bring division and dissension into the home.* If both parties to the marriage contract earn money, there should be an agreement beforehand as to how it is to be dispensed.

9. *The family altar must have a fixed position in the daily routine.* Couples that pray together stay together, and what God has joined together, He can certainly protect. One of the most frequently heard reasons given in divorce courts for the dissolution of the marriage contract is the word "incompatibility." Whether by this is meant physical or personality incompatibility matters little. The fact is that, in the great majority of cases, a little time, patience, and hard work could correct this; but few people have either the courage or staying power necessary to do so. This is where union with Christ is so important, for He imparts to us those necessary qualities to work at our marriages and make them stick. There is nothing automatic about happiness. There are laws that govern and safeguard hap-

piness, and these laws must be obeyed—or peace will forever flee our souls and our homes.

Another reason for divorce is jealousy. The Bible says that jealousy is as cruel as the grave. The FBI and other detective agencies are good for the nation, but are of little use in the marriage situation. Wives who check every move their husbands make, and vice versa, are courting disaster. Also, the disposition to believe any negative report brought to one about his mate is an injustice to that mate.

Another basic reason for divorce is neglect. We think of this in three respects:

a. The neglect of those personal attentions practiced during courtship. In certain Eastern countries couples marry first and court afterward. There are few divorces in these cases. In the West we court and then marry. But courtship must continue during marriage or the marriage will grow cold.

b. The neglect of one's personal appearance. It is no secret that men and women marry what they see in each other. There can be no taking of the other party for granted in this respect. The husband and the wife should not neglect their personal grooming after marriage on the assumption that it is no longer important.

c. Another frequently held cause for divorce is abuse. We live in a violent age, and men and women who discipline their feelings and their tempers are rare. But marriage is no boxing ring, no crucible of abuse. It is a disgrace to the marriage vow for the husband or wife to perpetrate a violent act on the other. But basically any marriage can be saved if the two parties are willing to make the sacrifice to save it. Neglect of one's spiritual life is certain to lead to a deterioration of human relationships. In the language of the spiritual, "A Wheel in a Wheel," the "Little wheel runs by faith, Big wheel runs by the grace of God." Yes, faith and the grace of God are the oil that makes the wheel of marriage run smoothly. It is not the will of God that marriages be dissolved. What God hath joined together, let not man put asunder.

"For the woman which hath an husband is bound by the law to her husband so long as he liveth; but if the husband be dead, she is loosed from the law of her husband. So then if, while her husband liveth, she be married to another man, she shall be called an adulteress: but if her husband be dead, she is free from that law; so that she is no adulteress, though she be married to another man" (Romans 7:2, 3).

But suppose the marriage is unbearable? Does the Bible give no relief to such? In a particular situation Paul counseled:

"Unto the married I command, yet not I, but the Lord, Let not the wife depart from her husband: but and if she depart, let her remain unmarried, or be reconciled to her husband: and let not the husband put away his wife" (1 Corinthians 7:10, 11).

If for reasons beyond human endurance the husband and wife must part, they are to remain unmarried (and this means no girl friends or boy friends), or be reconciled to each other.

But suppose the husband or wife is morally unfaithful? Does the mate have to continue to live with the unfaithful party? First of all it should be assumed that one party is faithful and the other is unfaithful to answer the question clearly. My counsel is to forgive him or her—as the case may be—if you possibly can and try to make your marriage work. If, however, you find this impossible and you are making your lives utterly miserable by cherishing the memory of this immoral act, then Matthew 19:9 gives you the answer: "And I say unto you, Whosoever shall put away his wife, except it be for fornication, and shall marry another, committeth adultery: and whoso marrieth her which is put away doth commit adultery."

So the innocent party in this matter does have the permission, though not the encouragement, of Christ to put away his wife and marry another. Let me repeat, there is no encouragement in this text for the offended party to do so. Furthermore, if the offended party has been guilty himself of the same act, but has not been caught, he should gladly forgive his mate, who was detected, and the two of them settle down to try to make a happy and successful marriage out of the remains.

The love of God is sufficient even to cover this transgression, and when that love is shed abroad in our hearts we do become miraculously forgiving human beings.

> Have faith in God,
> He teaches hearts to love.
> Have faith in God,
> Strife fleeth like a dove.
> Have faith in God,
> Peace cometh from above.
> Have faith, dear friend, in God.
>
> Have faith in God,
> His love will make you one.
> Have faith in God,
> Jehovah's will be done.
> Have faith in God
> Until life's setting sun.
> Have faith, dear friend, in God.

With this faith and the love of God in your hearts, you can make of your home a little heaven on earth.

339

Remember me when tears are falling down;
Remember me when troubles are all around;
Then, O, down at the river of Jordan
When calling the roll, O, Lord, remember me.

"Remember Me"

"MAN THAT IS BORN of a woman is of a few days, and full of trouble" (Job 14:1). "Man is born unto trouble, as the sparks fly upward" (chapter 5:7).

It is difficult to imagine, but true, that there was a time on this earth when the word *trouble* was unknown. It was when God put man in the Garden of Eden, at Creation. Then his day-to-day existence was totally without complication. You see, the will of God and the will of man were one, and man sought only to please his Maker. It was when Adam and Eve transgressed the holy law of God that trouble entered the experience of man. Perplexity, trial, and worry became the curse of the human family. Anxiety became a day-to-day experience, following man like his own shadow. Suddenly his untroubled existence vanished and due to his own perverse actions, man became a hunted and a haunted creature. His survival was no longer ensured by his sinless state. Even his environment became a threat to his existence. Extremes in weather of hot and cold, wild and ravenous animals that had been previously docile and submissive to the will of man, the earth itself that had so readily yielded her bounty—these became a test of man's energy and patience. In short, man's spiritual delinquency gave rise to economic, social, and spiritual ills that were hitherto foreign to his experience. Then came death. For the first time man had to face the fact of the cessation of life. He had lost his claim to eternal life when he yielded to temptation in the Garden of Eden. There was now to be a brief interlude when man would live and die, but if faithful in this life he could again receive eternal life through the glorious hope of the gospel at the coming of the Lord.

The religion of Jesus Christ does not promise man freedom from trouble. In John 16:33 we read, "These things I have spoken unto you, that in me ye might have peace. In the world ye shall have tribulation: but be of good cheer; I have overcome the world."

Tribulation is part of man's payment for transgression. Adam fully understood this before he committed sin. Now, all the sons and daughters of Adam are born to trouble as the sparks fly upward. It is a part of our experience because of our sinful human nature. So Christ promises that in spite of the tribulation we encounter in the world, we may still have peace. We may still "be of good cheer." The reason He gives is, "I have overcome the world." Thus it is faith in Jesus Christ that enables us to survive trouble, whatever its nature, however strong it is.

I stood in a pulpit one gray afternoon delivering the funeral eulogy for the son and daughter of a grief-stricken mother. I noticed, however, that she behaved herself with remarkable calm in spite of her double loss. I asked her after the ceremony just how she was able to maintain her composure under such conditions, to which she answered, "If religion is good at any time to anyone, it must be in the day of trouble. My faith in God kept me strong."

This is perhaps what David meant when he said, "Yea, though I walk through the valley of the shadow of death, I will fear no evil: for thou art with me; thy rod and thy staff they comfort me" (Psalm 23:4).

Again and again the Scriptures admonish us not to let this world's problems get us down. I know it gets a little rough sometimes, no matter who you are—saint, sinner, rich, poor, black, red, or yellow, leader or led, privileged or underprivileged, for all people, sooner or later, the cup of human sorrow fills and overflows. But for all the sorely tried there are solace and solution.

A young man stood one day watching two others play tennis. He noticed that again and again they knocked the ball into the net. Not understanding the game, he turned to another and said, "Why don't they take that net down—then it would not get in the way of the ball?"

Back came the answer: "It is the net that makes the game interesting."

The skillful player labors to knock the ball over the net. He has no desire for the obstacle to be removed. And so it is with a Christian and his trials. He does not pray for the removal of all difficulty, but day by day he prays for strength, faith, and courage to surmount any problem he may face during the day. This is the key to unbounded optimism. This is the secret of constant faith.

In these tension-filled times man, both individually and collectively, is subjected to constant crises. The danger in this situation is that we may become fatalistic. Assuming that certain problems are inevitable, we resign ourselves to endure them stoically. We permit the darkened horizon to deaden our hope and destroy our faith and to paralyze our energies. Yet others are moved to the opposite extreme. They become perennial problem solvers. So preoccupied are they with the difficulties that they have little time to work constructively or positively on their problems. With these men the devil has a field day. He keeps them burdened down with worry and care and thus wears away their physical, mental, and spiritual energies.

Christ has given us the only true solution to the trouble problem. We should not seek to bear our burdens alone. "Cast thy burden upon the Lord, and he shall sustain thee: he shall never suffer the righteous to be moved" (Psalm 55:22). Yes, the troubled in heart should learn the divine art of prayer. It is in this way that we share our burdens with the greatest Problem-solver of all times. "Casting all your care upon him; for he careth for you" (1 Peter 5:7). The knowledge that somebody cares gives a man a psychological lift, but enlisting the active aid of the God of heaven is an even greater blessing. He puts His broad shoulders under our cares, for He is able to bear them. Unaided we are not.

The promises of God are sure: "He that dwelleth in the secret place of the most High shall abide under the shadow of the Almighty" (Psalm 91:1). "The secret place of the most High" has been clearly defined by Jesus. He advised us, when we pray, to enter into our closet and shut the door and seek the Lord in secret. And the promise is that those who seek Him secretly

343

will be rewarded openly. But prayer must be our constant spiritual exercise; not just once or twice or thrice a day, but we must learn to pray as we breathe. Pray without ceasing. Let those who know the value of prayer tell you what it does. It lightens the burden, brings hope to the heart and wisdom to the mind. "He shall cover thee with his feathers, and under his wings shalt thou trust: his truth shall be thy shield and buckler" (verse 4). That last phrase is the key to ultimate deliverance. "His truth shall be thy shield and buckler." For the truth to shield us, we must know it, and we cannot know it unless we study. To this end, God in His merciful kindness has given us His Word, and daily we should search the Scriptures, for they are our assurance in the time of trouble.

"Because he hath set his love upon me, therefore will I deliver him: I will set him on high, because he hath known my name" (verse 14). Once again we are brought face to face with the fact that there is no other name under heaven whereby we must be saved except the name of Jesus. Knowing Him brings deliverance. "He shall call upon me, and I will answer him: I will be with him in trouble; I will deliver him, and honour him. With long life will I satisfy him, and shew him my salvation" (verses 15, 16).

But there is a reason why God permits trials to come to His children. You see, man has no other way of demonstrating his fitness for the kingdom of God than by manifesting the Spirit of God under duress. Trial drives a man to his knees and thereby increases his knowledge of how dependent he is on Christ. This in turn strengthens faith, for every deliverance makes us even bolder to trust in Christ in every emergency. The saints of Bible times knew what this meant. Their determination to serve the

Lord in face of death itself inspires confidence in the heart of the reader.

Said Dante: "Sorrow remarries us to God." Suffering helps develop spiritual insights. As one author put it, "It is a window through which man sees the glory of God and is satisfied."

Carl Knudsen said, "When we measure our eternal debt to the saints of earth who have forged our richest spiritual treasures out of their own suffering, we can imagine what an insane and barren world this would be without the spiritual illumination that comes from bearing a cross."

A number of years ago a friend brought Mr. McCartney a beautiful carving of the Lord's Supper cut out of mother of pearl. Mr. McCartney took it to a jeweler to have it mounted and told him that he thought it would appear best suspended against a light, so that its colors and beautiful figures could be revealed. But the practiced eye of the jeweler knew otherwise, and he said, "No, this must be mounted against something dark."

So the sorrow and grief and pain in the world often forms the background against which shine out the virtues of life and the graces of the Spirit. So we press on, knowing that a brighter day is indeed coming and the old spiritual will be fulfilled:

> There will be no more sorrow, no tomorrow;
> No more sighing, no more dying,
> When we bid farewell to every care
> And wipe our weeping eyes.

"Zion's Walls"

OLD JERUSALEM, chief city of Judea, was originally called Salem. When the Jebusites owned it they called it Jebus. Finally, David captured it. For the Jews the city of Jerusalem became a national symbol. Here was the sacred Mount Moriah. More than that, God intended it to be the center of all He wanted the world to become. Later, it became a symbol for Christians. It was a symbol of righteousness, of God's revealed will, and of worship.

By contrast, the city of Rome, on the banks of the Tiber River, became a symbol of apostasy and rebellion against God. Like Babylon in Old Testament times, Rome—first pagan and later papal—became a great enemy of the God of heaven. Here we have an intriguing tale of two cities, Jerusalem and Rome.

Now, because Jerusalem was a Jewish city, let us ask what Christians are indebted to Jews for. Down through the centuries Christians have talked much about the Jews being responsible

346

for the crucifixion of Christ, which in some instances has fostered a strange spirit of anti-Semitism, even of hatred for the Jews. But let Christians remember what the apostle Paul said about the Jews. Raising the question, "What advantage then hath the Jew? or what profit is there of circumcision?" he then answered his own question: "Much every way: chiefly, because that unto them were committed the oracles of God" (Romans 3:1, 2).

In Romans 11 he admonishes us Gentile Christians not to rail or boast against the Jews, because they were the original followers of Christ. Paul likens them to a natural branch of the olive tree. He speaks of some of those branches being cut off, and of Gentiles being grafted among them and partaking of the sweetness of the sap of the olive tree. We, then, become branches by adoption, whereas the Jews were natural branches from the very beginning.

Christianity today owes Judaism so much that no Christian minister should ever boast against the Jews. As a matter of fact, if it hadn't been for the Jews, I don't know if we would have a Bible, for the forty writers of the Bible, with one possible exception, were all Jewish. Furthermore, the law of God was handed down to a Jew for the entire world's benefit, and when Jesus Christ came, He took a Jewish body. Men and women who do not love Jews could not love Jesus, for the thirty-three years that Christ walked the earth, He was in a Jewish body, born of a Jewish mother with a Jewish lineage. Indeed, He was a child of Abraham. Obviously we owe the Jews much in this life, but what about the life to come?

In Revelation 21 we read about that great city toward which our weary footsteps tread. It has twelve great gates, and over the gates the names of the twelve tribes of Israel. In its twelve foundations are the names of the twelve apostles—all Jews. So, then, we do owe the Jews much, even in the world to come. But Jerusalem is symbolic of more than this. It is a symbol of salvation. As a matter of fact, we won't be able to get away from Jerusalem even when we go to heaven. There, we will still be going to Jerusalem. Not to a city built by human hand, of course, for the Bible says that there is a city "which hath foundations, whose builder and maker is God." Its name is New Jerusalem.

But there is still more that should claim our attention. Salvation from sin came from Jerusalem, for Christ began His ministry there. As a boy at the age of twelve He reasoned with the doctors and the lawyers about the Messiah and God's purpose for His people. Yes, the gospel was preached first in Jerusalem, and Jerusalem may be called the cradle of Christianity.

In Isaiah 53:5 we are told: "But he was wounded for our transgressions, he was bruised for our iniquities: the chastisement of our peace was upon him; and with his stripes we are healed."

A painter was once painting in a high place when the scaffold broke. As he hurtled toward the earth he said to himself, "This is the end," and he began to pray. Around the building a shepherd happened to be leading his sheep and as the painter hurtled toward the ground a sheep broke his fall. The sheep's body was split open, and its blood scattered in all directions. Indeed, the falling painter himself was covered with its blood. But the soft cushion of the sheep's body saved his life.

So it was that Jesus Christ, the Son of the living God, suffered, bled, and died at Calvary for our sins, and we may now be covered by His blood, cleansed from our sins, pardoned of our iniquities, and empowered to overcome them. This is the gospel of the Lord Jesus Christ, for by grace we are saved. Salvation is ours through faith, not of ourselves, but a gift of God. Jesus Christ is that gift, the Word made flesh that dwelt among us, and all who look to Him in repentant faith and confidence will be accepted at the throne of God.

So much for the city of Jerusalem. Much more might be said, but there is another city.

The second city is Rome, the symbol of apostasy, for centuries a symbol of all that was and is against God. Rome set itself up to extinguish the light that came into the world to enlighten every man. A Roman hammer drove the nails into the hands of our Lord. A Roman hand held the whip that lashed His back. It was a Roman governor who washed his hands and committed Christ to the cross. Roman hands pressed upon His brow a crown of thorns until innocent blood ran down, and a Roman centurion ripped a spear into His side, from which came blood and water. It was Rome that persecuted the apostles. James and Paul were beheaded; John was exiled to the Isle of Patmos; Peter was crucified upside-down. Yes, it is no wonder that the prophet Daniel referred to Rome as an iron monarchy. The historian Gibbon referred to the iron monarchy of Rome as committing so many sins that eventually the Lord God had to bring upon her the destructive power of ten nations.

Later, under the papacy, Rome chained Bibles to the desk, and put people in jail simply for having a Bible in their possession. It was a crime to own a Bible. It was Rome that changed the Sabbath from Saturday to Sunday. It was Rome that persecuted during the Middle Ages. Rome is the very antithesis of Jerusalem. Jerusalem—the symbol of light, of hope, of salvation,

349

of redemption, and Rome—the symbol of apostasy, of sin, of backsliding, of death.

This is the choice men have had throughout the Christian Era. Obedience to God, and a man will live; disobedience, and a man will die. Since Adam and Eve sinned in the Garden of Eden, this has, in principle, been our choice. What choice will you make?

A man was once faced with a fateful choice. The question was: His son had become a draft dodger, and that father was torn between love for his son and loyalty to his country. Should he deliver his son up to the authorities? He made his decision. He would not allow his son to live forever in shame. He notified the authorities where the young man was hiding. As the young man was led away, he looked at his father and said, "And to think, Dad, I felt you were my friend," to which the father replied, "I am your friend, and once you've cleared your name either on a far-flung battlefield or in a court of law, you will acknowledge that this was the better way, even though it was the hard way."

So it is with the Christian life. It is the better way even though sometimes it calls for persecution, privation, and sacrifice. It is still the better way. It may be a hilly pathway of battle and praise, but at the end there is a city, at the end there is a Saviour, at the end there is a land that is fairer than day. May God give us the grace to enter in by faith to the high privileges of divine grace now, and at last into the life to come.

We're soldiers in the army,
We have to fight and some may have to die.
We're holding up the blood-stained banner;
We have to hold it up until we die.

"We're Soldiers"

SOMEONE MAY ASK, "What's wrong with God's law?" We could easily answer, "Why, nothing, of course," and we would be telling the truth, for Romans 7:12 says, "The law is holy, and the commandment holy, and just, and good." But there is more to the story than this.

In Matthew 1:21 we read, "Thou shalt call his name Jesus: for he shall save his people from their sins." A man is saved from sin, not by the law, but by the saving grace of the Lord Jesus Christ. God bestows His unmerited favor on man. His blood covers our transgressions, and by it we are cleansed from our sins. Why then bother about the law at all if Jesus died to save His people from their sins? Romans 7:7 gives us a clue: "What shall we say then? Is the law sin? God forbid. Nay, I had not known sin, but by the law: for I had not known lust, except the law had said, Thou shalt not covet."

351

You see, the law simply makes clear what sin is. The law is an instructive agency. It tells a man about his deep need of cleansing, hence his deep need of Christ. The law, then, complements the mission of Christ, for all the law can do is to point out sin, and only the blood of Jesus Christ can cleanse from sin. But how can the blood cleanse us from something if we don't know we need cleansing? Another way of saying it is, Why would a man take a bath if he didn't know he needed it? Why would a person wash his face if he didn't know it was dirty? That's why we have mirrors—to tell us where to apply the soap and the water. In the same way, we need the law to tell us where to apply the blood of Jesus.

When we talk about being saved from sin we are talking about three things. We are talking about being saved from the penalty of transgression, we are talking about being saved from the power of transgression, and we are talking about being saved from the very presence of sin. John 3:16 says, "For God so loved the world, that he gave his only begotten Son, that whosoever believeth in him should not perish, but have everlasting life." Do you get the promise? To believe in Christ is not to perish! The penalty of sin, the wages of transgression is death. The great purpose and design of the gospel is to remove this penalty of death and to set us free, all by the grace of God.

The power of sin can be broken, and every reader ought to believe it. I know the word has gone out that sin is invincible, that it cannot be stopped, that whenever it attacks it conquers. I have news for you. Read Titus 2:11, 12: "For the grace of God that bringeth salvation hath appeared to all men, teaching us that, denying ungodliness and worldly lusts, we should live soberly, righteously, and godly, in this present world." So, then, there is in our world a power that can enable us to live soberly, righteously, and godly. The power of sin can be broken in the life. No matter how long the sinful habit has been indulged, it can be broken and the cycle ended with the past transgression.

Jeremiah asked: "Is there no balm in Gilead; is there no physician there?" (Jeremiah 8:22). An old spiritual gives the answer:

> There is a balm in Gilead
> To make the wounded whole;
> There is a balm in Gilead
> To heal the sin-sick soul.
>
> Sometimes I feel discouraged
> And think my work in vain,
> But then the Holy Spirit
> Revives my soul again.
> There is a balm in Gilead.

The song writer wrote:

> Come ye disconsolate, where'er ye languish;
> Come to the mercy seat, fervently kneel;
> Here bring your wounded hearts,
> Here tell your anguish;
> Earth has no sorrow that heaven cannot heal.

And yet another:

> O come, every soul, by sin oppressed,
> There's mercy with the Lord,
> And He will surely give you rest
> By trusting in His Word.
>
> For Jesus shed His precious blood
> The rich blessings to bestow;
> Plunge now into that crimson flood
> That washes white as snow.

When we talk about being saved, we are not talking about being saved from the law, for the law is not sin. The Bible says, "Thou shalt call his name Jesus: for he shall save his people from their sins" (Matthew 1:21), and it is from the penalty of sin that we are saved by grace. We're saved by grace from the power of sin, and ultimately we will be saved by grace from the very presence of sin (see Revelation 7:9). The grace of God literally brings the life of the sinner into harmony with the law of God. It is grace that makes Christians out of sinners, but what this really means is that it not only converts the heart and transforms the inner man but it alters the sinful habit pattern—visibly and definitely—so that the way we live every day, the way we think, talk, and treat other people is different.

Sin has made man a rebel. The grace of God that brings salvation makes him a son. Romans 3:31 asks, "Do we then make void the law through faith? God forbid: yea, we establish the law." Faith in Jesus Christ doesn't eliminate the necessity for obedience to the law of God, even though obedience doesn't save us. Faith in Jesus Christ literally establishes the law (Romans 3:31). Let me illustrate this.

A man walks up to me and says, "I know I owe you five dollars, and on the fifth of the month I am going to pay you." When the fifth of the month comes, that man walks up and hands me the five-dollar bill he owes me. This validates his promise. It naturally strengthens my faith in him. It says to me that he is a man of his word. Why? Because he does what he promises to do. It is thus that faith establishes the law of God, for, you see, the law of God commands obedience. Faith supplies the obedience that has been commanded. This is one sense in which faith establishes rather than destroys the law of God.

In Romans 8:3, 4 we read, "For what the law could not do, in that it was weak through the flesh, God sending his own Son in the likeness of sinful flesh, and for sin, condemned sin in the flesh: that the righteousness of the law might be fulfilled in us, who walk not after the flesh, but after the Spirit." You see, there is something the law cannot do. It cannot pardon, it cannot cleanse, it cannot empower. But what the law cannot do, thank God, the gift of Jesus Christ—grace—can do! When He came to this earth He brought that missing element with Him— that thing the law cannot do. So it is fair for Him to condemn sin in the flesh. All the law could do was point out sin in the flesh. It took the power of the righteous life of the living God to condemn sin in the flesh.

We use that word condemn, not in the sense that it is condemned verbally, for the law has already done that, but in the sense that a house is condemned that it might be torn down and a new house erected on the site. This is what Christ does for the sinful heart. He takes away the old heart of stone and inserts a new heart of flesh. This new creation in Christ Jesus makes it possible for the works of the law, the righteousness of the law, to be fulfilled in us.

Many of you may be thinking about Romans 6:14: "For sin shall not have dominion over you; for ye are not under the law, but under grace."

"Aha," somebody says, "if you're not under the law, that means you don't have to keep it."

The Bible uses the phrase, "under the law," in different ways. For instance, in Romans 7:1 we read: "Know ye not, brethren, (for I speak to them that know the law,) how that the law hath dominion over a man as long as he liveth?" Well, what do you think about that? As long as a man is alive the law has dominion over him. There is a sense in which the law has dominion. The law does not, however, condemn a man who is in Christ Jesus, and it is this function of the law—the condemnatory function—that ceases when a man becomes a Christian. "Ye are not under the law" may mean either that we're not under its *jurisdiction*, or that we're not under its *condemnation*. Romans 7:1, 2 makes it clear that as long as a man is alive he is under the jurisdiction of the law of God. But when he becomes a Christian and accepts Christ as personal Saviour, Lord and King, he is no longer under the condemnation of the law.

Many years ago when I was traveling in a Southern city I became so involved in my conversation that I forgot to observe the speed limit. An automobile pulled up beside me, and out stepped an officer of the law who wanted to know where the fire was. Well, I knew the problem, I confessed my sin, and asked for mercy. The officer said, "Well, you look like an intelligent man. I'm going to trust you this time. I'll let you go, but if you come back through this city and break the laws, you know where I'm going to take you."

Once that officer pardoned me, I was under grace. But as long as there was some question of my being fined, I was under the law. You know how I acted while I was under grace? I drove that car at thirty-five miles an hour even out on the highway where I could have gone faster. Finally my wife said to me, "Earl, you can do fifty-five now." But only gradually did I pick up speed to the limit. When we are under grace we are to act with reference to the law of God. "If ye love me, keep my commandments," Jesus said. "Ye are my friends, if ye do whatsoever I command you." "Why call ye me, Lord, Lord, and do not the things which I say?" "If thou wilt enter into life, keep the commandments." (John 14:5; 15:14; Luke 6:46; Matthew 19:17.) But you know, a man can't do it by himself.

Galatians 2:20 is the secret of all sanctified, purified, holy living. It says, "I am crucified with Christ: nevertheless I live; yet not I, but Christ liveth in me: and the life which I now live in the flesh I live by the faith of the Son of God, who loved me, and gave himself for me."

Yes, there is another life that can be implanted in our human hearts, and that life produces in us the divine attributes of the Spirit. The fruits of the Spirit are made manifest, and the world glorifies God because it sees God in us. Thus armed, the Christian is prepared like a soldier to "fight the good fight of faith" against the world and the devil. He submits to the discipline of training and the muscle-hardening processes that will ensure his spiritual survival. Through prayer and the study of the Word of God he fortifies himself daily for the struggle. This is the secret of victory. This is the key to the other world.

Steal away, steal away, steal away to Jesus.
Steal away; steal away home,
I haven't long to stay here.

"*Steal Away*"

ABOUT TWELVE YEARS AGO I
sat in the living room of an Indian
friend of mine in conversation with a Hindu priest. "Why do
you Christians pray?" he asked me. "God is too strong for you
to take anything from Him. He is too adequate for you to add
anything to Him. Since you can neither add to nor take from,
why do you pray?"

I had never been asked this question before and after some
prayerful thought, I spoke thus: "Sir, do you have any nephews
or nieces?"

He answered, "Yes."

"Well," I asked, "do they ever come to you and ask you for
money to buy an ice-cream cone?"

"Yes," he said.

"Do you give it to them?" I asked.

"I do," he answered.

359

Happy is the family that prays together!
Prayer opens hearts to God, brings peace,
and solves the difficult problems of life.

"How do you feel, being able to provide things they ask for?"

"It gives me a sense of satisfaction," he said.

"They can neither add to nor take from you, for you are too powerful to need and too strong to be overwhelmed."

"I get the point," he answered.

"And further," I asked him, "do they ever climb up in your lap, put their arms around your neck, kiss you, and say, 'Uncle, we love you'?"

He said, "Yes."

"We Christians on our knees sometimes just give thanks to God for His being God and our Father and express our love for Him," I said.

Prayer is communion with God. It is "the opening of the heart to God as to a friend." "Prayer is the key in the hand of faith to unlock heaven's storehouse, where are treasured the boundless resources of omnipotence." "Prayer does not bring God down to us but brings us up to Him." (*Steps to Christ,* pp. 93-95.) Whereas it was the privilege of man in his sinless state to commune with God face to face, which privilege is now denied us due to our sinful human nature, it is still our privilege to converse with God person to person through the exercise of prayer.

"Prayer is the breath of the soul."—*Gospel Workers,* p. 254. This being true, do you find it difficult to understand why there are so many expired and expiring Christian experiences? Some Christians breathe so seldom, what is there left to do but expire?

"Prayer is not to work any change in God; it is to bring us into harmony with God."—*Christ's Object Lessons,* p. 143. Small wonder, then, that the disciples would say to Christ on one occasion, "Lord, teach us to pray." But how often should we pray? "Pray without ceasing" (1 Thessalonians 5:17). Apparently the great God with whom we have to deal never wearies of hearing His children talk to Him. Human beings often become irritable at repeated requests, but not so with God. There is a spiritual which says, "King Jesus is listening all day long just to hear some sinner pray."

"Behold, the Lord's hand is not shortened, that it cannot save; neither his ear heavy, that it cannot hear" (Isaiah 59:1).

But there are conditions to answered prayer just as there are conditions to meaningful and productive conversation between human beings. But with God we must first believe.

"Wherefore, when I came, was there no man? when I called, was there none to answer? Is my hand shortened at all, that it cannot redeem? or have I no power to deliver? behold, at my rebuke I dry up the sea, I make the rivers a wilderness: their fish stinketh, because there is no water, and dieth for thirst. I clothe the heavens with blackness, and I make sackcloth their covering" (Isaiah 50:2, 3).

God wants to be believed; in fact, He insists on it.

"Verily, verily, I say unto you, He that believeth on me, the works that I do shall he do also; and greater works than these shall he do; because I go unto my Father. And whatsoever ye shall ask in my name, that will I do, that the Father may be glorified in the Son" (John 14:12, 13).

Whatever we seek of the Lord must be in the name of His Son Jesus Christ. There is a reason for this. It is found in Acts 4:12: "Neither is there salvation in any other: for there is none other name under heaven given among men, whereby we must be saved."

We must make our requests according to the will of God, and submit ourselves to His answer, recognizing it to be for our best good whether or not it accedes to our request. "If we ask any thing according to his will, he heareth us" (1 John 5:14).

We must pray out of repentant hearts. The preamble to every prayer should be repentance and confession of sin. We must humble ourselves before God, acknowledging our unworthiness of His goodness, and make our petitions on the merits of His Son. He will hear us. And while we acknowledge our unworthiness to seek the face of our Lord, we need not make our approaches to Him infrequent or timid.

"Let us therefore come boldly unto the throne of grace, that we may obtain mercy, and find grace to help in time of need" (Hebrews 4:16). The word "boldly" as here used implies frankness, confidence, and outspokenness. All three words are important to prayer, but they are descriptive of an attitude. First of all, we are commanded to voice our desires and deep needs to our Maker. This is outspokenness. We are admonished to be honest or frank with Him. It is useless to try to conceal anything from the all-seeing eye of the Almighty. We should approach the throne with the confidence a child would exhibit toward a loving father, and expect our prayers to be answered.

Earlier we mentioned that a man when praying should not pray from a guilty conscience. "And whatsoever we ask, we receive of him, because we keep his commandments, and do those things that are pleasing in his sight" (1 John 3:22).

Our hearts must be brought into a covenant relationship with Christ. We must agree with Him not only in those things that are pleasing to us but also in those things that cut across our grain.

What should we pray for?

1. High on the list should be the salvation of our own souls and those of our fellow men. "But seek ye first the kingdom of God, and his righteousness; and all these things shall be added unto you" (Matthew 6:33).

2. We should pray for our daily needs. "Give us this day our daily bread" (verse 11). Our Lord taught His disciples how to pray.

3. We should pray for physical health. It is significant that when Christ was on earth He never turned down one earnest plea for physical healing.

4. We should pray for the rulers of the nations. "I exhort therefore, that, first of all, supplications, prayers, intercessions, and giving of thanks, be made for all men; for kings, and for all that are in authority; that we may lead a quiet and peaceable life in all godliness and honesty" (1 Timothy 2:1, 2).

5. We should pray for the coming of Christ. Did not our Lord enjoin His disciples to say, "Thy kingdom come" (Matthew 6:10)?

6. We should pray for peace in this world (Psalm 122:6; Jeremiah 29:7).

I still believe that prayer changes things and that more things are wrought by prayer than this world ever dreams of. My own life has been saved many times through intercessory prayer, and when the saints of God get into the kingdom of God, perhaps the greatest revelation they will ever have is of the many dangers, seen and unseen, from which they were delivered through prayer.

"See Abraham holding back the lifted arm of God in behalf of guilty Sodom. See Jacob wrestling with God and overcoming

Him. See Joshua arresting the heavens. See Elijah praying a dead child to life and calling down fire and sealing up and then opening clouds. See Hezekiah by prayer adding fifteen years to his life and keeping Zion from being plowed like a field. See Daniel compelling secrets from God. See the 120 disciples in Jerusalem praying into birth the pentecostal revival. See Peter liberated from prison by the breath of a beseeching church, and finally see Paul and Silas by their midnight supplication shaking the foundation of the jail at Philippi, bursting open the doors and rending the stocks that held them fast."—H. C. Fish.

Yes, God answers prayer. But Job raised the question: "What profit should we have, if we pray unto him?" (Job 21: 15). Thank God, there are many good answers to this question.

1. There is the psychological relief that comes with the privilege of communing freely and frankly with a friend. Any psychiatrist will testify that this alone has therapeutic values.

2. There is the removal of guilt that accompanies prayer, for it is the promise of the Saviour to cleanse us from all unrighteousness if we repent of our sins.

3. There is the added advantage of the constant companionship of Christ. This is assured to all who commune with Him and who welcome Him into their hearts—"Christ in you, the hope of glory" (Colossians 1:27).

4. There is the many-faceted blessing of answered prayer.

5. Prayer strengthens confidence in God, in our fellow man, and in our ability to overcome whatever obstacles may confront us.

6. Prayer sharpens the intellect, refreshes the spirit, and increases a reverential attitude toward God and a respectful attitude toward one's fellow man.

7. Prayer awakens in man a sense of his own worth before God, and there follows in consequence an increase in dignity and discipline that is apparent to all. No man should attempt to negotiate the jungle that is our world without constant dependence on God through the medium of prayer.

> What a friend we have in Jesus,
> All our sins and griefs to bear.
> What a privilege to carry
> Everything to God in prayer!
>
> . . . . .
>
> Can we find a friend so faithful
> Who will all our sorrows share?
> Jesus knows our every weakness,
> Take it to the Lord in prayer.

Go tell it on the mountain,
Over the hills and everywhere;
Go tell it on the mountain,
That Jesus Christ is born.

"Tell It on the Mountain"

"AND HE SAID unto them, Go ye into all the world, and preach the gospel to every creature" (Mark 16:15).

On a New Orleans television panel in 1968 it was my privilege to discuss the mission of the church in the world with a group of fellow ministers. One of them said, "I think the church should provide an example to the world of what it [the world] should be. Therefore, in my ministry I concentrate on making my church an example to the world rather than leading the church out into the world aggressively."

With this position I took issue, and I do today. The Christian church is by nature aggressive. The gospel commission makes it so. All followers of Christ are commanded to make disciples of all men. That is why Christianity has fared so harshly at the hand of dictators. They have correctly read the nature of Christianity. They know that Christianity cannot co-

Dr. Martin Luther King, twentieth-century dreamer, said, "Tell it on the mountain." He foresaw the day when all would be free.

exist peacefully with evil. It must attack evil. It must always seek converts for, and to, its Master.

You see, the church has a purpose for its existence on earth, namely, the conversion of every creature, and with the population explosion the demands on the church's energies always exceed the supply. The business of the church, therefore, is its all-consuming passion. The message of Christ must greet the ears of every living creature. How else is this possible without a constant program of intensive evangelism?

It is said that a group of Chinese came one day to see the editor of a church journal, aglow as the result of reports covering the year of the most anti-Christian persecution China had seen for a long time. "We can plainly see," they said, "that Christianity is non-downable," adding, "We've come to call you Christians the Bu Tao Yung"—a Chinese term for little puppet dolls filled with lead at the bottom that always bob up when knocked over. It seems that the Christian church in China had clearly demonstrated its resiliency and its vitality by growing in spite of the persecution. The religion of Jesus Christ is truly "non-downable."

During His three years of public ministry on earth Christ gave a clear demonstration of what the ministry of the church should be in all aspects of its operation. The New Testament resounds to His ringing sermons, and the Record teems with the evidence of His service. He is seen healing the sick, raising the dead, preaching the gospel. Christ was aggressively evangelistic. He neglected no opportunity to draw a lost soul to His own life-giving ministry of love. In this the church must imitate its Lord. This we must do because:

1. We love God. This would indicate that our messages must

368

reflect the love of God. Love is the main spring of all true Christian service. It is because we love Christ that we tell others about Him with such enthusiasm and happiness. Love for God leads men to make sacrifices for Him and for their fellow man that cannot be explained in human language. We think of the cultured Schweitzer, the talented Livingstone, giving their lives in the heart of Africa. Only love divinely implanted in the human heart could produce this Heaven-born response. That a man would isolate himself from his own culture and find his deepest satisfaction living among those who are physically and culturally different, while at the same time experiencing genuine happiness, is indeed a manifestation of the miracle of grace. Divine love imparted and implanted produces this miracle. And it is also true of us that when we truly love God we will seek out the needy and minister to their suffering.

2. Those who are truly Christian share the gospel with their fellow man because of their love for him. The gospel offers the only permanent cure for the many and complex ills that afflict the human family. The Christian knows this and, surrounded by the overabundance of human need, his conscience cannot rest until he has shared with others the good news of salvation. This certainly motivated our Lord. "And Jesus went about all the cities and villages, teaching in their synagogues, and preaching the gospel of the kingdom, and healing every sickness and every disease among the people" (Matthew 9:35).

"And he said unto them, Let us go into the next towns, that I may preach there also: for therefore came I forth. And he preached in their synagogues throughout all Galilee, and cast out devils" (Mark 1:38, 39). "I must preach the kingdom of God to other cities also: for therefore am I sent" (Luke 4:43).

24

And does it pay? In front of me is a letter from E. J. Mavanza. It reads: "It was in 1963 that you were in Dar es Salaam with the wonderful message of Christ. My wife and I attended most of your meetings conducted in that city. We were convinced of the truthfulness of what you said, and by the grace of God made up our minds to follow Christ and join the church. But this involved the loss of my job. After praying and studying the promises of God, we decided to give up the job and go back to our village, three hundred and ninety miles away. I secured a position as an accountant that gave me the privilege of observing God's holy day of rest, which job I held until I was called by the administrators of our mission field as an accountant, where I am serving at this moment.

"But while at home in my village, I taught the message of Christ to my brother, who was converted. He became a religious book salesman, and today there are thirty-five Christians in the village where there were none three years ago."

From the pen of Pastor Hancock comes this story: "Augustine Cusi Tite is a nineteen-year-old boy who lives about twenty-five miles from the Broken Stone Mission on the shores of Lake Titicaca in Peru. He is an Amara tribesman with only a sixth-grade education. He has had visions and dreams of the second coming of Christ. He went forth preaching in fifty different places. He has only two sermons—the second coming of Christ, and the Lord's day. The other young people in his church follow up the interest he stirs up with his Bible messages. He began preaching about 1964 and has now been preaching for more than two years. In one and a half years of preaching, one hundred and eighty-one people became Christians. By the end of 1966 the total had reached two hundred."

Yes, every man is involved in the gospel commission. During the Reformation, even little children carried the message.

3. We must become witnesses to save our own souls. It is a fact that while teaching the message of Christ to others our own hearts are strengthened and our own confidence grows.

In the speech of a certain West African tribe the word for missionary means "the man who brings the ember." Yes, into the darkened lives of the lost the Christian brings the ember.

It is said that a Chinese baby girl, three days old, was abandoned in the street because she was the third daughter of parents who did not want another girl. Missionaries picked her up and cared for her and educated her. She became a Christian and married a Chinese pastor. Her first child was a daughter who is known far and wide as a great physician, Dr. Li Bi Cu, a graduate of Woman's Medical College in Philadelphia, and head of the hospital at Ngucheng. Some missionary, thousands of miles from his natural habitat, carried an ember, and with it blessed the world.

Not every member of the church will operate in the same way as his brethren. Some can teach the gospel verbally, others will have to carry Christian literature. Still others will carry machines on which the gospel has been recorded by other voices. Yet others will perform a ministry of medicine in the care of the sick. Others will become involved in a welfare ministry that includes attention to economic problems. The important thing is to become involved.

The world has become a neighborhood, thanks to communications, and has shrunk to the point that no man is an island, and no man can walk alone. We have now, in a very real sense, become a community. The question is: Will it be a Christian

371

community? The Christian's answer is: I shall not rest until I have at least exposed the world to the love of Christ. "Ye are my witnesses" (Isaiah 43:10).

But we are not alone in this awesome task. "Ye shall receive power, after that the Holy Ghost is come upon you: and ye shall be witnesses unto me both in Jerusalem, and in all Judaea, and in Samaria, and unto the uttermost part of the earth" (Acts 1:8).

Yes, Christ offers the supreme power of the Godhead to anyone who will embark upon the work of soulsaving. The Holy Spirit gives us power to witness, and this witnessing testifies to the presence of the Spirit. In short, no man can possess the Spirit of the Lord in his heart and remain silent concerning the love of God. The world desperately needs the message of salvation. It needs the reassurance that comes with a message of love. It is divine love that makes a saint out of the sinner. It is the lack of awareness of being loved that makes men delinquents. This insecurity reflects itself in aggressiveness on the part of the unloved. Therefore, at least in part, the fractious relationship now existing between men and nations may be directly attributable to the slow spread of the gospel. "Ye are the salt of the earth" (Matthew 5:13), Jesus said. Then let us become the true preservers of the earth by sowing the seeds of the gospel in the hearts of men—all men everywhere—for therein is the hope of the world.

Yes, "Go tell it on the mountain, over the hill and everywhere; Go tell it on the mountain that Jesus Christ is born."

Great day—
Great day, the righteous marching;
Great day—
God's going to build up Zion's walls.

"Great Day"

WHICH DAY is the Lord's day?

"There is therefore now no condemnation to them which are in Christ Jesus, who walk not after the flesh, but after the Spirit" (Romans 8:1).

The whole question of the observance of the Ten Commandments is rooted in love for Christ and in the desire to follow His example. The Hebrew nation provides us an example of a nation that rejected Christ despite being meticulous about obeying His laws. You see, the Bible is full of requirements as well as provisions, but to discuss a requirement independent of Biblical provision is true legalism. The question of the Lord's day resolves itself in our knowledge of, and love for, the Lord. John said, "I was in the Spirit on the Lord's day" (Revelation 1:10). Those who are in Christ Jesus will discover just which day is the Lord's day, and like John—though in a different sense—be in the spirit on that day.

Romans 8:7, 8 says: "Because the carnal mind is enmity against God: for it is not subject to the law of God, neither indeed can be. So then they that are in the flesh cannot please God." The whole problem of pleasing God is rooted in a man's state of mind. If he has a carnal mind, then he is not only against God, but refuses to be subject to the law of God. Consequently he cannot please God. But those who are in Christ Jesus are not condemned, for to be in Christ Jesus is not only to experience and enjoy transformation of heart, but also to manifest a reformation in the life. Another way of putting it is that we ought to be able to demonstrate by the way we live just what has taken place inside our hearts, and if our experiences with God are genuine and valid there will indeed be a visible manifestation of that change. Romans 8:3, 4 describes the nature of that change:

"For what the law could not do, in that it was weak through the flesh, God sending his own Son in the likeness of sinful flesh, and for sin, condemned sin in the flesh: that the righteousness of the law might be fulfilled in us, who walk not after the flesh, but after the Spirit."

You see, the righteousness of the law has to be fulfilled in us, and God sent His own Son in the likeness of sinful flesh to make this possible. So when we talk about the Lord's day, we are talking about one manifestation of inner transformation. We are talking about one bit of evidence, visible to man, that God has indeed transformed our lives and changed our hearts.

Mark 2:27 and 28 goes right to the heart of the question: "The sabbath was made for man, and not man for the sabbath: therefore the Son of man is Lord also of the sabbath." Jesus is the Son of man. He is Lord of man because He created man, and He is Lord of man because He redeemed man. Christ is not only Lord of man but Lord of the day, and that is why John the revelator referred to the Sabbath as the Lord's day. Mark identifies that day as the Sabbath. What Mark writes is in remarkable agreement with the Old Testament prophets. For instance, Isaiah 58:13 says: "If thou turn away thy foot from the sabbath, from doing thy pleasure *on my holy day.* . . ." You see, the Bible, Old and New Testaments, identifies the seventh-day Sabbath as the Lord's holy day. This is in agreement with the fourth commandment, which says, "Remember the sabbath day, to keep it holy. Six days shalt thou labour, and do all thy work: but the seventh day is the sabbath of the Lord thy God" (Exodus 20:8-10). So once again we are face to face with the Sabbath, the Lord's day. God calls it "my holy day." He says it is the Sabbath of the Lord thy God, and Mark says that the Son of man is Lord also of the Sabbath.

There should be no problem, then, in identifying which day is the Sabbath day, for the Sabbath commandment itself identifies it—"the seventh day is the sabbath of the Lord thy God." We can go back to the Genesis story of Creation to find which day is the seventh day. You can read the story in the first two chapters of Genesis: In six days God created Himself a world. He made light, He made the firmament, He separated the waters from the dry land, caused vegetation to appear, He made the sun, moon, and stars, the fish of the sea, the fowl of the air, He made man, He made woman, and He made the beasts of the earth. Thus Creation was finished, and the world was a place of perfection and beauty.

In Genesis 2:2, 3, we come face to face with the first blessed day in all human history: "And on the seventh day God ended his work which he had made; and he rested on the seventh day from all his work which he had made.

"And God *blessed the seventh day,* and sanctified it: because that in it he had rested from all his work which God created and made."

It does not say that God blessed the Sabbath as an institution. Had He done that, one day of the week could be the Sabbath as well as another. But there is only one day in the week that can ever be the seventh day, and that is the seventh day. The Bible says that God blessed *the seventh day,* and that is why, when we discover which day the seventh day is, we would recognize it as the unchangeable, immovable Lord's day of all human history. That seventh day of Creation week is the same seventh day of the week that we know. It is the Sabbath of the Lord, and thus the only day the Bible knows as the Lord's day.

But how can we be sure, absolutely sure, that the day we now call Saturday is the true seventh day of the week? In the third chapter of Ecclesiastes, verses 14 and 15, we read: "I know that, whatsoever God doeth, it shall be for ever: nothing can be put to it, nor any thing taken from it: and God doeth it, that men should fear before him. That which hath been is now; and that which is to be hath already been; and God requireth that which is past."

Genesis tells us that God made the seven days of the week and set them in their sequential order, and Ecclesiastes says that whatever God does is done forever. Someone may ask: "But what about the calendar? Hasn't the calendar been changed?" Yes, the calendar has been changed, more than once. But such changes affected the date—the day of the month—but not the sequence of the days of the week. Man made the calendar, but

376

the Bible says that God made the week, and that what God does remains forever. He never gave man permission to tamper with the week.

In Genesis 2 God gave man the privilege of naming everything He created—every beast of the field, every fowl of the air. He created the elephant, but let man name it. He made the first day of the week and allowed man—centuries later, of course—to name it "Sun's day," or Sunday. He made the second day and man called it "Moon's day," or Monday. He made the third day and man named it "Tiu's day," or Tuesday. He made the fourth day and man named it "Woden's day," or Wednesday. He made the fifth day and man called it "Thor's day," or Thursday. He made the sixth day and man called it "Frigg's day," or Friday. He made the seventh day, and called it His own Sabbath day, though men later named it "Saturn's day." That is what "Saturday" means.

The seventh day of the week is, without question or quibble, the day God has commanded men to observe. He said, "Remember the sabbath day, to keep it holy." At this point someone asks, If Saturday is the true Sabbath of the Lord, how did men ever begin to keep Sunday with such startling unanimity around the world? History has not been silent on this question. Very few people have taken the pains to look it up, but it is right there to read and understand.

According to Luke 4:16, 31, Saturday was the day on which Christ worshiped. It was the day the apostles used as their weekly day of worship and spiritual refreshment (Acts 13:42-44; 17:1, 2; 18:4). As late as A.D. 125 there was only one day of worship for the Christian and that was Saturday, the seventh day, called by the Bible "the Lord's day." It is the day John referred to when he said, "I was in the Spirit on the Lord's day."

In A.D. 125 a man named Sixtus, out of his love for Christ and the resurrection of the Lord, proposed that an annual holiday be observed in honor of the resurrection. This proposal was accepted and rather widely observed, but in A.D. 200, seventy-five years later, a man by the name of Victor decided that not enough people were observing the yearly Sunday in honor of the resurrection of the Lord and proposed that civil and ecclesiastical penalties be imposed on anyone failing to observe it. This, of course, brought more people into the fold, and somewhere between A.D. 200 and A.D. 321, this annual observance of the resurrection became a weekly observance.

In A.D. 321 Emperor Constantine decreed a total public rest from work for all but farmers on the first day of the week. This was the first civil Sunday law ever passed. Successive church councils imposed more and more burdens on those who would keep the seventh day as the Sabbath, and extended more and more privileges to those who observed the first day of the week. In an address to the Council of Trent the Archbishop of Reggio said that tradition is of equal force with Scripture, and used as an example the fact that men had been able to substitute Sunday as the day of worship for the true Sabbath of the Lord, and that this substitution was then universally accepted.

This is the history of how Sunday became a universally respected day of worship, and how Saturday, the seventh day of the week, has been relegated to relative obscurity. But the Word of the living God will stand forever, and throughout history there have always been men and women who have clung tenaciously to the Sabbath of the Bible, the Lord's day of the New Testament.

Today on a round world there are millions of men and women who look to the Lord as their Saviour and who still observe the Sabbath of the fourth commandment of the Decalogue.

Nineteen hundred years ago Jesus said: "If ye love me, keep my commandments" (John 14:15). It is out of love and esteem and respect for Him who loved us first, and who on a cruel Roman cross paid with His life for our sins; it is out of respect for Him that whatever He tells the loving child of God to do, he does it. It is this love that brings our lives into conformity to His righteous law. I used to sing a little song when I was a small boy:

> 'Tis love that makes us happy,
> 'Tis love that smooths the way;
> It helps us mind, it makes us kind
> To others ev'ry day.

Love brings the life into harmony with the revealed will of God.

Nearly twenty-eight years ago I was alone and apparently friendless in the city of Toledo, Ohio. I attended a Sabbath church service and noticed one of the elders staring at me intently. Later, at the door, he took me aside and asked my name. When I told him, he asked me, "Are you Bill Cleveland's son?" I told him I was.

He said, "Where are you living?"

I said, "I don't have a place to live."

"What do you do for food?"

"I don't have any food," I told him.

He said, "Then you come to my house, for anyone who is a son of Bill Cleveland's is a friend of mine, and I'll do anything for him."

This man respected me because of my father and treated me with kindness because years before he had received kindness from my father. The Sabbath is the Lord's day, and I respect it because it is the Lord's, and I respect Him.

"Blessed is the man that doeth this, and the son of man that layeth hold on it; that keepeth the sabbath from polluting it, and keepeth his hand from doing any evil. . . . Even unto them will I give in mine house and within my walls a place and a name better than of sons and of daughters: I will give them an everlasting name, that shall not be cut off. . . . Even them will I bring to my holy mountain, and make them joyful in my house of prayer: their burnt offerings and their sacrifices shall be accepted upon mine altar; for mine house shall be called an house of prayer for all people" (Isaiah 56:2-7).

"Great Change"

WHEN GOD created the world He placed the Sabbath day at the end of the week as the cornerstone of that Creation. Man, created on Friday, the day before, was the beneficiary of everything God made. Jesus said, "The sabbath was made for man, and not man for the sabbath: therefore the Son of man is Lord also of the sabbath" (Mark 2:27, 28). Just as the vegetation, the water, the light, and the air were all made for man's benefit, so on the last day of the week God gave man a day for rest and spiritual refreshment, that he might remember the goodness of God.

God put the Sabbath at the end of the week as a perpetual memorial to the creative and redemptive power of God. Said the wise man, "I know that, whatsoever God doeth, it shall be for ever: nothing can be put to it, nor any thing taken from it: and God doeth it, that men should fear before him. That which hath been is now; and that which is to be hath already been;

381

and God requireth that which is past" (Ecclesiastes 3:14, 15). What God has done man cannot undo. In the beginning He created the birds, the beasts, the vegetation, the atmosphere, light, planets—and all these things are still here for God placed them here. Thus it is with the Sabbath, the memorial of Creation.

The seventh day He designated as the Sabbath, the day of rest and worship, a day of joy and gladness, a memorial of the creative power of the great beneficent Father of all mankind. The seventh day of the week is still God's Sabbath day. It is "the Lord's day."

During the time of John a Roman emperor would visit a city, and thereafter the day of his visit was proclaimed a holiday —because the emperor was considered lord of the people. This is apparently the background of John's declaration, "I was in the Spirit on the Lord's day." That Saturday as the Sabbath is the Lord's day is further attested by the Sabbath commandment itself: "Remember the sabbath day, to keep it holy. Six days shalt thou labour, and do all thy work: but the seventh day is the sabbath of the Lord thy God" (Exodus 20:8-10). In fact, in all of the Bible the only day designated as the Lord's day is the Sabbath, Saturday, the seventh day of the week.

The first occurrence of the expression "the Lord's day" in reference to Sunday is in the apocryphal Gospel of Peter about A.D. 150. By that time the last Bible writer had died, and the inspired portions of Scripture had already been completed. That Saturday was the Sabbath as late as New Testament times is expressly clear from the following passages of Scripture: "And now when the even was come, because it was the preparation, that is, the day before the Sabbath" (Mark 15:42). If the day of the crucifixion and the preparation which the world recognizes as Good Friday was the day before the Sabbath, then Saturday was the Sabbath day in New Testament times.

The following passage locates the Sabbath from a different point of view: "And when the sabbath was past, Mary Magdalene, and Mary the mother of James, and Salome, had bought sweet spices, that they might come and anoint him. And very early in the morning the first day of the week, they came unto the sepulchre at the rising of the sun" (Mark 16:1, 2).

These two verses clearly indicate that the first day of the week comes after the Sabbath is past, and verse 9 makes it clear that the first day of the week is the day of the resurrection. So the resurrection day follows the Sabbath, and the Bible calls the Sabbath the "Lord's day."

But why do most Christians go to church on Sunday? It will interest you to know that the Bible predicted that this day would come. In Daniel 7:25 we read: "And he shall speak great words against the most High, and shall wear out the saints of the most High, and think to change times and laws: and they shall be given into his hand until a time and times and the dividing of time."

This text predicts the rise of a power on earth that would speak against God and try to change His law, and that is exactly what history reports as taking place. The first evidence of Sunday observance by Christians occurred under Sixtus, a bishop of Rome, about A.D. 125. But the occasion was an annual observance of Easter. Easter comes once a year, near the beginning of spring. By that time Christians had formed the habit of celebrating annually, in the spring, the memorable closing events of the life of Christ. Christ was crucified on Friday and died about the time of the slaying of the Jewish Passover lamb.

383

It became a tradition among early Christians, both Jew and Gentile, to celebrate the crucifixion of Christ at the time of the Passover season. But this was also once a year. For this practice there was no Biblical authorization; it was simply a custom that developed into a tradition. During New Testament times all Christians observed the Saturday Sabbath as the weekly day of worship (Acts 18:4; 13:42-44; 17:1, 2). But the Roman bishops decided to emphasize the celebration that honored the resurrection in place of emphasizing the crucifixion. Their celebration would thus not coincide exactly with the Jewish Passover on the 15th of Nisan. Also, Rome insisted that the celebration always be on Sunday, the first day of the week, regardless of the exact date. The church of Rome won out in this endeavor, and the reasons are not hard to find:

The Jews had always been opposed to Christianity. They had rejected Christ when He was on earth. They had brought about His crucifixion at the hands of the Romans, and had tried to discredit the fact of His resurrection. So it was easy to argue against a seemingly Jewish tradition such as the celebration of the crucifixion. Also, because the Jews seemed constantly to be in revolt against Rome, and because the Romans considered Christianity a Jewish sect, and thus presumably a threat to the empire, Gentile Christians sought in every way possible to dissociate themselves from Judaism. Thus in A.D. 125 Bishop Sixtus of Rome decreed the annual observance of the resurrection. About A.D. 200 Bishop Victor caused to be excommunicated any man who refused to observe the annual Easter. In time the day of the resurrection became so popular that the annual observance became a weekly one. It should be noted that the observance of the seventh-day Saturday Sabbath continued right along through this period. The Roman church and state from this point forward united in trying to stamp out the Saturday Sabbath and to establish Sunday as the Lord's day. Daniel the prophet was right when he said that the Roman power would "think to change times and laws." The word "think" clearly indicates that this power would try to change the law but implies that he could not really do so. "I know that, whatsoever God doeth, it shall be for ever" (Ecclesiastes 3:14). Remember? After A.D. 321 church laws began to multiply, as the Roman clergy sought to push the Sabbath further and further into the background and to exalt the weekly Sunday as the day to be observed. This activity reached its climax at the Council of Trent when the Archbishop of Reggio made his famous speech, declaring tradition to be of equal authority with the Scriptures.

To further illustrate the attitude of the Church of Rome toward the Sabbath, as late as A.D. 600, we quote Pope Gregory of Rome in Book Thirteen of his epistles, Letter One, in which he says in great bitterness of soul: "It has come to my ears that certain men of perverse spirit have sown among you some things that are wrong and opposed to the holy faith so as to forbid any work being done on the Sabbath day. What else can I call these but preachers of antichrist." Preachers of antichrist indeed! Was Paul a preacher of antichrist? The Bible says he went into the synagogue every Sabbath day. Was Christ against Himself? Luke 4:16, 31 indicates that He went into the synagogues on the Sabbath day as a matter of custom. No, it is not anti-Christian to remember the Sabbath day to keep it holy.

The Church of Rome has made no secret of its efforts to change the Sabbath, and writers of church history clearly indicate that we may look to Rome as the reason most people observe

Sunday today. It was at the Roman Church's Council of Laodicea late in the fourth century that Christians were admonished not to work on Sunday and forbidden to be idle on the Sabbath.

In his commentary on the Psalms the church historian Eusebius writes: "All things whatsoever that it was the duty to do on the Sabbath, these we have transferred to the Lord's day as more appropriately belonging to it because it has a precedence and is first in rank and more honorable than the Jewish Sabbath."

Thus man transferred all the solemn injunctions the Scriptures apply to the seventh-day Saturday Sabbath, to Sunday. But, thank God, not everybody bowed the knee to this human ordinance. Christians in scattered parts of Europe held onto the Sabbath of the Bible. They recognized that though man had changed, God had not. "For I am the Lord, I change not" (Malachi 3:6). As late as the fifth century Socrates says in his book, *Ecclesiastical History,* book 5, chapter 22, "For although almost all churches throughout the world celebrate the sacred mysteries on the sabbath of every week, yet the Christians of Alexandria and at Rome, on account of some ancient tradition, have ceased to do this."

Finally the day came when the religious persecution in Europe grew so intense that many people sought to escape to other parts of the world. Some of them reached the far-off shores of what is now the United States of America. They brought with them Sundaykeeping and established it as a part of the laws of the States. In New England men were publicly flogged for working on Sunday. It is ironic that while fleeing from persecution of a religious nature in Europe, they would install their own special brand of it in the new world. It is to our everlasting credit that our national Constitution forbade legislation on matters of religion, and those Sunday blue laws were eventually repealed.

On a hot day in August, 1619, a ship appeared off the coast of Jamestown, Virginia, with twenty black people from Africa. They were sold to the colonists in exchange for some New England rum and silverware. These slaves were the first black men to inhabit the North American continent. We have the names of three of them: Anthony, Petro, and Isabella. Anthony married Isabella, and the first black child born in America was their son. As it was the custom of the white inhabitants to observe Sunday, they taught this to the new black people who had arrived, and they were allowed to observe at least a portion of Sunday as a religious day of worship. As the continent was populated, the custom of Sunday observance followed and the slave taught his children to observe Sunday. Thus respect for that day was passed down from generation to generation, until today very few people know how the custom began. And once again Sunday laws are being enacted in some of the States of the United States of America. There are laws that prohibit the selling of certain drugs and the performing of certain services on Sunday even now. Will history repeat itself? Let us pray that it will not.

In closing let us turn our attention once again to the true Sabbath of the Lord. In spite of all the religious and political pressures against it, the Word of God has stood, and the true Sabbath of the Lord has not been blotted out. The fourth commandment of the Decalogue still says, "The seventh day is the sabbath." A casual glance at your calendar will clearly indicate that the seventh day is Saturday.

Thousands of men and women around the world are hearing this message and accepting it, embracing it with all their hearts. In at least one hundred and ninety-three countries of the earth you will find men and women still observing the true Sabbath of the Lord, the Sabbath of Creation, the Sabbath of all the Old Testament prophets, the day on which Christ Himself worshiped while He was on earth, the day all the apostles of the New Testament period kept. One day they will receive the blessing pronounced by Isaiah in the fifty-sixth chapter of his book: "Blessed is the man that doeth this, and the son of man that layeth hold on it; that keepeth the Sabbath from polluting it, and keepeth his hand from doing any evil. . . . Even unto them will I give in mine house and within my walls a place and a name better than of sons and of daughters: I will give them an everlasting name, that shall not be cut off. . . . Even them will I bring to my holy mountain, and make them joyful in my house of prayer: their burnt offerings and their sacrifices shall be accepted upon mine altar; for mine house shall be called an house of prayer for all people" (verses 2-7).

I'm going to sing and never get tired;
I'm going to sing and never get tired,
One of these days.

"Sing and Never Get Tired"

EVERYBODY wants to be happy.

Everything we do is in search for some form of satisfaction. The Bible holds the key to happiness. Jesus said, "These things I have spoken unto you, that in me ye might have peace" (John 16:33). The Author of happiness must operate within the human heart or there can be no genuine, lasting, deep-down satisfaction.

Let us read how the wisest man who ever lived searched for happiness. Let us see how he failed, and there will be no need for us to repeat his mistakes.

"And I gave my heart to seek and search out by wisdom concerning all things that are done under heaven," he wrote, "this sore travail hath God given to the sons of man to be exercised therewith. I have seen all the works that are done under the sun; and, behold, all is vanity and vexation of spirit" (Ecclesiastes 1:13, 14).

You see, we have picked a prime subject to study. Here is a man who examined everything done under the heavens. Let us follow this man in his exciting search for happiness and see if he found it.

In Ecclesiastes 7:29 Solomon tells us what he discovered: "Lo, this only have I found, that God hath made man upright; but they have sought out many inventions." You see, God made man upright, God made man happy, God placed within man natural satisfaction, rest of soul, and peace of mind. But man sought out many inventions—sinful practices, that is—and developed substitute sources of happiness that bring no permanent satisfaction.

Now Solomon, in his search, built a Temple for God. He thought that if he built this Temple it would somehow give him satisfaction, peace of mind, and rest of soul. So he built it (1 Kings 5). But, you know, he wasn't happy after all. As a matter of fact, he says of his vast construction projects, "I hated life" (Ecclesiastes 2:17). It is possible to have your name on a church roll; but if your relationship with Christ isn't what it ought to be, you're not going to be happy, for all happiness is rooted in our relationship with Christ. As someone put it: Going to a garage doesn't make a man an automobile, neither does going to church make a man a Christian. We become Christians by entering into a living relationship with Christ. When He comes into the heart, takes control of the life, digs deep into the inner man, and removes the root causes of apostasy and transgression—then we find peace.

Then Solomon thought he would try something else. We read in 1 Kings 4:22 and 23, that he attempted what a lot of people are trying today, but he didn't derive any more happiness from this than he had from building a church. He tried food. He said, "If I could just fill my stomach with everything to satisfy the taste, certainly I would be happy." We read that Solomon's provisions for one day were "thirty measures of fine flour, and threescore measures of meal, ten fat oxen, and twenty oxen out of the pastures, and an hundred sheep, besides harts, and roe-bucks, and fallowdeer, and fatted fowl" (verses 22, 23). What a feast! Certainly enough to delight any man, to satisfy any man's appetite and craving. But not so. After he had all that to choose from he said he hated his life. About all he got out of it was a bad case of indigestion. He made the interesting discovery that happiness does not reside in the stomach. It is a matter of the heart, a state of mind, and you do not feed the mind through the stomach.

Well, he failed to find lasting satisfaction with food as he had failed by building a temple, so he set out to try something else. We read about it in Ecclesiastes 2:1: "I said in mine heart, Go to now, I will prove thee with mirth, therefore enjoy pleasure: and, behold, this also is vanity." He decided to paint the town red. If there were nightclubs in those days, he probably decided to go to them. He had comedians come in and tickle his sense of humor. He tried everything—pleasure, money, laughter—but he discovered that when he finished laughing all he had had was a bit of emotional exercise, and the gloom began to settle around his heart again. The cloud came over, obscuring the sun, and he was an unhappy man. All of this, he said, is vanity.

He said, "I know what I'll do. I'll get away from it all. I'll go out to the farm, and do a little farming. The devil is in the cities; I'm going to the country." So we read in Ecclesiastes 2:4-6: "I made me great works; I builded me houses; I planted me vineyards: I made me gardens and orchards, and I planted trees in them of all kind of fruits: I made me pools of water, to water therewith the wood that bringeth forth trees." All of this he did, but in Ecclesiastes 2:17 he said again, "I hated life."

He tasted the fruits of royal living, but he found all of it vanity and vexation of spirit.

He built a temple and that wasn't it; he tried food, and that didn't satisfy him; he tried all kinds of high living, and that didn't help; he planted a farm, and that didn't do it.

"I know what I'll do," he said, and in Ecclesiastes 2:7 we discover what he did. "I got me servants and maidens, and had servants born in my house; also I had great possessions of great and small cattle above all that were in Jerusalem before me." Now that's supposed to make a man happy—to have someone wait on him. He doesn't have to do any work. He doesn't even have to put on his clothes in the morning. There is someone to bathe him, someone to feed him. What Solomon discovered is what we already know, and that is that there certainly is no satisfaction in idleness. Peace of mind does not come from sitting around doing nothing and having everybody wait on you. "I hated life; . . . all is vanity and vexation of spirit," he said.

Then in Ecclesiastes 2:8 he tried something else: "I gathered me also silver and gold, and the peculiar treasure of kings and of the provinces: I gat me men singers and women singers, and the delights of the sons of men, as musical instruments, and that of all sorts." Money and music! Money to satisfy his needs and music to soothe his emotions. He found while counting his shekels what he tells us in Ecclesiastes 5:10: "He that loveth silver shall not be satisfied with silver; nor he that loveth abundance with increase: this is also vanity."

If there is a poor man reading this, don't worry about getting rich. That is not going to bring you happiness. If you are unhappy while you're poor, you will be unhappy while you are rich. The poor man is worried about getting money, and the rich man is worried about keeping what he has and getting more; so there's no satisfaction with money. All is vanity and vexation of spirit. If you have enough to live on, be content. It's no sin to be rich, but there's certainly no satisfaction in it.

As for music, he called in his orchestra. He had men singers, women singers—all of this to bring satisfaction and peace of mind. But it didn't work. So he decided to turn to women. We read the tragic story in 1 Kings 11:3, 2: "And he had seven hundred wives, princesses, and three hundred concubines: and his wives turned away his heart." "Of the nations concerning which the Lord said unto the children of Israel, Ye shall not go in to them, neither shall they come in unto you: for surely they will turn away your heart after their gods."

Solomon went into immoral living on a scale that no other record surpasses. He wound up with a thousand women, and they turned his heart away from God. Of course, he could cry out, "I hate life! All is vanity and vexation of spirit!"

Well, he tried one more thing. He tried wine. He thought he'd drown his sorrows. Ecclesiastes 2:3: "I sought in mine heart to give myself unto wine, yet acquainting mine heart with wisdom; and to lay hold on folly, till I might see what was that good for the sons of men, which they should do under the heaven all the days of their life."

The next morning, with pouches under his eyes and a heavier pouch of guilt on his heart, he said, "I hate life. All is vanity and vexation of spirit."

What then is the solution to the problem? It is found in John 16:33, the words of our text: "These things I have spoken unto you, that in me ye might have peace. In the world ye shall have tribulation: but be of good cheer; I have overcome the world."

Yes, Christ has overcome the world. We may indeed be of good cheer. He is the answer to our problem of peace of mind and rest of soul—if we'll repent of our sins and turn to Him with all our hearts, if we'll stop being self-centered, selfish human beings, if we'll give ourselves in service to God and service to our fellow men, if we'll share with others the abundance of our inheritance. If we have two coats, we will give our brother one. We will watch for human misery and do what we can to relieve it. We will stop feeding on novels and unreal fictional situations that drain us emotionally. This is the path of peace, the path to the cross, the path to the side of the Saviour. Let us find out which way God is going and go that way ourselves. Then we can expect to find peace.

Some of the happiest people in the world are poor. Some of the most miserable are rich. So look not to the building of temples or to the multiplication of food, farm, servants, money, music, women, or wine. Simply turn to the true and living God. Kneel at the cross, leave every care. Yes, let us kneel at the cross, for Jesus will meet us there. True happiness comes with daily surrender of the will to Christ, from putting our lives in His hands and trusting Him to do for us, to us, and through us that which is best for us. Then the troubled subsurfaces of the soul assume a heavenly, mysterious quiet, a calm that remains undisturbed in the midst of trouble; a quiet that is rooted in faith in Christ. Said the poet: "There is a place of quiet rest,

Near to the heart of God, A place where sin cannot molest, Near to the heart of God."

Wrote the prophet Isaiah: "O that thou hadst hearkened to my commandments! then had thy peace been as a river, and thy righteousness as the waves of the sea" (Isaiah 48:18).

There can be no peace of mind for a man with a guilty conscience, and the heaviness of the heart can only be lifted through sincere, repentant prayer. Day by day we must roll our burdens and sins upon the Lord and allow Him to take them. Freely we must yield them to Him. Such a course will pave the highway of our lives with the sweet fragrance of peace and happiness.

Soon one morning
Death came creeping in my room.
O, my Lord, what shall I do?

"*Soon One Morning*"

WHAT IS a man's soul? Is it an invisible man within a man? Does the soul live on after the body dies? The Bible clearly answers all these questions, and we dedicate this chapter to its answer.

As to the definition of the word *soul,* Genesis 2:7 gives us the most comprehensive one that can be found anywhere. "And the Lord God formed man of the dust of the ground, and breathed into his nostrils the breath of life; and man became a living soul." If someone should ask me what is the soul of a man, my answer would be that man himself is a soul, for the Bible says "man became a living soul." We acknowledge this in everyday speech. If you see an older person walking along, deformed or carrying a heavy burden, you say, "Poor old soul," and this is true. It is Biblically true.

The only thing God put into man after forming him from the dust of the ground was breath, that is, life. The Bible says,

397

"If a man die, shall he live again?" Job answers: "I know that my redeemer liveth, and that . . . in my flesh shall I see God."

"The Lord God . . . breathed into his nostrils the breath of life" (Genesis 2:7). God did not put a soul into man. All He put in was the breath of life that we breathe in and out every day. This is the only new element He inserted into His newly formed man. The Bible calls the breath "spirit" in Job 27:3: "The spirit of God is in my nostrils." This is repeated in Isaiah 2:22. The Hebrew term for spirit is used 378 times, but never once is the spirit said to be immortal. The Bible usually refers either to a man's breath or to his attitudes. Three hundred and eighty-five times the Greek word for spirit is used, and never is this spirit said to be immortal or not subject to death.

The first great Bible fact about the soul is that the soul is mortal. It is subject to death, as we read in Ezekiel 18:4: "Behold, all souls are mine; as the soul of the father, so also the soul of the son is mine: the soul that sinneth, it shall die." "For all have sinned, and come short of the glory of God" (Romans 3:23). "For the wages of sin is death; but the gift of God is eternal life through Jesus Christ our Lord" (chapter 6:23).

Proverbs 6:32 says, "But whoso committeth adultery with a woman lacketh understanding: he that doeth it destroyeth his own soul." The soul can die. The soul can be destroyed. The soul is never referred to in the Bible as being immortal.

One popular old song sung by many sincere Christians is simply not true according to the Bible. It says:

> A charge to keep I have,
> A God to glorify,
> A never-dying soul to save,
> And fitted for the sky.

We do not have never-dying souls. The soul that sins shall *die*. And all souls have sinned. When a soul dies, is it really dead? Is it dangerous to go through the graveyard at twelve o'clock at night? When a man is dead, is there a spirit from the man that can come back to haunt the living? What does the Bible say about death?

Psalm 146:4 describes death thus: "His breath goeth forth, he returneth to his earth; in that very day his thoughts perish." Now that's really all there is to the man—his breath, his thoughts, and his body. This constitutes the living soul. It is this man, this soul, that dies, and these three things happen in death. According to Ecclesiastes 9:5, 6, "The living know that they shall die: but the dead know not any thing, neither have they any more a reward; for the memory of them is forgotten. Also their love, and their hatred, and their envy, is now perished; neither have they any more a portion for ever in any thing that is done under the sun."

Or take verse 10: "Whatsoever thy hand findeth to do, do it with thy might; for there is no work, nor device, nor knowledge, nor wisdom, in the grave, whither thou goest." This text even tells the dead man where he is headed. It says we are headed for the grave. We neither love nor hate; we are neither wise nor unwise after we are dead. All of this comes while we are still alive.

Then read Ecclesiastes 3:20: "All go unto one place; all are of the dust, and all turn to dust again." You see, when a man dies, he is altogether *dead*. Period. The only thing that leaves his body is the life God originally put into him, and when you put a man in the grave, all of the man is in the grave. He is not in heaven, praising the Lord, if he is a Christian, and he is not in hell, being roasted by the devil, if he is a sinner. The Bible says that when a man dies he goes to the grave.

399

Job raises the question, "If a man die, shall he live again?" Then he answers his own question: "All the days of my appointed time will I wait, till my change come" (Job 14:14). Two things are pointed out here. 1. If a man dies he *will* live again. 2. But he will have to wait until his change comes. The change is not instantaneous with death. There is a cessation of life at death. Man is mortal, which simply means that he can die. Death is not a friend but an enemy, according to 1 Corinthians 15:26. If a man's soul went to heaven when he died, then death would be a friend, for it would deliver a man from this world into the immediate presence of God. But according to the Bible, that is not what happens. Death cuts off life at the point that life leaves the body. Death is a cessation of life, and therefore death is an enemy. When we read in 1 Corinthians 15:26 that the last enemy to be destroyed is death, let us understand the nature of this enemy. It is not the entrance into the land of fadeless day; it is not a commencement of a new life on a higher plane; it is not fellowship with angels and with Jesus and with the spirits of departed saints, as we've heard for so many years. Death cuts off life, and the body goes to the grave.

1 Timothy 6:16 clearly states that only God has immortality. Only God is not subject to death. All of His created creatures are, especially those who have sinned against Him. Death is their sure lot. Hebrews 9:27, 28 says it is appointed unto all men once to die and after that the judgment.

Yes, the Grim Reaper with his icy fingers is scheduled to visit every life, and it is our solemn duty and responsibility to live with reference to death, to live knowing we must die, for it is appointed unto all men once to die. The Bible speaks of death as water being spilled upon the ground, which cannot be gathered up again (2 Samuel 14:14). It speaks of death as seed being planted in the earth, where it dies before it brings forth again—wheat, corn, tomatoes, or what have you. The seed must die before it can yield its best fruit.

But there will be a gathering up again, and this is the good news. I would be remiss as a minister of the gospel if I did not point out that just as death is sure, the resurrection from the dead is also sure. In Job 19:23-27 we read, "Oh that my words were now written! oh that they were printed in a book! That they were graven with an iron pen and lead in the rock for ever! For I know that my redeemer liveth, and that he shall stand at the latter day upon the earth: and though after my skin worms destroy this body, yet in my flesh shall I see God: whom I shall see for myself, and mine eyes shall behold, and not another; though my reins be consumed within me." It is wonderful to know that one day our loved ones will rise from the grave that now constitutes their prison, that this corruptible shall put on incorruption, that this mortal shall put on immortality, and that death is not the end but a mere resting from one's labors. It is the time between the cessation of life and the return of the Life-giver. It is that rest from toil, surcease from suffering. Death is an enemy, yet relief from the trials of this life comes with the approach of this enemy.

Oh, but what a glorious day it will be when the dead are raised to life! Job says he knows that his Redeemer lives. He ties the fact of the resurrection to the fact of the death of Jesus Christ, for it was His death that accomplished our redemption. It was the shedding of His blood that opened before the sinner a great and effectual door. It was His suffering, bleeding, and dying for my sins that inspires hope, that implants faith, that creates confidence, and that gives me and all who read these blessed words reasons for living.

I would appeal to each reader to have faith in God. Believe in Him. You can trust Him. He has never told a lie, and He has never let His followers down. He has certified His love by the shedding of His blood. He has authenticated His promises by the giving of His life. Even as He rose from the dead, in that very fact there is promise that we who go down to the grave shall rise again. Meanwhile the Grim Reaper continues to take his toll.

I am a poor pilgrim of sorrow,
Tossed in this wide world alone;
No hope have I for tomorrow;
I've started to make heaven my home.

"A City Called Heaven"

"HERE HAVE WE no continuing city, but we seek one to come" (Hebrews 13:14). Yes, there are better days ahead!

Our present insecurity in this world makes it necessary that we pin our hopes on something more stable, permanent, lasting. Thousands of years of human history clearly indicate that there has been no such thing as a permanent civilization on this earth. Powerful races have arisen, established themselves and their cultures with a view to never-ending domination, only to be torn apart either by internal dissension or invasion from without. Archeologists have unearthed irrefutable proof that anything to which man sets his hand is temporary. It will pass away.

This hope for a better world has been shared throughout the ages by believers in the true and living God. Abraham "looked for a city which hath foundations, whose builder and maker is God" (chapter 11:10).

403

In our anticipation of a better world we should not neglect this present one, but hope of life in the hereafter should make us better here. This was shown in the life of Abraham, for when invading armies conquered Sodom and Gomorrah and took his closest friends and relatives away as captives, Abraham assembled an army and recaptured not only his friends and relatives but the spoils that had been taken. Abraham was a prosperous cattleman. His was a bountiful herd. He was also a great statesman. He was very much interested in the here and now, but as he went about his daily tasks he was inspired by a preoccupation with the world to come. Yes, Abraham looked for a city which hath foundations, whose builder and maker is God.

A young man came to me before my sermon on this subject in a certain city, wanting to know, if there is such a city, where it is. Of course, I pointed upward to the sky. "Well," he said skeptically, "when is up down and down up? This world is a sphere, and it is in constant motion. It revolves on its own axis, and it orbits the sun. So there are times when down is up and up is down. Now, where is the city?" he demanded.

"Well, the best I can do for you," I said to him, "is to turn to the Scriptures." I read from Acts 1:11: "Ye men of Galilee, why stand ye gazing up into heaven? this same Jesus, which is taken up from you into heaven, shall so come in like manner as ye have seen him go into heaven."

When Jesus left the earth, He went to that city, and the Bible says that He went up into heaven, simply stating that He left the earth. In Hebrews 1:3 we read that after He left the earth, "he . . . sat down on the right hand of the Majesty on high." "Now of the things which we have spoken this is the sum: We have such an high priest, who is set on the right hand of the throne of the Majesty in the heavens. A minister of the sanctuary, and of the true tabernacle, which the Lord pitched, and not man" (Hebrews 8:1, 2). "Christ is not entered into the holy places made with hands, which are the figures of the true; but into heaven itself, now to appear in the presence of God for us" (chapter 9:24).

From these passages it is clear that when Christ left the earth He went to that city, and furthermore, He tells us why—in John 14:2, 3: "I go to prepare a place for you. And if I go and prepare a place for you, I will come again, and receive you unto myself; that where I am, there ye may be also." And in that same text He refers to that city as "my Father's house."

But what of the city itself? Has anybody ever seen it? What is it like? Hebrews 11:16 says, "But now they desire a better country, that is, an heavenly: wherefore God is not ashamed to be called their God: for he hath prepared for them a city." The apostle John, who wrote the Revelation, says, "And I John saw the holy city, new Jerusalem, coming down from God out of heaven, prepared as a bride adorned for her husband" (Revelation 21:2).

So the city *is* out there. It was prepared by God and is called the dwelling place of God, and that is exactly where Jesus is now, preparing a place for us.

Not only does the Bible say that the city is there, but it has given many of the measurements. As to its size, Revelation 21:16 says, "And the city lieth foursquare, and the length is as large as the breadth: and he measured the city with the reed, twelve thousand furlongs." The city is a perfect square. Its circumference is twelve thousand furlongs, or about fifteen hundred miles. A furlong is one eighth of a mile. The city is a square, which means that there are three hundred and seventy-five miles along each of its four sides. In short, if that city were set down on the East Coast, large portions of the States of Ohio, Pennsylvania, West Virginia, Maryland, Virginia, and North Carolina would be covered. The city has a great wall around it. Of this we read in Revelation 21:17, 18: "And he measured the wall thereof, an hundred and forty and four cubits. . . . And the building of the wall of it was of jasper." A cubit is about eighteen inches. That would make the wall two hundred and sixteen feet high. The wall is made of solid jasper, with radiance and beauty beyond description. It is nearly twenty stories high. No wonder the slaves sang, "Oh, what a beautiful city; twelve gates to the city, four-square wide, Hallalu!"

There were twelve gates to the city according to John's description in Revelation 21: It had "twelve gates. . . . On the east three gates; on the north three gates; on the south three gates; and on the west three gates" (verses 12, 13). "And the twelve gates were twelve pearls: every several gate was of one pearl." We even know what the streets are paved with: "The street of the city was pure gold, as it were transparent glass" (verse 21). The city has foundations. We read about them in Revelation 21:14, 19, 20: "The city had twelve foundations, . . . garnished with all manner of precious stones. The first foundation was jasper; the second, sapphire; the third, a chalcedony; the fourth, an emerald; the fifth, sardonyx; the sixth, sardius; the seventh, chrysolyte; the eighth, beryl; the ninth, a topaz; the tenth, a chrysoprasus; the eleventh, a jacinth; the twelfth, an amethyst."

It is interesting to know that those who enter the city will find eternal vigor and youth, like Adam and Eve in the Garden of Eden, for we read in Revelation 22:2: "In the midst of the street of it, and on either side of the river, was there the tree of life, which bare twelve manner of fruits, and yielded her fruit every month: and the leaves of the tree were for the healing of the nations."

The language of man is too feeble to describe the glories of the world to come. In the presence of its awesome glory the pen of the poet is still. The canvas of the painter cannot reflect more than a weak facsimile of its beauty. Simply contemplating it leads us to exclaim with the apostle Peter: "Blessed be the God and Father of our Lord Jesus Christ, which according to his abundant mercy hath begotten us again unto a lively hope by the resurrection of Jesus Christ from the dead, to an inheritance incorruptible, and undefiled, and that fadeth not away, reserved in heaven for you" (1 Peter 1:3, 4).

Charles Spurgeon has said, "Land birds greeted Columbus long before his eyes saw the green coastline of the new world. Sailors feel the influence of the fresh waters of the Amazon River long before they enter the mouth of that great body of water. We are also told in history that when the northern barbarians—the Huns and the Goths—had once tasted the delicious wines of Italy, they could not rest satisfied until they themselves were quartered in that sunny land. And before Israel crossed Jordan they had the grapes of Eschol and the testimony of those who had viewed the land. Lo, too, the believer has his foretastes of heaven, and his soul is fired with resolve to go up and possess it in the strength of his God."

A little child said to her mother, "Mother, my teacher tells me that this world is only a place in which God lets us live a while that we may prepare for a better world. But, Mother, I do not see anybody preparing. I see you getting ready to go to the country and Aunt Liza preparing to come here, but I do not see anyone preparing to go to the better world. Why don't they try to get ready?"

In another incident, Ben's master died, and they told Ben he had gone to heaven. Ben shook his head and said, "I'm afraid he hasn't gone there."

"But why, Ben?" he was asked.

"Well," he said, "when my master went up north or journeyed to the springs, he talked about it a long time before he left. I never heard him talk about going to heaven, and I've never seen him getting ready to go there. That's why I know he isn't there."

You who read these pages, are you ready to go there? In your daily conversation, do you show any interest at all in the world to come? Or are you so burdened down with things transpiring here that you have lost sight of the hereafter?

Said Jesus, "Take heed to yourselves, lest at any time your hearts be overcharged with surfeiting, and drunkenness, and cares of this life, and so that day come upon you unawares. For as a snare shall it come on all them that dwell on the face of the whole earth. Watch ye therefore, and pray always, that ye may be accounted worthy to escape all these things that shall come to pass, and to stand before the Son of man" (Luke 21:35, 36).

Take me to the water
To be baptized.

"Take Me to the Water"

IS BAPTISM necessary? Mark 16:16 answers that question. "He that believeth and is baptized shall be saved; but he that believeth not shall be damned." It is clear from this text that baptism is indeed a necessity. In 1 Peter 3:21, 22 we read: "The like figure whereunto even baptism doth also now save us (not the putting away of the filth of the flesh, but the answer of a good conscience toward God,) by the resurrection of Jesus Christ: who is gone into heaven, and is on the right hand of God." "Then why be baptized?" someone asks.

This text does not mean that salvation is dependent upon baptism. As a matter of fact, in the great process of finding salvation, a man is forgiven and cleansed of his transgressions and is saved—even before his baptism by water.

As to the significance of baptism, it is, I believe, the first test of conversion. In Acts 22:16 we read, "And now why tar-

riest thou? arise, and be baptized, and wash away thy sins, calling on the name of the Lord." Baptism is the outward symbol of inward cleansing, an inward cleansing that must take place before participation in the outward symbol. Baptism also commemorates the resurrection of Christ. We read about that in Romans 6:3, 4: "Know ye not, that so many of us as were baptized into Jesus Christ were baptized into his death? Therefore we are buried with him by baptism into death: that like as Christ was raised up from the dead by the glory of the Father, even so we also should walk in newness of life."

Not only does baptism symbolize the death, burial, and resurrection of the Lord; it also symbolizes our own death and burial to sin, and our resurrection in the Lord. It is a symbol of the total program of salvation for the human being. The water symbolizes the blood, the burial (or immersion) symbolizes the entrance of Christ into the tomb and also the burial of our old man of sin. The coming up out of the water not only symbolizes the resurrection of Christ but the rising to walk in newness of life. Paul says, "For if we have been planted together in the likeness of his death, we shall be also in the likeness of his resurrection: knowing this, that our old man is crucified with him, that the body of sin might be destroyed, that henceforth we should not serve sin" (verses 5, 6).

You will notice that baptism even talks to us about the crucifixion. It talks about what happened that Friday as well as what happened that Sunday: "Christ was raised up from the dead by the glory of the Father" (verse 4). That talks about what happened Sunday. The words, "planted together in the likeness of his death," talk to us about what happened Friday afternoon through Saturday. "Knowing this, that our old man is crucified

411

"He that believeth and is baptized shall be saved." The Ethiopian treasurer entered upon a new life when Philip baptized him.

with him"—talks to us about what happened Friday. It teaches us that "henceforth we should not serve sin."

It is by the authority of Christ Himself that we baptize. "Go ye therefore, and teach all nations, baptizing them in the name of the Father, and of the Son, and of the Holy Ghost: teaching them to observe all things whatsoever I have commanded you: and, lo, I am with you alway, even unto the end of the world" (Matthew 28:19, 20). But before baptism you will notice there must occur the preparation of the head. "Go ye therefore, and teach." Furthermore, teach men to observe all things, whatsoever is commanded.

The man who baptizes is not authorized to do so until he has taught the candidate all the commandments and requirements, as well as the promises, of God. The candidate for baptism should know about his privileges after baptism. He just might change his mind and decide he is not ready yet. So, in all fairness, all things must be taught the man who asks baptism. If you are initiating a man into a club and fail to tell him the rules, once he gets in and finds out what the rules are, he may quit with the accusation that you didn't level with him. Something was kept hidden, and you tricked him. Christianity doesn't operate like that. The Head of Christianity said not to baptize a man until you have taught him to observe all things.

That is preparation of the head. But there must also be preparation of the heart. Peter said, "Repent, and be baptized every one of you . . . for the remission of sins, and ye shall receive the gift of the Holy Ghost" (Acts 2:38).

Proverbs 28:13 says, "He that covereth his sins shall not prosper: but whoso confesseth and forsaketh them shall have mercy." Repentance is the initial step in the preparation of the

412

heart. A man is not ready for baptism until he has repented. He is not ready for the inner as well as the outer manifestation of cleansing until in humble submission he kneels at the cross and leaves every care and unburdens himself of his load of guilt. This is repentance; this is the first requirement of the man who would be saved. Belief leads to repentance. Living faith makes a man sorry for his sins. The man who believes will bow in humble submission to God's will and will acknowledge his own sinfulness. Further, he will acknowledge his helplessness to better his own condition.

Then there is conversion. Acts 3:19 says, "Repent ye therefore, and be converted, that your sins may be blotted out, when the times of refreshing shall come from the presence of the Lord." A man must be converted before he is baptized. Baptism will never convert him. He must be forgiven under God's terms of repentance. He must be cleansed under the terms of conversion. These are inner experiences, accomplished by grace through faith in the Lord Jesus Christ. It is the Lord who applies His blood to the human heart. It is Christ who cleanses. It is Christ who converts. It is Christ who pardons. It is Christ who empowers. This is an inner work of grace done by our blessed Lord through the agency of the Holy Spirit. Once a man's head and heart have been prepared, he is then ready for baptism, that sacred symbol of inward cleansing that says to the world that the man baptized is a follower, a disciple, of Christ.

Lengthy arguments have been held about the correct method of baptism. Is it sprinkling or immersion? There was once a man who used to baptize people by turning the fire hose on two or three hundred of them in the street on a hot day! What is the Biblical requirement with reference to baptism? In Matthew 3:16 we discover that Christ was baptized by immersion, for it says He went down into the water and He came up out of the water.

The word *baptize* in the New Testament, especially in Ephesians 4:5, literally means "to immerse." One Lord, one faith, one baptism, one immersion. It literally means a burial, according to Romans 6:3 and Colossians 2:12—we are "buried with him."

In John 3:23 we read this interesting statement: "And John also was baptizing in Aenon near to Salim, because there was much water there: and they came, and were baptized." What is the need for "much water" if there is not an immersion rather than a sprinkling or a pouring taking place here? In Acts 8:38, 39 we read even further indication that Bible baptism is indeed immersion: "And he commanded the chariot to stand still: and they went down both into the water, both Philip and the eunuch; and he baptized him. And when they were come up out of the water, the Spirit of the Lord caught away Philip, that the eunuch saw him no more: and he went on his way rejoicing."

This black man was riding along in his chariot reading the fifty-third chapter of the book of Isaiah, but he understood nothing of what he read. The Spirit of the Lord led Philip to his chariot, where Philip explained to him the Word of God. Following that, Philip baptized him. The Bible makes it clear that both of them went down into the water.

My dear Christian reader, this is no real problem for a converted man. There are some people who refuse baptism out of fear. They think they are going to be drowned. May I suggest to you that in all my years of baptizing we have never had

414

a near fatality. No problem at all. The immersion is quick, almost instantaneous, when properly done. What the Christian really says is, "I'm burning all my bridges behind me. I am one with Christ, and He is one with me. I am saying by this public act that the world will never again stake its claim on my life."

As a man who had stopped drinking passed the tavern his friends said to him, "Oh, you'll be back down here. Come on in now. Take another drink." He said, "No, I've been baptized. I can't do that anymore." They all ganged up on him, threw him down, and forced the liquor bottle to his lips. But you've heard the old statement, "You can lead a horse to water, but you can't make him drink." Well, they couldn't make him drink, so they just poured it on him and left him there immersed in the foul-smelling liquid he had forsaken. As he was lying there, somebody shouted, "Well, you're all right now, but what about the future? Don't you think you'll be back down here with us?" He answered, "I don't know. But the Lord is in the future, and I'm in the Lord. I'm sure that as long as I am with Him, He'll be with me, and I'll never go back to my old habits and sins."

Baptism is a public testimony that you have fully and finally broken with the old life, and that the old man of sin is crucified with Christ, buried in the watery grave. A new man rises to walk in newness of life, a new creature in Christ Jesus. Baptism burns all the sinful bridges behind us, leaving before us the green fields of Canaan.

Let us break bread together on our knees;
Let us fall down on our knees,
With our face to the Father and Son;
O, Lord, have mercy on me.

"Break Bread Together"

"WHEREFORE THE LAW was our schoolmaster to bring us unto Christ, that we might be justified by faith. But after that faith is come, we are no longer under a schoolmaster" (Galatians 3:24, 25).

The Bible here speaks of the ceremonial system of Old Testament times as a tutor whose objective was to instruct the people in regard to the will of God and the character of Christ. In this sense it was an instrument of conversion. "The law of the Lord"—God's will as revealed in the Old Testament—"is perfect, converting the soul: the testimony of the Lord is sure, making wise the simple" (Psalm 19:7). Christ becomes our teacher, and the Bible becomes our textbook. "This is the covenant that I will make with the house of Israel after those days, saith the Lord; I will put my laws into their mind, and write them in their hearts: and I will be to them a God, and they shall be to me a people" (Hebrews 8:10).

For four thousand years the law pointed forward to the coming of Christ as man's supreme Teacher. But the Hebrew people made the law, which had been their schoolmaster for fourteen hundred years, an end in itself, and as a result of this they did not recognize the Christ toward which it had pointed for these many years. Consequently, their religion became one of legalism and spiritual oppression, and it was this against which Christ warred while on earth. Again and again He asserted Himself as the object toward which the law pointed. Standing on the porch of the Temple, watching the priests carrying their golden buckets of water during the Feast of the Tabernacles, and thereby commemorating the great miracle of the water coming from the rock during their wilderness journeys, Christ said, "If any man thirst, let him come unto me, and drink" (John 7:37). "I am the way, the truth, and the life" (John 14:6).

Christ was not fighting against the law, which He Himself had given to Israel. He was fighting against the Hebrew concept of law—obedience for obedience' sake, the old concept of "let us work our way to heaven, let us obey that we may please God." This pharisaical concept could only produce a generation of slaves. It drained all of the joy and exuberance out of Christian living. Had not God Himself declared, while Christ stood with Moses and Elijah on the Mount of Transfiguration, "This is my beloved Son . . . ; hear ye him" (Matthew 17:5)?

So, for fourteen centuries, the law was man's divinely appointed teacher, and Christ was the textbook. The teacher was to bring man to Christ. This is the meaning of the text: "The law and the prophets were until John: since that time the kingdom of God is preached, and every man presseth into it" (Luke 16:16). The meaning is clear. Until John the Baptist came, the prophets were man's only teacher about righteousness and about God. Since that time the God toward which the law pointed has made His appearance on the earth. The Word made flesh has now dwelt among men, and all the law said concerning Christ was fulfilled in Christ. The Author of the law has now come. He is the new Schoolmaster. The lesser cannot overshadow the greater. The law is but a pale reflection of the living reality of God in the flesh. This is no reflection on the moral law, which Paul describes as "holy, and just, and good" (Romans 7:12). It merely says that a book is never greater than its author, and that while the book may say much about its author, when the author comes he can always say more about himself. He will not deny what has been written in the book. He may explain it and then lead us into even deeper revelations of himself. This is exactly what Christ did.

It is to the ceremonial law of the Bible I would like to give special attention at this time. These laws pointed forward to Christ. They were a temporary expedient, in force until the Saviour should come. In a sense that is not true of any of the other laws; the ceremonial law literally functioned until Christ came, at which time all of its functions ceased. Unlike the Ten Commandments, it was written by Moses (Deuteronomy 31:24) in a book and placed in the side of the ark (verse 26). The Ten Commandments were written by God (chapter 4:12, 13) on tables of stone, and later, under the new covenant, they were to be written in the heart (Hebrews 8:10). The ceremonial law specifically enjoined the practice of certain rituals that pointed to some aspect of the ministry of Christ. Hebrews 9:9, 10 explains much of this in detail: They were "a figure for the time then present, in which were offered both gifts and sacrifices, . . .

which stood only in meats and drinks, and divers washings, and carnal ordinances, imposed on them until the time of reformation." These ordinances prefigured the life and ministry of Christ on earth for sinners. They were like a signpost hundreds of miles from a city telling the driver how far he is from the city. But once he arrives in the city, he no longer needs the signpost to point him to it. He is there. That is the meaning of Colossians 2:14: "Blotting out the handwriting of ordinances that was against us, which was contrary to us, and took it out of the way, nailing it to his cross."

To continue to offer lambs as burnt offerings and sacrifices to God in the presence of the Lamb "slain from the foundation of the world" would dishonor the Lamb of God. It is not in our interest to dally with substitutes in the presence of the genuine. It would be living a lie to be in, let us say, the city of New Orleans and fool ourselves into thinking we are one hundred miles from New Orleans. This would be contrary to our best interests, for we might begin to drive inside the city, which has a posted speed limit of thirty-five miles an hour, as though we were one hundred miles from the city with a posted speed limit of sixty-five miles an hour. This certainly would be contrary to us.

When Christ came and lived and died, the ceremonial provisions of the law died at His crucifixion. In their stead Christ instituted an ordinance that would point them back to His crucifixion, resurrection, and ministry in heaven for the Christians who would live thereafter.

"And he took bread, and gave thanks, and brake it, and gave unto them, saying, This is my body which is given for you: this do in remembrance of me. Likewise also the cup after supper,

419

saying, This cup is the new testament in my blood, which is shed for you" (Luke 22:19, 20).

Jesus not only commanded His disciples to do this, but told them also that as often as they did it they would show forth Christ's death until He comes. This ceremony inaugurated just before the crucifixion was to serve the same purpose this side of the cross as the ceremonial law served before the cross. The ceremonial law was a promise to all God-fearing people who lived before the crucifixion that Christ would one day die for their sins. The Lord's Supper says to every Christian born this side of the cross that Christ did die for man's sins. The first was a promissory note; the last, the fulfillment. Both were educational; both led men to Christ. Most of the people who lived before the cross never saw the Lord. The same is true of those who have lived since the cross. Before the cross men needed the ceremonies specified in that great law as an education, as a promise, an encouragement to look forward to the coming of the Messiah. We who live this side of the cross need the Lord's Supper to remind us that Christ did die for our sins; for our problem, like theirs before the cross, is a problem of faith in Him.

Following the supper, the Lord did something that serves as an example of humility for all succeeding generations. "He riseth from supper, and laid aside his garments; and took a towel, and girded himself. After that he poureth water into a bason, and began to wash the disciples' feet, and to wipe them with the towel wherewith he was girded" (John 13:4, 5).

"So after he had washed their feet, and had taken his garments, and was set down again, he said unto them, Know ye what I have done to you? Ye call me Master and Lord: and ye

The blessings of salvation come to humble believers when they take bread and wine, symbols of the sacrifice of Christ on Calvary.

say well; for so I am. If I then, your Lord and Master, have washed your feet; ye also ought to wash one another's feet.

"For I have given you an example, that ye should do as I have done to you" (verses 12-15).

Another problem of the human family is the problem of pride. So often differences between believers are allowed to go unresolved for years. The ordinance of humility in connection with the communion service virtually assures the sincere participant the high privilege of reconciliation with his brother. "Let us break bread together on our knees."

I'm going to walk up the milky, white way,
My Lord, some of these days.
I'm going to walk up and take my stand.
I'm going to join that Christian band.
Yes, when I walk up the milky way,
My child, one of these days.

"The Milky, White Way"

PEOPLE WHO TALK about one day leaving this world and going to another to live have become a much-maligned minority. The derision and ridicule remind one of Columbus asking for money to travel west and come back from the east, on the assumption that the world was round. At last his vision paid off, and the unbelievable became reality. In his day men thought the world was flat, and that if you sailed far enough you would simply drop off the edge. The voyage of Columbus told the world that there were vast new stretches of rich land awaiting settlement.

In the light of this discovery, is it unreasonable to believe that beyond the skies, as beyond the sea, there are other lands than these awaiting the tread of human footsteps? Those who believe this are not dreamers. Nor are they scientists in an advanced stage of preparation to establish a base on the moon from which to probe the outer universe. Man's exploration of space will at best be limited. But we know there is a city out there in space the Bible calls the New Jerusalem, and that one day the saved of earth will live there. Yes, we're going to walk up the milky, white way some of these days. In the next chapter we will examine this city in more detail.

About twenty-five years ago I was riding a bus with a traveling companion who was deeply interested in the Scriptures. He turned to me and said, "You look like a minister."

I answered, "I am."

He said, "What are you teaching people about heaven? Are you telling people they can go to heaven?"

I said, "Yes, I teach some of them that they'll go to heaven; others, that they'll go to hell."

"Well," he said, "that statement about heaven is false, for the Bible says, 'flesh and blood cannot inherit the kingdom of God,'" and he showed me 1 Corinthians 15:50.

I suggested to him that he should read on in the chapter: "Behold, I shew you a mystery; we shall not all sleep, but we shall all be changed, in a moment, in the twinkling of an eye, at the last trump: for the trumpet shall sound, and the dead shall be raised incorruptible, and we shall be changed. For this corruptible must put on incorruption, and this mortal must put on immortality" (1 Corinthians 15:51-53).

I told him that before we are taken to heaven, we will all be changed.

"But," he interrupted, "where do you find that business about going to heaven?"

I referred him to 1 Thessalonians 4:16, 17: "For the Lord himself shall descend from heaven with a shout, with the voice of the archangel, and with the trump of God: and the dead in

Christ shall rise first: then we which are alive and remain shall be caught up together with them in the clouds, to meet the Lord in the air: and so shall we ever be with the Lord."

Yes, those who have made Christ their Saviour on earth will probe the secrets of the universe in space travel; not in man-made capsules propelled by rockets, but on angels' wings we'll literally fly away. "They that wait upon the Lord shall renew their strength; they shall mount up with wings as eagles; they shall run, and not be weary; and they shall walk, and not faint" (Isaiah 40:31).

One may take a giant telescope and scan the heavens while still on earth, and look with awe upon the vast expanse that is our universe. Planets in orbit around the sun, and stars—some near and some far—add their glitter to the silver-spangled sky. Orion, the Milky Way, Jupiter, Mars, Saturn, Venus; to name a heavenly body is like picking up one grain of sand on a wide beach. "The heavens declare the glory of God; and the firmament sheweth his handywork. Day unto day uttereth speech, and night unto night sheweth knowledge" (Psalm 19:1, 2).

One cloudless night when Napoleon Bonaparte was on his way by boat to exile on the island of St. Helena, some of his traveling companions were arguing in favor of atheism. "There is no God," they exclaimed one to another. But Napoleon, who had been intently studying the sky, quieted them with a wave of his hand, and asked simply, "Then who made all of this?"

Now to be sure, the mass exodus that will take place at the second coming of Christ will not be the first time human beings have penetrated to the very center of the universe.

In 2 Kings 2:11 and 12 we read: "And it came to pass, as they still went on, and talked, that, behold, there appeared a

PAINTING BY ROBERT BERRAN AND RUSSELL HARLAN
© BY REVIEW AND HERALD

Christ will come, raise the sleeping saints, and take faithful ones of all nations to live and abide with Him forever and ever.

chariot of fire, and horses of fire, and parted them both asunder; and Elijah went up by a whirlwind into heaven. And Elisha saw it, and he cried, My father, my father, the chariot of Israel, and the horsemen thereof. And he saw him no more: and he took hold of his own clothes, and rent them in two pieces."

But even Elijah was not the first space traveler to penetrate the innermost secrets of the universe, for the Bible says Enoch walked with God, and "he was not; for God took him." So history affords us a precedent for what is going to happen at the end of the world.

In John 14:1-3 Jesus said, "Let not your heart be troubled: ye believe in God, believe also in me. In my Father's house are many mansions: if it were not so, I would have told you. I go to prepare a place for you. And if I go and prepare a place for you, I will come again, and receive you unto myself; that where I am, there ye may be also."

You see, Jesus wants all of His children to be where He is. As of now He is in heaven, but soon that will change:

"And then shall appear the sign of the Son of man in heaven: and then shall all the tribes of the earth mourn, and they shall see the Son of man coming in the clouds of heaven with power and great glory. And he shall send his angels with a great sound of a trumpet, and they shall gather together his elect from the four winds, from one end of heaven to the other" (Matthew 24: 30, 31). Paul says we will be caught up to meet the Lord in the air, and that we will never be separated from Him again.

But where will we go from there? In Revelation 7:9, 10 we read, "After this I beheld, and, lo, a great multitude, which no man could number, of all nations, and kindreds, and people, and tongues, stood before the throne, and before the Lamb, clothed with white robes, and palms in their hands; and cried with a loud voice, saying, Salvation to our God which sitteth upon the throne, and unto the Lamb."

Psalm 11:4 indicates that the Lord's throne is in heaven. Accordingly, those who are caught up to meet the Lord in the air will proceed with Him to the very throne of God, which is in the City of God in heaven.

In Revelation 14:2, 3 we read: "And I heard a voice from heaven, as the voice of many waters, and as the voice of a great thunder: and I heard the voice of harpers harping with their harps: and they sung as it were a new song before the throne, and before the four beasts, and the elders: and no man could learn that song but the hundred and forty and four thousand, which were redeemed from the earth."

So some people who are now on this earth are going to heaven. Let the scoffers scoff and the mockers mock. They will not have the last laugh. Those who hear about, dream about, and talk about a city in heaven do not think, talk, and dream in vain. This world is not the end for man. The dismal conditions that exist here would be enough to depress and discourage anyone if there were no hope of life in the hereafter. But there are those who say that men who look forward to a place in heaven are practicing a form of escapism, when they ought to be doing something to better things on the earth. They say that all talk and dreams of heaven serve as an opiate and render one useless in this present world. Nothing could be further from the truth. Men and women who believe in another world work their hardest in this one to prepare themselves and others to live with angels. They have read in the Bible that there are disciplines required of those who would be citizens of the world to come, and that they must practice those disciplines here. The ten-commandment law is the moral code that forms the basis of their behavior in this world.

Those who expect to be citizens of that other world clean up their lives down here. They become easier to deal with. They do not lie, steal, commit adultery, kill. They respect God and their fellow men. They are energetic, productive, helpful. They visit the sick, clothe the naked, feed the hungry, and shelter the homeless. These are the people who have a heart. These are Christians. They recognize this world as preparatory to the one to come. They are not depressed by the discouraging outlook here, for they have a vision of the hereafter, and this gives them a reason for living and working and being sons of God and brethren to their fellow men.

A peanut vendor was selling his nuts on a rainy day. He was soaked to the skin. A friend said, "You're fairly miserable, old man. Why don't you come in out of the rain?"

Said the peanut vendor, looking skyward, "It is miserable now, but by and by—think of that." Yes, the by and by makes more bearable the here and now.

O, fix me. O, fix me.
O, fix me; Fix me, Jesus, Fix me.

"Fix Me"

DEATH IS AN ENEMY, and nobody really wants to die. Not even the person contemplating suicide wants to die. He just can't discover any reason for continuing to live. Our lives were intended to be a harmonious development of our physical, mental, and spiritual natures. This is the more abundant life spoken of by Jesus Christ our Lord. When there is an imbalance, either in the physical, mental, or spiritual nature of man, there is unhappiness, disease, and even death. Because of this curious yet certain interrelationship between man's three natures, let us discuss the physical part of man and how man may enjoy physical well-being.

Doctors say that a lot of people who come to them are not physically sick but mentally disturbed, and because of the close interrelationship between the physical and the mental, the body is affected by the mental condition. It is also true that physical distress may cause mental illness. This, too, is because of the

431

close interrelationship between body, mind, and spirit. I need not add that spiritual pathology or sickness can also lead to physical and mental sickness. The mental and the physical can affect the spiritual as well.

So man is an entity. He is a combination of body, mind, and spirit; and he must guard all three if he is to prosper and be in health—physical, mental, and spiritual health.

We read in 3 John 2: "Beloved, I wish above all things that thou mayest prosper and be in health, even as thy soul prospereth." We have discovered here that God equates the right treatment of our body with any other spiritual virtue mentioned in the Scriptures.

"If any man defile the temple of God, him shall God destroy; for the temple of God is holy, which temple ye are" (1 Corinthians 3:17).

"Know ye not that ye are the temple of God, and that the Spirit of God dwelleth in you?" (verse 16).

The defilement of the temple of God brings upon man the anger of the Lord, for the temple of God, or the body, is the residence of the Spirit of God, and if any man defiles that body temple, God will destroy him.

"Whether therefore ye eat, or drink, or whatsoever ye do, do all to the glory of God" (chapter 10:31).

You see, God is either honored or dishonored by the things we do, whether it be eating, drinking, or anything else. We are to ask God's blessing on whatever we do. We are to ask His sanction. We are to seek His presence. To have God with us always, we must keep the body temple clean. The Bible speaks of certain things we do that defile the body temple. Consider the question of eating.

Leviticus 11 mentions many creatures God placed on this earth, never intending that they be used as food. But man began to eat them, and they are contributing to the physical disease of the human family. Swine's flesh is one of these things. Some may object that since this ban on swine as food is in the Old Testament, perhaps it is no longer binding on Christians. But listen to Paul in 2 Corinthians 6:17: "Wherefore come out from among them, and be ye separate, saith the Lord, and touch not the unclean thing; and I will receive you."

The New Testament agrees that there are certain unclean things that are not to be eaten. But the Old Testament specifically names these unclean things.

The Bible pronounces a curse on people who eat unclean meat: "For, behold, the Lord will come with fire, and with his chariots like a whirlwind, to render his anger with fury, and his rebuke with flames of fire. For by fire and by his sword will the Lord plead with all flesh: and the slain of the Lord shall be many. They that sanctify themselves, and purify themselves in the gardens behind one tree in the midst, eating swine's flesh, and the abomination, and the mouse, shall be consumed together, saith the Lord" (Isaiah 66:15-17).

This prophecy points all the way down to the second coming of Christ. It specifically states that people who eat swine's flesh, mice, and other abominable animals will be consumed together at the end of the world. So the laws governing the treatment of the body, even though first given in the Old Testament, have not been abolished.

Let's think about drink. Some people will drink anything from hair tonic to wood alcohol. This is a defilement of the body, and no drunkard will enter the kingdom of God.

"Wine is a mocker, strong drink is raging: and whosoever is deceived thereby is not wise" (Proverbs 20:1).

I know this to be true. I had an uncle who drank himself to death, and I have never seen a more pitiful creature than a man reduced mentally, physically, and spiritually by the demon alcohol. Billy Sunday used to fight John Barleycorn at all his meetings, and he did not fight in vain. I'd like to lift my voice with that chorus of faithful witnesses and add my testimony to theirs, that wine does make a fool out of the one who consumes it. Strong drink is raging, and a man is not wise who drinks it.

"Who hath woe? who hath sorrow? who hath contentions? who hath babbling? who hath wounds without cause? who hath redness of eyes? They that tarry long at the wine; they that go to seek mixed wine. Look not thou upon the wine when it is red, when it giveth his colour in the cup, when it moveth itself aright. At the last it biteth like a serpent, and stingeth like an adder" (Proverbs 23:29-32).

The use of tobacco is another debilitating habit. Tobacco has at least twenty-seven poisons in it, and a person who smokes a cigarette is likely to subject himself to a variety of ills in addition to lung cancer. It has an effect on the blood pressure, on the nerves, and on the brain. The man who persists in using it will have his name blotted out from under heaven. Narcotics, drugs, alcohol, and unclean meats all render the body unfit for the residency of the Holy Spirit. By using them a man sins against his own body.

But what about the mind? "Let this mind be in you, which was also in Christ Jesus" (Philippians 2:5). The mind, like the stomach, is affected by what goes into it. To fill the mind with

434

filth is to reap a harvest of filth in thought, in word, and in deed. Many magazines, movies, and television shows belong in this category. One should also be careful of the friends with whom he associates. Avoid worry, read the Bible, pray, keep the mind clear, for the mind as well as the body has to be guarded against filth.

What about man's spiritual nature, since the three natures are inseparably intertwined? Man is born without a spiritual nature. We read this in John 3:7: "Marvel not that I said unto thee, Ye must be born again." The new birth first begins with the mind. Often when the Bible talks about the heart it is really talking about the mind. A man's spiritual nature has to be bestowed. It is a gift of God: "For by grace are ye saved through faith; and that not of yourselves: it is the gift of God" (Ephesians 2:8).

Thank God, nineteen hundred years ago, on Calvary's hill far away the Son of the living God suffered, bled, and died that we might experience the new birth, that our new spiritual nature might be activated. Thank God we are not born derelicts without hope, without God, without the high privilege of progressing, without the opportunity of climbing. Mankind may be bettered. You can be bettered; I can be bettered. There is saving grace in this old sinful world for human betterment. The prayer of our hearts should be, "Lord, lift me up, and I shall stand By faith on heaven's tableland; A higher plane than I have found; Lord, plant my feet on higher ground." As we pray this prayer and sing this song, we should have in mind higher ground for the treatment of our bodies, higher ground for the way we treat our minds, and higher ground in the development of our spiritual nature.

One day my little boy and I were out playing a game of tennis. As we hit the ball to and fro across the net, he seemed to be getting the better of me. I knew he was inexperienced and he needed a bit of help with his game, but the more successful he was against his daddy, the more sure of himself he became until he began to laugh and tease me. It was then I decided to end his false security. I began to bear down and hit the ball harder and harder until suddenly he looked at me in bewilderment and said, "Daddy, I thought I was beating you!"

You know, we can have this false sense of security with some of the things we eat and drink and do. It is an inexorable law of nature that when we do things that destroy the body, we are certain to reap what we sow. We deceive ourselves into believing we are winning the game of life even though we are taking into our body and mind and spirit those things that would destroy, debase, and delude.

Some of our habits are cultivated and never reach the point of being chronic. Others are compulsive habits that fasten onto the soul and seemingly refuse to let go. Some habits can be overcome by the mere exercise of the will. Others are deeper, and require agonizing fasting and prayer and sometimes a lifelong struggle. But let none give up the fight. Let none retire before the awesome specter of an overwhelming desire. Let it be understood here and now that there is a balm in Gilead. There is a Physician there, and help is available twenty-four hours a day from an all-seeing God who neither slumbers nor sleeps. He is always ready to help each of His children, and will indeed help them when they turn to Him with all their hearts. Christ alone can isolate the virus of sin. Christ alone can insulate our souls against internal passion and external seduction. Christ has overcome in His own flesh. If we will let Him, He will do the same in ours.

The days ahead for our nation are fraught with peril, and the question of black-white relations is far from being settled. The black man can ill afford the luxury of liquor while he seeks to drive safely toward his desired destiny of full citizenship in the kingdom of man and God. Slavery has many forms. Men may be dominated by other men, or they may be dominated by debasing habits. It is difficult to know which is worse. One fact is certain: No prize is possible to men who will not sacrifice. Nations have been surrendered on the altar of alcohol. The night ancient Babylon fell, her guards and soldiers were drunken with wine. Belshazzar himself drank wine from the sacred goblets of the Lord's Temple. Tradition has it that Greece's greatest military genius died as the result of a drunken orgy.

Will our nation, conceived in liberty and dedicated to the equality of every person under God, turn upon itself and become the instrument of its own destruction? Will the black man who has traveled so far over the tortuous journey toward freedom, now surrender it to the debauchery of undisciplined living? How long will the statistics of the land trumpet to the world the sad tale of black men destroying themselves with narcotics and alcohol, which lead to crimes of violence, thievery, and prostitution? It is true that men of all races, in far too great numbers, indulge in these sinful practices. But the underprivileged man can least afford to practice these vices.

"Then said Jesus unto his disciples, If any man will come after me, let him deny himself, and take up his cross, and follow me" (Matthew 16:24).

"The Old Ship"

FOR THIRTY years Christ attended the Jewish synagogue as a member of the established religion of His day. God in the flesh, as truly God was and is, grew up in the church of His mother and father. But on the day the nation fully and finally rejected Him, He walked out of the Temple never to re-enter it. As He left He said, "Behold, your house is left unto you desolate. For I say unto you, Ye shall not see me henceforth, till ye shall say, Blessed is he that cometh in the name of the Lord" (Matthew 23:38, 39).

On the ruins of Judaism Christ established His own church. One day He took a sampling of opinion from His disciples as to what the public thought of Him. "Whom do men say that I the Son of man am?" He asked. "And they said, Some say that thou art John the Baptist: some, Elias; and others, Jeremias, or one of the prophets. He saith unto them, But whom say ye that I am? And Simon Peter answered and said, Thou art the Christ, the

Fellowship with others who love Jesus imparts courage and strength to overcome the problems and temptations of this life.

Son of the living God. And Jesus answered and said unto him, Blessed art thou, Simon Barjona: for flesh and blood hath not revealed it unto thee, but my Father which is in heaven. And I say also unto thee, That thou art Peter, and upon this rock I will build my church; and the gates of hell shall not prevail against it" (Matthew 16:13-18).

"And being made perfect, he became the author of eternal salvation unto all them that obey him" (Hebrews 5:9).

So Christ built the church. Christ authored the plan of salvation. "I will build my church," He said.

"Whom say ye that I am?" Christ asked. Peter acknowledged Him to be the Christ, the Son of the living God. On this sure foundation of Peter's acknowledgment, Christ built His church. He is the Author and Finisher; He is the True Foundation.

"For other foundation can no man lay than that is laid, which is Jesus Christ" (1 Corinthians 3:11).

Thus the spiritual house of Christianity is indeed founded upon a rock. It is this that guarantees it against the onslaughts of the gates of hell. But why join the church? Is it essential to salvation? And having joined, is there any sound reason for attending regularly? "And they, continuing daily with one accord in the temple, and breaking bread from house to house, did eat their meat with gladness and singleness of heart, praising God, and having favour with all the people. And the Lord added to the church daily such as should be saved" (Acts 2:46, 47).

According to this text, those who should be saved joined the church. The church has the keys to the kingdom of heaven. To be out of the church, then, is to be out of the spiritual family of Christ. The church is the custodian of spiritual truth.

To Timothy Paul wrote: "But if I tarry long, that thou mayest

440

know how thou oughtest to behave thyself in the house of God, which is the church of the living God, the pillar and ground of the truth" (1 Timothy 3:15).

The church is the house of God. Here one becomes familiar with the teachings of God as they are contained in the Scriptures. The church is a place of spiritual fellowship. "Not forsaking the assembling of ourselves together, as the manner of some is; but exhorting one another: and so much the more, as ye see the day approaching" (Hebrews 10:25).

The assembling of ourselves together becomes a more urgent necessity as we near the end of the world. Christians can truly sing, "Blest be the tie that binds Our hearts in Christian love." It is through fellowship with Christ and with one another that Christians are bound together in an indissoluble union that the gates of hell cannot break. Each Christian draws strength from his fellows. They are companions in trial and triumph. Thus an instrument of God is forged that will bring liberty to the captive and cause the legions of hell to tremble. Is not the church pictured as being "fair as the moon, clear as the sun, and terrible as an army with banners" (Song of Solomon 6:10)?

In all Christian communions there are saved men and women, redeemed by the blood of the Lamb. Even among the heathen there are those whom God numbers as His chosen ones. But this is true only when the person has not been exposed to the full gospel message. Jesus Christ did not establish the vast number of differing religious faiths that exist today. In fact, He established only one. There is only "one Lord, one faith, one baptism" (Ephesians 4:5). It was His prayer that His believers would always be one.

In 1 Corinthians 1:10 the apostle exhorted, "Now I beseech

you, brethren, by the name of our Lord Jesus Christ, that ye all speak the same thing, and that there be no divisions among you; but that ye be perfectly joined together in the same mind and in the same judgment." It was therefore never the will of God that schisms develop among His people, that they differ with one another in matters of doctrine. Viewing the widespread confusion resulting from the differences that have developed among Christians, one can only conclude that "an enemy hath done this."

But the Bible says, "Ye shall know the truth, and the truth shall make you free" (John 8:32).

Thank God, His truth has remained on earth in spite of the machinations of men. Man can, if he will, find his way to the true church of God through a study of the Scriptures.

And what are the characteristics of the true church of God in these last days?

1. It will teach the divinity of Jesus Christ and His office as Saviour and Redeemer of mankind (Acts 16:30, 31; Isaiah 9:6, 7; John 1:1 and 14).

2. It will teach that a man is saved from sin by grace through faith in the Lord Jesus Christ (Ephesians 2:8).

3. It will teach obedience to the law of God as a consequence of faith in God (James 2:18; 10-12).

4. It will teach the observance of the true Lord's day (Mark 2:27, 28; Luke 4:16, 31).

5. The true church of God will possess the spiritual gifts mentioned in the Scriptures (1 Corinthians 12).

6. The true church of God in these last days will be a world church (see Matthew 28:19, 20).

7. The true church of God is a tithing church. It believes in

the support of the world mission program through financial liberality (Matthew 23:23).

8. The true church of God teaches the truthfulness of the Scriptures, both the Old and the New Testament (John 5:46, 47; 17:17).

9. The true church of God teaches its members the disciplines of grace in relation to recreation, fashion, and appetite. These are but a few Bible characteristics of the true church of God, and one may measure his own religion against that of Jesus Christ and the Bible by these standards. Occasionally the objection is made that some church members do not adhere to the principles of the faith. To be sure, this has always been true. Among the first twelve members of the church was one who betrayed his Lord. This, however, does not detract from the obligation that rests upon every man to find truth at its source and to walk in its enlightening precepts. For every hypocrite who misrepresents the faith, there are hundreds of men and women who love the Lord and are sincerely walking in His steps.

Another asks: In lands where men practice their own pagan religions, what right have you Christians to invade their privacy and disturb their peace? The answer lies in the command of our Lord: "Go ye into all the world, and preach the gospel to every creature" (Mark 16:15). What the gospel is and what it does for human beings impels us to carry it to the ends of the earth. The gospel of Christ combats the listlessness of paganism and the fatalism of predestination. Wherever the gospel goes, men come alive to their own possibilities and become energetic achievers. The value of human life increases, men take better care of themselves, are more careful toward one another here, and become heirs to the life to come.

The religion of Jesus Christ offers the highest and best form of human existence in this world. Thus it is that we preach it with zeal, and by radio and television, as well as the personally spoken word, we communicate it. We can do no less in view of what Christ has done for us.

I agree with one author who states that the church, feeble and defective though it is, is the object upon which Christ bestows His supreme regard.

It is said that once a man came to Charles Spurgeon and asked that great preacher if his church was a pure church. The man stated that he was looking for a pure church that he might belong to it. Mr. Spurgeon told him that he did not know if his church was pure, but he did know that many good people belonged to it, saintly people, and truly Christian people. But he admitted that there might possibly be a Judas among them as there was in the company of Jesus and the first apostles, and there might be some deceivers and idolaters and those who walk ungodly, as there seem to have been in the churches of Rome, Corinth, Galatia, Ephesus, Colossus, Philippi, Thessalonica, and all the others to which the New Testament Epistles were written. On the whole he thought that his church was not the one the brother was looking for. In fact, he did not know whether there ever had been such a church.

"But," said Mr. Spurgeon, "if you happen to find a pure church, I beg you not to join it, for you would spoil the whole thing."

Yes, the church is the old ship of Zion. "It has landed many a thousand; it will take you home to glory. Get on board; yes, get on board."

"Free at Last"

MEN ARE PRISONERS of their own limited goals. They fall short of their earthly aspirations when they have no heavenly ones. Men should always dream beyond their expectations. We need not sacrifice the hereafter for the here. There are some who in the hot passion of the present dismiss the future as pie-in-the-sky promises. They would gamble all on the here and now.

To all such I say, look at history. Freedom movements have always undershot or overshot their marks. New conquerors have repeated the mistakes of the old. The struggle for power has never been resolved nor will it be. The contest here may be resolved in compromise, but not the one hereafter. In the hereafter all men will be given the privilege of limitless development. There will be no jockeying for advantage, for God will be ruler, and goods and services will be ample. None of the problems that plague the here will affect the hereafter. What a joy to escape a world of slums, sin, crime, unemployment, ostracism, and war. "And God shall wipe away all tears from their eyes; and there shall be no more death, neither sorrow, nor crying, neither shall there be any more pain: for the former things are passed away" (Revelation 21:4).

So let us cherish our dream of the hereafter. It will make more bearable the burden we bear here. Man cannot live without hope, and when, because of broken promises or hope deferred, the dream dies, there follows the orgy of rioting with its destruction of life and property. When hope dies, man dies. This book says that hope need not die, that man may live abundantly in spite of political procrastination or outright oppression. It says that the moral force of right in the bosom of hope will triumph both here and hereafter. Truth crushed to the earth has always risen again. No form of human tyranny can survive. What of Napoleon, the Kaiser, Hitler, and countless others? For the most hopeless is there not hope in this?

But the frightening specter of the here is that the endless cycle of hate will bury all hope, black and white, in a sea of blood. It is this madness that must not prevail. We have little to choose from—black or white hate. It is all self-defeating. We have come too far too long to lose hope now. White intransigence and black recklessness can only ruin us both. The nation and the world need the master touch of Christ the great Reconciler.

On the Sea of Galilee stormy winds lashed the waters into a stinging storm. Men did all they could think of to keep the ship afloat. When all seemed lost they turned to Christ. He solved the insoluble. The wind ceased and there was a great calm. Christ is the only hope of this troubled world today. Without Him, our earthly peril defies description.

446

Thank God, there is another world, the thought of which fires our hopes and colors our dreams. I am a better man here because there is a hereafter. Let the cynical limit man with ball and chain to this earth. Mine is a dream unconfined, of better things in a better place. By faith my soul has scented the heady elixir of Paradise. And now no storm cloud, dark though it be, can hide the guiding star that beckons me. The slavery that was will tint the freedom that is to be with a golden glow. All pain will be swallowed up by that which satisfies. And in the bright glow of tomorrow's sunrise, man—the crowning act of God's creation—comes at last into his own.

Mahalia
Jackson

Booker T.
Washington

George
Washington
Carver

Jackie
Robinson

Mary
McLeod
Bethune

Marian
Anderson

Jesse
Owens

Dr. Charles
S. Johnson

Ralph
Bunche

Lt.
Leo
Joh

Dr. Mo
W. Joh

Walter A.
White

Roy
Wilkins

Robert R.
Moton